personal representation
the neglected dimension of electoral systems

Edited by
Josep M. Colomer

© Josep Colomer 2011

First published by the ECPR Press in 2011

Paperback first published by the ECPR Press in 2013

The ECPR Press is the publishing imprint of the European Consortium for Political Research (ECPR), a scholarly association, which supports and encourages the training, research and cross-national cooperation of political scientists in institutions throughout Europe and beyond.

The ECPR Press
University of Essex
Wivenhoe Park
Colchester
CO4 3SQ, UK

All rights reserved. No part of this book may be reprinted or reproduced or utilised in any form or by any electronic, mechanical, or other means, now known or hereafter invented, including photocopying and recording, or in any information storage or retrieval system, without permission in writing from the publishers.

Typeset by ECPR Press
Printed and bound by Lightning Source

British Library Cataloguing in Publication Data
A catalogue record for this book is available from the British Library

Hardback ISBN: 978-1-9073011-6-2

Paperback ISBN: 978-1-907301-57-5

www.ecpr.eu/ecprpress

ECPR – Studies in European Political Science

Series Editors:
Dario Castiglione (University of Exeter) and
Vincent Hoffmann-Martinot (Sciences Po Bordeaux)

ECPR – Studies in European Political Science is a series of high-quality edited volumes on topics at the cutting edge of current political science and political thought. All volumes are research-based offering new perspectives, with contributions from leading scholars working in the relevant fields. Most of the volumes originate from ECPR events including the Joint Sessions of Workshops, the Research Sessions, and the General Conferences.

Books in this series

The Domestic Party Politics of Europeanisation: Actors, Patterns and Systems
(ISBN: 9781907301223)
Edited by Külahci Erol

Interactive Policymaking, Metagovernance and Democracy
(ISBN: 9781907301131)
Edited by Jacob Torfing and Peter Triantafillou

Perceptions of Europe: A Comparative Sociology of European Attitudes
(ISBN: 9781907301155)
Edited by Daniel Gaxie, Jay Rowell and Nicolas Hubé

Personal Representation: The Neglected Dimension of Electoral Systems
(ISBN: 9781907301162)
Edited by Josep Colomer

Political Trust: Why Context Matters
(ISBN: 9781907301230)
Edited by Sonja Zmerli and Marc Hooghe

Please visit www.ecpr.eu/ecprpress for up-to-date information about new publications

contents

List of Figures and Tables — vi

Contributors — ix

Chapter One: Introduction: Personal and Party Representation
JOSEP M. COLOMER — 1

Chapter Two: Candidate Selection
NIR ATMOR, REUVEN Y. HAZAN AND GIDEON RAHAT — 21

Chapter Three: Single Seat
HELEN MARGETTS — 37

Chapter Four: Closed Party List
PEDRO RIERA — 55

Chapter Five: Primary Elections
JOHN M. CAREY AND HARRY J. ENTEN — 81

Chapter Six: Mixed Systems
LOUIS MASSICOTTE — 99

Chapter Seven: Preferential Vote in Party List
LAURI KARVONEN — 119

Chapter Eight: Ordinal Rank
MICHAEL MARSH — 135

Chapter Nine: Open Ballot
GEORG LUTZ — 153

Bibliography — 175

Index — 187

list of figures and tables

Figures

Figure 2.1: Candidacy requirements and party/personal representation	24
Figure 2.2: The selectorate and party/personal representation	26
Figure 2.3: Voting vs appointment and party/personal representation	27
Figure 2.4: Decentralisation and party/personal representation	28
Figure 2.5: Dimensions of candidate selection and party/personal representation	29
Figure 2.6: Personal and party representation between and within parties	34
Figure 3.1: Relative use of 'MPs' expenses' as a search term 2009–2010	49
Figure 4.1: Ratios of parachutists by party and election	70
Figure 4.2: Ratios of parachutists by district magnitude and election	70
Figure 4.3: Ratios of ministers strategically allocated by birthplace and election	72
Figure 4.4: Ratios of ministers strategically allocated by district magnitude and election	72
Figure 5.1: Closing prices for Democratic candidates on the Iowa Electronic Market as of the day before primary elections	89
Figure 5.2: Closing prices for Republican candidates on the Iowa Electronic Market as of the day before primary elections	89
Figure 5.3: Uncertainty and turnout over time among open primaries in 2008	93
Figure 5.4a: Turnout vs national uncertainty – open primaries	96
Figure 5.4b: Turnout vs national uncertainty – semi-closed primaries	96
Figure 5.4c: Turnout vs national uncertainty – closed primaries	97
Figure 6.1: Party and personal representation in mixed electoral systems	112
Figure 8.1: Disproportionality for FF and FG 1923–2007	141
Figure 9.1: Frequency of rank correlations between alphabetical order and actual order of candidates on the ballot	164
Figure 9.2: Box-plots of Spearman's rho alphabetical order of the ballot per cantons	165
Figure 9.3: Frequency of percentage of unchanged party ballots per ballot	167
Figure 9.4: Frequency of mean lost votes to other party per ballot	168

Tables

Table 1.1: A two-dimensional classification of electoral systems	10
Table 3.1: Seats, votes and disproportionality for Great Britain 2010	40
Table 3.2: How MPs should and do spend time	44
Table 4.1: Electoral performance by district, UCD (1977–1979), AP (1982–1986), PP (1989–2008) and PSOE (1977–2008)	68
Table 4.2: Descriptive statistics – candidates in Spain	69
Table 4.3: Mean comparison tests by birthplace	73
Table 4.4: Mean comparison tests by membership of the national government	73
Table 4.5: Determinants of personal vote in Spain, PSOE (1977–2008), UCD (1977 and 1979), AP (1982 and 1986) and PP (1989–2008)	75
Table 4.6: Determinants of personal vote in Spain, PSOE (1977–2008)	76
Table 4.7: Determinants of personal vote in Spain, UCD (1977 and 1979), AP (1982 and 1986) and PP (1989–2008)	77
Table 5.1: OLS regressions of turnout on measures of competitiveness, by party and type of primary.	94
Table 6.1: The effect of individual preferences in Lithuanian legislative elections	107
Table 7.1: Preferential list systems. Theoretical range of variation	121
Table 7.2: Existing variants of preferential list systems	123
Table 7.3: The origins of preferential list systems compared with closed-list systems	130
Table 8.1: Election count, Cork NW 2007	139
Table 8.2: How did incumbents lose? (1927–2007)	144
Table 8.3: Who should TDs represent?	145
Table 9.1: Number of ballots presented by parties in the 2007 election	162
Table 9.2: Relative advantage of preference votes for candidates between last elected on a ballot and first not elected on a ballot	166
Table 9.3: Multi-level model explaining the number of unchanged party ballots, mean votes lost and won per list	170
Table 9.4: Multilevel model explaining the number of preference votes for candidates	173

contributors

JOSEP M. COLOMER is Research Professor in Political Science at the Higher Council for Scientific Research, Institute for Economic Analysis, in Barcelona, and Prince of Asturias Distinguished Visiting Professor at Georgetown University, in Washington, DC. He is an elected member of the Academia Europaea. He has published on political institutions, electoral systems, democratisation, empire- and state-building, and European politics. He is the author, among other books, of *The Science of Politics. An Introduction* (Oxford University Press, 2010), *Political Institutions: Democracy and Social Choice* (Oxford University Press, 2001), and editor of the *Handbook of Electoral System Choice* (Palgrave Macmillan, 2004).

NIR ATMOR is Research Assistant at the Israel Democracy Institute and a PhD candidate in Political Science at the Hebrew University of Jerusalem. He works on comparative politics, electoral systems and candidate selection methods.

JOHN M. CAREY is the John Wentworth Professor in the Social Sciences, Dartmouth College, Hanover, New Hampshire. He works on comparative politics, elections, representation and Latin American politics. He is the author, among other publications, of 'The Electoral Sweet Spot: Low-magnitude Proportional Electoral Systems' (with Simon Hix), (*American Journal of Political Science*, 2011), 'The Reelection Debate in Latin America' (in *New Perspectives on Democracy in Latin America: Actors, Institutions and Practices*, William C. Smith (ed.) Blackwell, 2010), and *Legislative Voting and Accountability* (Cambridge University Press, 2009).

HARRY J. ENTEN is a graduate at Dartmouth College, Hanover, New Hampshire, working on American government, elections and statistics methods.

REUVEN Y. HAZAN is Professor of Political Science at the Hebrew University of Jerusalem. He works on elections and electoral systems, political parties and party systems, legislative studies and Israeli politics. He is the author of *Democracy Within Parties: Candidate Selection Methods and their Political Consequences* (with Gideon Rahat) (Oxford University Press, 2010), *Cohesion and Discipline in Legislatures: Political Parties, Party Leadership, Parliamentary Committees and Governance* (Routledge, 2006), and co-editor of 'Understanding Electoral Reform' (with Monique Leyenaar) (a special issue of *West European Politics*, 2011).

LAURI KARVONEN is Professor of Political Science at the Åbo Akademi, Helsinki. He works on comparative politics, including parties, voters, electoral systems, democracy and democratisation. He is co-editor of *Party Systems and Voter Alignments Revisited* (with Stein Kuhnle) (Routledge, 2001) and author of *The Personalisation of Politics* (ECPR Press, 2010).

GEORG LUTZ is Project Director of the Swiss Electoral Studies (Selects) at the Social Science Research Centre (FORS) in the University of Lausanne. His work focuses on political institutions and political behaviour from a comparative perspective, as well as Swiss politics. His recent publications include 'First Come, First Served: the Effect of Ballot Position on Electoral Success in Open List PR Elections' (*Representatio,* 2010), and 'The Electoral Success of Beauties and Beasts' (*Swiss Political Science Review*, 2010).

HELEN MARGETTS is Professor of Society and the Internet at the Oxford Internet Institute and a professorial fellow of Mansfield College, University of Oxford. She is a political scientist currently researching government, public policy and political behaviour in digital environments. Her recent publications include: *Paradoxes of Modernization: Unintended consequences of public policy reform* (with Hood and Perri 6) (Oxford University Press, 2010), 'The Latent Support for the Extreme Right in British Politics' (with Peter John) (*West European Politics*, 2009), and *Digital-Era Governance: IT Corporations, the State and E-government* (with Patrick Dunleavy) (Oxford University Press, 2008).

MICHAEL MARSH is Professor of Political Science at Trinity College, Dublin. He works on electoral behaviour, elections, parties and Irish politics. He is the author, among other publications, of *The Irish Voter* (with Richard Sinnott, John Garry and Fiachra Kennedy) (Manchester University Press, 2008).

LOUIS MASSICOTTE is Professor of Political Science at the Université Laval, Québec. He works on electoral systems, legislatures and federalism. His publications include 'Canada: Sticking to First-Past-the-Post, for the Time Being' (in Michael Gallagher and Paul Mitchell (eds) *The Politics of Electoral Systems*, Oxford University Press, 2005), *Establishing the Rules of the Game. Election Laws in Democracies* (with André Blais and Antoine Yoshinaka) (University of Toronto Press, 2003) and 'Electoral Reform in Canada (in André Blais (ed.) *To Keep or to Change First Past the Post? The Politics of Electoral Reform*, Oxford University Press, 2008).

GIDEON RAHAT is Associate Professor of Political Science at the Hebrew University of Jerusalem. He works on political parties, candidate selection and electoral reform. He is author of *The Politics of Regime Structure Reform in Democracies: Israel in Comparative and Theoretical Perspective* (State University of New York Press, 2008), and *Democracy within Parties: Candidate Selection Methods and their Political Consequences* (with Reuven Y. Hazan) (Oxford University Press, 2010).

PEDRO RIERA is a Researcher at the European University Institute, Florence. He works on comparative politics, electoral systems and political behaviour. He is the author of 'Non bis in idem: voto escindido en sistemas electorales mixtos. Los casos de Nueva Zelanda en 1999 y 2002' (*Revista Española de Ciencia Política*, 2009).

chapter one | introduction: personal and party representation
Josep M. Colomer

THE COUNTY ELECTION (1852), BY GEORGE C. BINGHAM

An efficient electoral system for a representative democratic government must include appropriate rules for both *party representation* and *personal representation*. Many classifications and analyses of electoral systems focus on the distinction between majority and proportional rules. By having this focus, they address only party representation, but neglect the second essential element of any electoral system: personal representation. Some basic elements of an electoral system, mainly district magnitude (or number of seats to be elected in each district) and the electoral formula, are tools to allocate *seats to parties*, that is, to produce party representation. The voting procedure as shaped by the ballot form, which is to be studied here, deals with the allocation of *seats to persons* in order to produce personal representation. An electoral system can include rules to allocate both seats to parties and persons in order to produce both party and personal representation.

The aim of this book is to clarify the importance of these two elements of electoral systems and, given that voting formulas for personal representation are under-studied, to present a basic analytical framework and a number of applied analyses on the following aspects: the different *procedures of voting for individual candidates*, their origins and consequences, their degree of compatibility with formulas for party representation, and the contexts, strategies and normative criteria for the choice of personal representation formulas.

The systematic study of procedures for personal representation, together with the previously accumulated knowledge on those for party representation, should advance the discussion about 'the best' electoral system. Of course, this discussion may never finish because it is strongly linked to different values and criteria held by different scholars, practitioners and voters (whether correspondence between votes and seats, political pluralism, government effectiveness, policy consistency or change, etc.). However, a fine analysis of the different formulas, their expected consequences, and the trade-off among them should reduce the disparity of evaluations, make some people reconsider their opinions or change their minds, and differ less on the basis of yet unsolved differences in scientific analysis than on difference of values.

THE ORIGINS OF PARTY REPRESENTATION

The origins of the tension between personal and party representation are remote. They can refer to the most primitive emergence of organised political factions, later called political parties, when they began to run in elections, which were conventionally organised with traditional rules favouring personal representation by means of the selection of individual candidates.

Traditional elections focus on the choice of the best individual representatives to defend the interests or values of the community or group. Cases include elections in small towns and communities, in local constituencies for ancient regime assemblies and parliaments, as many elections in current times for housing condominium-, school-, university-, professional organisation- and corporation-boards, and students' and workers' unions. This kind of election is conceived and broadly accepted in the intention to produce 'personal representation', that is the selection of the best individual representatives. This focus is based on the assumption that there is broad agreement or consensus in the group regarding the common interests to be protected and the priority of public goods to be provided by the action of the elected representatives.

In particular, many elections in local communities or small groups were held in the past and are still held today by a set of rules composed of *multi-member districts, open ballot* and *majority rule*. Basically, people vote for the individual candidates they prefer and those with higher numbers of votes are elected. This set of electoral rules indeed appears as almost 'natural' and 'spontaneous' to many communities when they have to choose a procedure of collective decision-making based on votes, especially because it permits a consensual representation of the community. Many formulas are compatible with the essentials of the electoral system just mentioned, including oral or written ballot, assembly or booth voting, variants of approval voting, as well as plurality or second round rules.

The combination of multi-member districts with majority rule has been neglected in recent political science literature on elections. Virtually all studies of electoral systems distinguish two basic types: one combining single-member districts with majority rules and another combining multi-member districts with proportional rule. However, the type of traditional electoral system just mentioned was used very widely in local and national assemblies in pre-democratic or early democratic periods before and during the nineteenth century. It has survived in a number of local elections, and has also been adopted in a few new democracies in recent times.

Specifically, two- or three-seat districts by plurality rule were largely used in English shires, towns and boroughs from the thirteenth century onwards and for the election of the House of Commons until 1935. Multi-member districts have survived in most English local elections. The English model of elections in multi-member districts by plurality rule was adopted in all the British colonies in North America for the lower houses of their legislatures. With independence, it was used for most seats in state congresses, the U.S. Presidential College and the House of Representatives (in some cases until the 1960s). At state and local levels, most representatives have, most of the time, been elected in multi-member districts. In France, the tradition of using multi-member districts in indirect elections for municipalities and medieval provincial and general Estates was maintained for post-revolutionary national assemblies during most of the nineteenth century. This system has survived in small French municipalities with less than 3,500 inhabitants. It was also still evident in Spain, where multi-member districts with individual-candidate ballots were used in indirect elections of anti-French invasion Juntas in the early nineteenth century, and in the Spanish colonies in the Americas of the time, and in most constitutional elections until 1936. Nowadays, they are used for the election of the Spanish Senate, as well as in small towns with less than 250 inhabitants.

Variants of the above-identified electoral system with multi-member districts, vote for individual candidates and majority rule were also used in medieval German and Swiss communes and cantons, in Italian communes, as well as for the election of the single or lower house of state parliaments and assemblies in some thirty countries in all parts of the world from the early nineteenth to the mid-twentieth century. They are still widely used in local elections in a number of countries (see detailed data and sources in Colomer 2004, 2007).

The Emergence of Political Parties
The focus on personal representation in elections with traditional rules was challenged with the emergence of organised factions or political parties running lists of candidates and acting as compact groups in the subsequent councils and assemblies. In recent times, political parties emerged partly endogenously from the previously existing elections and assemblies, and partly exogenously to represent or promote the interests or values of different groups in new, larger and more complex societies.

In historical terms, voting 'in block' for a partisan list of candidates was not an institutionally-induced, but a strategy-induced behaviour. In the old-fashioned way, certain men who were judged to be distinguished for their professional or other activities were announced as being eligible by newspapers or offered themselves as candidates. Gradually, elected representatives moved to organise their supporters and present lists or tickets of candidates. The success of this new way may lie in the fact that 'party' candidacies and labels provide the voters with very cheap information about their candidates, which, in large constituencies and complex societies may be more difficult to obtain on those candidates who are not labelled in this way. This may move voters to vote in block rather than to choose their most preferred individual candidates.

Party inducements to voting in block were crucially aided in some countries and periods by the form of the ballot, which is, of course, an institutional feature of elections. In the earliest times alluded to above, oral voting or handwritten ballots facilitated the voting for individual candidates regardless of their possible grouping or factional allegiance. At some time, approximately the 1830s and 1840s for Britain, the United States of America and a few countries in Western Europe, the parties began to print their own ballots, listing only their own candidates. The voter needed only to cast the paper in the ballot box without marking any candidate in order to vote for the entire list (the 'general ticket'). Typically, party ballots were of various sizes, colours and shapes, and thus distinguishable to the election officials, the candidates, the party organisers and the voters.

Still, splitting the vote between candidates from different parties was possible by crossing out and writing in names or by turning in multiple party ballots with votes marked on each. In fact, in nineteenth century England, about half of the districts with two seats rendered 'split' representation of two different groupings (Cox 1984). But in the United States of America, by about 1890, a single party swept all the seats in almost 90 per cent of elections in multi-member districts (Calabrese 2000).

The so-called 'Australian ballot' again made non-partisan voting for individual candidates relatively easier. The new ballot, which was now printed and distributed by the electoral authority, listed the candidates of all parties instead of only one. As its name indicates, this new form of ballot was first introduced in the British colonies of Australia in 1856, expanded to New Zealand, Britain, Canada, Belgium, and several states in the USA during the second half of the nineteenth century, and was later adopted by most other countries with democratic experience.

The Australian ballot ensures a secret vote if the procedure includes a booth where the voter can mark the ballot unobserved. In some cases, the ballot requires the voters to vote for each candidate for whom they want to vote, which facilitates the choice of individual candidates regardless of their party affiliation; but in other cases it is also possible to vote for all candidates of a party with a single mark, which still favours block voting.

Initially, factions and parties tended to be loose and fluctuating groupings of individuals who joined together to support a particular leader or policy, but from the beginning they were viewed with suspicion as being destroyers of previously existing unity and consensus. In seventeenth and eighteenth century Britain and North America, there is much evidence of a considerable degree of hostility towards parties and partisanship. Political actors eventually acknowledged that in mass elections in large societies, where the homogeneity of interests and values that had prevailed in small, simple communities during the previous eras was decreasing, the formation of political factions was unavoidable and perhaps even necessary to make the political representation of a diversity of groups possible. Gradually, tension was developing between the recurring suspicion of partisan divisions and the seeming inevitability of partisan organisation. Parties were eventually conceived as 'unavoidable evils'.

Under traditional electoral rules conceived for the selection of individual candidates, the formation of electoral factions or parties introduced biased and partial representation. In comparison with the open ballot system, 'voting in block' for a list could change election results radically, typically producing a single party 'sweep' based on a minority of votes, or two-party polarisation. Traditional formulas of voting and elections, using plurality rule, majority run-off or other procedures supposedly based on the majority principle, were unable to guarantee actual majority support from voters' first preferences for the winner and, in a context of increasing social complexity and political pluralism, tended to produce minority winners and socially or ethnically strongly biased governments. In some crucial cases, it was largely as a consequence of this type of experience that different political leaders, candidates and parties began to seek alternative, less intuitive, or 'spontaneous' electoral rules likely to be less advantageous for the best organised faction or party. In more recent times, this has also induced some party members and politically motivated scholars to devise and choose new electoral and voting rules and procedures.

The Invention of New Electoral Rules
To the extent that parties and factionalisation were accepted as unavoidable, the re-establishment of broad voting support for the elected required the invention and introduction of new electoral rules different from the traditional system based on multi-member districts and majority rule. Different electoral rules and procedures for voting and elections were then invented to try to satisfy fair or suitable 'party

representation'. Some of these new inventions managed to combine new party representation with traditional or new forms of personal representation. But others threw away the baby with the bath water and neglected or just discarded any form of personal representation.

Virtually all the new electoral rules and procedures that were created from the mid-nineteenth century onwards and that are widely used nowadays can be understood as innovative variations of the simple, traditional system identified above. They can be classified into three groups, depending on whether they changed the district magnitude, the ballot, or the rule.

The first group of new electoral rules implied a change of the district magnitude from multi-member to single-member districts, keeping, of course, both individual-candidate voting and majority rule. With smaller, single-member districts, a candidate that would have been defeated by a party sweep in a multi-member district could be elected. Thus, this system tends to produce more varied representation than multi-member districts with party block vote or closed lists, although less varied than multi-member districts with open ballot. However, when more than two parties or candidates run, single-seat districts can also produce minority winners. In addition, most candidates running in individual districts have tended to be nominated by political parties, thus replacing the traditional system of personal representation with one in which party representation strongly prevails.

The second group of new electoral rules implied new forms of ballot favouring individual-candidate voting despite the existence of party candidacies, while maintaining the other two essential elements of the traditional system: multi-member districts and majority rule. By 'limited vote', each voter can vote for a lower number of candidates than seats to be filled so that one party can sweep as many seats as the voter has votes, but it is likely that the rest of the seats will be won by candidates of different political affiliation. The 'cumulative vote', by which voters can give more than one vote to some candidates, can also permit minority voters to elect some representatives. This kind of procedure may produce some representation for minority candidates, whether they are presented by a party or not, but they cannot prevent a single party 'sweep'. They were experimented with in Spain, Britain and Brazil, among other places, in the second half of the nineteenth century, but in most cases were soon abandoned.

Finally, the third group of new electoral rules implied the introduction of proportional formulas, which permit the maintenance of multi-member districts and, in some variants, open or individual-candidate ballot as well. Contrary to what well-established classifications may suggest, it can be argued that majority rule and proportional representation are not opposite stances in terms of the most basic principles when political parties are central political actors. The two corresponding types of rule cover different stages of the electoral process. With elections by majority rule, the winning party takes all and can usually access government. In contrast, assembly elections by proportional representation are not usually able immediately to produce a winning board or government, but they are just the first step in a process including further negotiations among parties in parliament or council to create a multi-party majority and the corresponding winner. Hence, in terms of general principles of governance, both majority and proportional electoral systems are based on the majority principle: both attempt to make the principle of majority government operational.

Actually, proportional formulas were invented in Europe in the late nineteenth century precisely with the aim of favouring majority rule. Traditional consensus vanished with the emergence of new political demands in large states and newly complex societies, the politicisation of new issues and the shaping of incompatible policy proposals, as alluded to above. Although proportional systems have been interpreted as a device to permit minority representation, they were strongly motivated by the aim of preventing actual minority rule as it could be produced by a single party sweep under usual procedures inspired in majority principle. It is precisely by including varied minorities in the assembly that proportional representation can facilitate the formation of an effective political majority to legislate and rule.

All these voting formulas – single-seat districts, limited or cumulative vote, proportional representation – and their variants, were invented at a time when electorates were enlarged and political parties emerged in a number of developed countries. They focus on party representation. The expected outcome of elections with the new rules was the production of an adequate representation of political parties in order to facilitate consistent, representative government.

However, many of these inventions, by focusing on party representation, neglected personal representation, which had been the only or main element in previous voting systems. This was particularly unfortunate, since the effects of ballot forms on personal representation, according to the analyses presented in several contributions to this book, would seem to be independent from the influence of electoral formulas on party representation. Reintroducing procedures for personal representation which can be compatible with fair party representation has therefore become a major challenge to achieving satisfactory electoral systems.

PERSONAL REPRESENTATION

Party representation is necessary in order to select the most relevant issues in the public agenda and to design public policy when different interests enter into conflict and people develop significantly different policy preferences. But, in turn, personal representation or the choice of individual representatives is also necessary to achieve a high quality of representation and effectively promote the preferences of the community once these are well defined.

For 'personal representation' we refer to the personal quality of representatives, that is, their reliability and ability to fulfil electoral promises and respond to voters' demands. The presumption may be that fair party representation can be satisfactory for achieving consistent political parties and clear-cutting policy design, but adding some degree of personal representation can improve legislative and policy performance.

The personal quality of individual representatives has been a traditional concern for the quality of representative democracy. John Stuart Mill (1865), for instance, already referred by the mid-nineteenth century to the 'grade of intelligence in the representative body', complained that 'it is becoming more and more difficult for any one who has only talents and character to gain admission into the House of Commons', and remarked on the importance of voting procedures, together with internal party rules in the selection of electoral candidates.

In order to fulfil the classic aspiration to be 'governed by the best', democracy requires that talented and skilful people should run in elections. In current times, the complexity of the public agenda, the concentration of political communication into unilateral messages from politicians through the mass media, and certain institutional complications have raised new concerns about the 'distance' between citizens and representatives and the quality of the latter. In certain democratic regimes, the decision to run for public office in elections, can largely depend on the potential candidate's opportunity costs. Skilful individuals with alternative attractive jobs may decline a political career..

In many elections, the selection of candidates and likely office-holders greatly depends on a party's internal procedures. Furthermore, both in single-seat districts, such as in Britain, and in closed party list systems with proportional representation, such as in Spain, most seats are 'safe', that is, they are always allocated to the same party in successive elections. This means that the choice of representatives by the voters is largely replaced with the nomination of candidates by internal party processes. With single-seat districts and closed lists, 'party selection is equal to election', as remarked by Nir Atmor, Reuven Y. Hazan and Gideon Rahat in Chapter 2 of this book.

From the point of view of citizens' participation in the selection of representatives, therefore, the electoral ballot is crucial. It can be expected that the greater the opportunities for voters to choose individual candidates, the better the personal qualities of the elected can be. Some classifications and analyses of voting formulas for individual candidates have focused on the degree of either the party-centred or candidate-centred nature of elections and forms of 'intra-party' competition, the degree of either localistic issues or large-scale public goods that they tend to promote, and other aspects of the electoral *supply* (most notably Katz 1994; Shugart and Carey 1995; Grofman 2005). A different point of view from the *demand* side, that is, from voters' opportunities to choose high-quality representatives, is adopted in this book. In this respect, procedures for personal representation can be classified for the opportunities of choice and the proportion of seats for which the voter can choose political parties and individual candidates.

Ballot Forms

We propose a new classification of voting procedures for its ability to produce different degrees of party representation and personal representation. Two elements of the ballot form can be taken into account: the number of choices available to the voter and the opportunity to vote for either political parties or individual candidates. Three groups of ballot forms can be distinguished, which can be called 'closed', 'semi-open' and 'open', respectively.

First, 'closed' voting procedures give voters only one choice, which is for a party candidacy. They include the single-seat system (like, for instance, the British

House of Commons), as well as some mixed systems permitting the voters to choose only one candidate (as in Mexico), and the party closed list system (as in Spain). All these systems, in spite of their differences, coincide in that they give the voters one single choice. It happens that the systems giving the voter only one choice always involves one party candidacy, since even if in the two first aforementioned forms of ballot the voter votes nominally for an individual candidate, in fact every candidate is appointed by a party, and the voter merely votes for the candidate appointed by the party. The voter chooses only a party, even if the names of the candidates might be written in the ballot. Actually in some cases the names of the candidates does not even appear in the ballot, both in single-seat systems (as, for instance, in some states in India) and in closed list systems (as in Portugal). Thus, ballot forms with only one choice implies the choice for a political party: all these procedures serve to produce party representation, but not direct personal representation of voters separated from party representation.

A second group of 'semi-open' forms of ballot gives the voters more than one choice, which always involves both a party and one or more individual candidates. Several procedures can be included in this category. The two-round system (as used, for example, in France) gives the voter two choices, separated in time, each for a candidate, typically nominated by a party. Likewise, the primary election system for the selection of candidates (as implemented in most states of the USA for most elections) also gives the voter two choices for individual candidates involving a party choice.

The other procedures we propose to include in this category give the voter two simultaneous choices for party and for candidate. The double vote (as in Germany and Hungary) gives the voter two choices, respectively, for a party and for a candidate who may not be of the party. Preferential list systems enable the voter to choose a party and one or more candidates from that party. Variants of this ballot form can be distinguished depending on whether voting for some individual candidate is compulsory (as in Finland) or optional (as in Belgium). But the two variants give the voter two choices, even if with the second variant a voter, whose preference order for individual candidates may coincide with the order in which they are presented by the party, exerts only one choice.

Finally, the 'open' systems offer the voter more than two choices for both party and individual candidates. In ordinal rank ballots (as in Australia and Ireland), the voters can order some or all of the candidates according to their preferences, regardless of the party for which they are presented. In some mixed systems, the voters can choose a party and a candidate who may not be of the party, but they can also select some candidates within the chosen party by a preferential list system (as in Lithuania). Finally, the open ballot (or 'panachage') allows the voter to choose as many candidates as seats up for election, regardless of the party to which they are affiliated (as in Switzerland). So, with all these forms, the voter can vote for more than one party and more than one candidate at the same time.

It should be noted that this classification of ballot forms is independent from the one usually derived from the elements for party representation mentioned above: district magnitude and electoral formula. 'Closed', 'semi-open' and 'open' ballots are compatible with 'majority', 'mixed' and 'proportional' rules. It happens that some majority rule systems, for example in Australia, can produce better results regarding the selection of candidates for personal representation than some proportional systems, for example in Spain, because the former example uses an ordinal rank ballot and the latter example uses a closed list. Likewise, a proportional system with a preferential list, like in Finland, can be better for personal representation than a majority rule single-seat system as in Britain, and so on. We are dealing, thus, with a two-dimensional issue, producing, in our simplified classification, up to nine categories, all with illustrative cases in current democratic regimes. As the studies collected in this book focus on assembly or presidential elections, the analysis could be extended to council, mayoral and other single-person office elections, and to new rules and procedures (as proposed, in particular, by Brams 2008). See Table 1.1 for the two-dimensional classification and Table 1.2 for data on forty-five major democracies.

Table 1.1: A two-dimensional classification of electoral systems

Personal representation

	Majority	Mixed	Proportional
Open	**Ordinal rank** (all candidates) Australia, San Francisco	**Open mixed** (1 candidate + some party candidates) Bavaria, Lithuania	**Open ballot** (all candidates) Luxembourg, Switzerland
Semi-open	**Two rounds** (1 party candidate +1 party candidate) France, United States	**Double vote** (1 candidate + 1 party) Germany, Hungary	**Preferential list** (some party candidates) Brazil, Netherlands
Closed	**Single seat** (1 party candidate) Great Britain, Canada	**Single candidate** (1 party candidate) Mexico, Senegal	**Closed list** (1 party) Israel, Spain

→ Party representation

Note: A long the horizontal axis, electoral systems are classified for their formulas in favour of party representation, whether based on majority, mixed or proportional rules. The vertical axis classifies electoral systems for their different ballot forms for personal representation, whether closed, semi-open or open.

introduction: personal and party representation | 11

Table 1.2: Party and Personal Representation in electoral systems

Party representation	Personal representation	Lower house
	CLOSED	
Majority	Single seat	Great Britain, Canada, India
Mixed	Single candidate	Mexico
Proportional	Closed list	Bulgaria, Italy, Portugal, Romania, Spain, Argentina, Costa Rica, Israel
	SEMI-OPEN	
Majority	Two rounds Primary	France United States of America
Mixed	Double vote	Germany, Hungary, Japan, Korea, New Zealand
Proportional	Open list (preferential vote)	Austria, Belgium, Cyprus, Czech Republic, Denmark, Estonia, Finland, Greece, Latvia, Netherlands, Norway, Poland, Slovakia, Slovenia, Sweden, Brazil, Chile, Peru, Indonesia
	OPEN	
Majority	Ordinal rank	Australia, Malta
Mixed	Open mixed	Lithuania
Proportional	Ordinal rank	Ireland
	Open ballot (panachage)	Luxembourg, Switzerland, Uruguay

Note: Author's own elaboration with data as for the end of 2009.

CHOICES AND CONSEQUENCES: A RESEARCH AGENDA

A number of suggestions on the origins and consequences of different ballot forms are presented in the following pages. Most of the hypotheses and empirical findings offered here, as they are based on the contributions collected in this book, are innovative or have not been previously subjected to systematic exploration. Therefore, they may become platforms for further research rather than conclusive statements. First, some political and institutional contexts for the choice of different rules for personal representation are discussed. Second, a focus is cast on certain 'proximate' political consequences of ballot forms that can be observed on party and candidate strategies, as well as on voters' behaviour and their relations with the elected representatives.

Choosing Ballot Forms

In order to deal with the choice of ballot forms for personal representation, we should approach the relations between voting rules and political parties by not focusing on the number of these parties, as in so many studies of electoral systems, but rather focus on the relative strength of organised parties and individual candidates. As has been studied for many decades, the choice of electoral rules for party representation depends on the party system. As stylised by the 'Micromega rule', which states that 'the larger prefer the small, and the small prefer the large', a dominant party or two large parties tend to prefer small districts, particularly with a single seat each, by majority rule, while multiple small parties tend to prefer large districts with proportional rules. With this approach, we have been dealing with the relations between the rules for party representation and the numbers of parties.

In order to explain the choice and maintenance of rules for personal representation, the relevant variables are different. From the chapters compiled in this book, some tentative hypotheses can be formulated, respectively for old and new electoral democratic regimes.

First, for countries and communities with long traditions of voting and elections, typically using the kind of electoral system with multi-member districts and majority rule discussed at the beginning of this introductory chapter, the adoption of the Australian ballot, which is provided not by the parties as under the previous system, but by the electoral authority, seems to have been a crucial moment. The Australian ballot was conceived to ensure the secrecy of the vote. But its design can vary immensely.

If the model adopted by the electoral authority somehow respects a previous tradition of open voting for individual candidates, the new ballot may include the names of the candidates and give the voter the choice of voting for some of them. This may imply more institutional continuity, as the historical experience of the cantons in Switzerland presented in this book by George Lutz (see Chapter 9), in particular, would seem to suggest. The open ballot used in Switzerland, which was made compatible with new rules of proportional representation by the early twentieth century, implies, in fact, strong continuity with the choice of individual representatives typical of previous periods with majority rule. Other cases can be identified in the corresponding survey.

Alternatively, in other contexts in which political parties are sufficiently strong as organisations and are interested in promoting only those candidates previously selected by their own internal procedures, they can make the new ballot an institutional instrument for their strategy of inducing voters to vote in block for a closed list of candidates. In this case, previously informal party ballots would have become the only available form of legally available ballot. Indeed the introduction of the Australian ballot in the late nineteenth century coincided with the moment in which many of the new electoral rules above reported were invented.

In other cases in continental Europe and elsewhere, some decisions on the electoral system made at the time of introducing this typically mid- or late-nineteenth century institutional reform in favour of the secret vote may have reflected the relative strength of political parties and individual candidates. The alternative variables to consider are consistently structured parties versus fluid and unstable candidacies, respectively implying significant leadership capacity to control party candidates and members of parliament or not. While this is a greatly understudied subject, a focus on this period of innovation in electoral institutions is certainly worth exploring in further research. In the absence of sufficient data on party organisation in past historical periods, a first provisional suggestion may be to take the age of the parties as a rough proxy for their relative strength.

A second hypothesis can be more appropriate for most current democracies. As electoral rules and voting procedures (including the Australian ballot) have been established in recent times, they may have implied lower institutional creativity. Most institutional designers tend to learn from others' experience or the existing literature. In his survey of open list systems in this book, Lauri Karvonen considers the hypothesis that sudden democratisation from a dictatorial regime can favour the adoption of closed party lists strongly favouring party representation. Some institution-makers in this kind of context typically argue that, with relatively new and weak parties in a just improvised and fragile democratic regime, personal representation might become a factor of political instability. Consequently, preferential list systems, and possibly other semi-open or open forms of ballot, can be introduced more easily by political parties when the party system has been significantly well structured over a period of sound democratic experience, or perhaps just after some previous electoral experience by political parties under an authoritarian regime. Thus, there would be a line of succession from non-democratic to soft-authoritarian, semi-democratic or democratic systems which would, first, favour party representation, and would bring about semi-open or open forms of personal representation at some later stage as the process moves ahead.

Some significant connection between party procedures for candidate selection and forms of ballot can also exist and contribute to create long-term stable sets of equilibrium formulas. For instance, openness at the stage of selecting the candidates, by means, for example, of primary elections, may be an alternative to the openness of the ballot, thus making the adoption of the latter less likely. In another instance, closed party lists may induce party leaders to strengthen their grip over the organisation and make the parties more rigid, closed and reluctant to open the system. As suggestive as these hypotheses look and can be illustrated with a few outstanding cases, they certainly require further empirical verification.

Political Consequences

Many political consequences have been attributed to different rules on district magnitude and electoral formula, but not always with neat assumptions or solid empirical support. In order to deal with the consequences of different ballot forms, we suggest focusing, first, on the 'proximate' political consequences that can be observed on party and candidate strategies, as well as on voter behaviour and voters' relations with the elected representatives. The rest of the consequences should be considered relatively 'remote', indirect, and perhaps identifiable in terms of constraints, limits, and opportunities, rather than determining specific decisions or outcomes, especially as regards to the quality of representation, legislative and policy-making performance, the scale of public goods, and people's degree of satisfaction with the democratic regime.

Let us start with party and candidate strategies. In an experimental exercise, it has been found that the different personal quality of candidates can affect the electoral equilibrium in the direction of producing greater policy distance between the contenders. The rationale for this is that relatively low quality candidates have to differentiate their policy positions in order to try to compete with other candidates who enjoy an advantage on the personal dimension. Likewise, relatively high quality candidates can exploit the opponent's weakness by adopting the opponent's policy position. As long as the candidates match each other on policy positions, the better candidate in terms of personal quality will have the advantage; as long as they differ in their policy positions, this advantage may count for less in the eyes of the voter. An implication of this observation is that higher quality candidates should be expected to be associated to more moderate policy positions than lower quality ones. (Aragonès and Palfrey 2004).

Different personal quality of candidates competing for the same seats can emerge in voting systems strongly favouring personal representation. This is consistent with the correlation between high levels of personal representation as induced by ordinal rank ballot and the predominance of valence policies in the public agenda, as noted by Michael Marsh in his analysis of the Irish system in Chapter 8 of this book. To the extent that party representation prevails, party competition can develop on the basis of position issues, which imply competition between distant policy proposals (such as in school or foreign policies). In contrast, if personal representation prevails, candidates may tend to focus on valence issues, that is, those on which there is broad consensus and almost everybody wants more of (such as peace or prosperity). Precisely, electoral competition on valence issues consists of claiming credit or getting blamed for them, mostly on the basis of candidates' credibility and effectiveness.

With other ballot systems not favouring personal representation, the differences in personal quality of the candidates can more likely depend on different parties' procedures for candidate selection. In the absence of homogeneous regulation of internal party processes to select electoral candidates, different parties in the same institutional context can choose different formulas (including, for instance, primary elections, party conference nomination, or leadership appointment). Higher quality candidates would be those who would have been able to replace pressures from internal party's activists and militants, usually in favour of extreme policy positions, with the appeal of voters. Thus, diversity of internal party procedures may lead to greater policy divergence among candidacies than in contexts with homogeneous party rules.

The other interesting proximate consequence of different ballot forms refers to the relations between voters and the elected representatives. Note that we are dealing with likely effects of institutional rules, which should be explained in terms of incentives provided for different types of behaviour. A different subject would be the analysis of voter's motivations, which may be conceived as mediations between institutions and choices. There is, in particular, an extensive literature on the 'personal vote' focusing on voter's motives which is not going to be reviewed here. In some analyses it is presumed that re-elected representatives in single-seat systems tend to maintain close contacts with their voters and be more accountable in their endeavour, while the opposite happens in proportional systems. This presumption implies, however, a blatant confusion between proportional rules and closed party lists. While closed party lists indeed discourage close relations between voters and the elected representatives, semi-open and open forms of ballots with proportional rules may create opportunities for both personal vote and party vote and make personal and party representation not mutually exclusive, but to some extent harmoniously compatible.

In contrast to long-transmitted assumptions, Helen Margetts argues in Chapter 3 of this book that the system of single-seat districts in Great Britain does not serve 'personal representation' well. Most of the interactions between representatives and their constituents deal with private goods rather than collective goods (of the type usually labelled 'pork barrel' in the United States). Margetts goes so far as to compare a large portion of representatives' work with that of social workers rather than legislators. She puts her hopes for improved personal representation in alternative electoral systems, including ordinal rank ballots that are already used in the United Kingdom for other types of elections.

More along the lines of conventional wisdom, Pedro Riera documents in Chapter 4 the overwhelming weight of party choices with the system of closed party lists. By using innovative hypotheses and new data from Spain, Riera is able to show tiny variations in amounts of party votes across districts in different elections when the top candidates in the party closed list change to well-known persons, such as prime ministers, members of regional cabinets, mayors, and incumbent members of parliament with long experience in it. The slight effect of the candidate decreases for lower places in the list. His findings can be interpreted as revealing some wishes from the voters to select the best individual representatives, even if the ballot system does not permit them to do so explicitly. But he concludes that, all in all, Spanish voters vote for parties rather than for candidates.

In comparison, personal representation thrives with semi-open and open forms of ballot. Some accumulated knowledge and the contributions to this book include the following empirical observations. Semi-open ballot forms with two rounds of voting by majority rule seem to encourage relatively high participation of voters in the choice of individual candidates. In particular, with the two-round system, as in France and other countries, the levels of participation in the two rounds of voting is very similar, with differences between the two rounds mostly depending on the expected competitiveness between the two surviving candidates in the second round. Participation in primary elections in the United States has also increased over time, reaching more than 60 per cent of the voters in the final election during the presidential season of 2008. In his thorough analysis, of presidential primary elections in the United States and several Latin American countries in Chapter 5, John M. Carey and Harry J. Enten conclude that for parties using primary elections, 'increasing personal representation appears to be complementary with the overall partisan goal of winning elections, not at odds with it'.

Regarding mixed systems, in Chapter 6 Louis Massicotte emphasises that whenever the voters have a chance to express preferences for individual candidates, 'they seize the opportunity', including modifications in the ranking of candidates, the defeat of candidates who otherwise would have been elected thanks to their prime positions in the party lists, and the election of candidates who do not enjoy this advantage. With double vote, it has been observed that in Germany increasing amounts of voters split their choices between a party and a candidate from another party (Klingemann and Wessels 2003; Gschwend et al. 2006)

With preferential lists, Lauri Karvonen shows different tendencies in Chapter 7. In some countries, very large portions of the electorate tend to make use of the opportunity to vote for individual candidates, as in Belgium and Brazil, and in these as well as in others in which the amounts of voters making those choices are relatively lower, such as Austria and the Netherlands, there is a tendency towards increasing numbers of preferential votes in successive elections. In some other countries, in contrast, the amounts of preferential votes are stable, as in Denmark and Sweden. But this may reflect the adaptation of political parties to use more open formulas of internal selection of candidates in order to be able to offer lists that can be accepted by most voters as they are, an indirectly induced effect of ballot rules which can also improve personal representation in the system.

With ordinal rank ballot, in Ireland, according to Michael Marsh in Chapter 8, more than one third of voters say that they vote for the candidate rather than for the party, while about one another third of them shifts between the two dimensions of representation at different elections. However, the voters who take the opportunity to change the order of candidates as given in the ballot are a smaller percentage of the total, which suggests that, also in this case, political parties try to do their best to present the candidates in an order that can be accepted by people that care about personal representation.

With open ballot, in Switzerland, as documented by Georg Lutz in Chapter 9, voters introduce many changes in the order of candidates and very few vote for the party lists as given. But people vote mostly for candidates from one party and only a few from other parties, even if the ballot permits them to do so.

Let us remark again that we are dealing with institutional opportunities and incentives, not with observed actual behaviours, which always involve a limited sample of relevant cases to study. The real outcomes in some institutional systems may indeed not coincide with the expected effects, as also happens with electoral rules for party representation and other institutional devices. For instance, the degree of proportionality between party votes and seats in the relative majority rule system for the House of Representatives of the United States is on many occasions significantly higher than, for example, in Spain, where proportional rules are officially enforced. The explanation for the former is that very high disproportionalities between votes and seats at district level (since the single winner takes all, whatever his share of votes) can be compensated across districts in favour of each of the two larger parties, while on some other occasions the distortions can accumulate and even make the winner in votes the loser in seats. Analogously, in a closed system of personal representation, it may happen that some highly qualified leaders can reach the top of the party by some chance events and process and produce better results than could be expected from the incentives provided by the system. This kind of possible empirical observations, however, does not deny the validity of institutional analysis for long-term predictions in a high number of cases, as well as for prudent institutional design and advice.

All in all, there seems to exist, as is logical to expect, significant empirical correlations between high opportunities for *personal representation* in the ballot form and the electoral system, the adoption of *moderate policy positions* by parties and candidates, the use of *open internal procedures by political parties*, and the actual *choice of individual candidates by voters*.

More specifically, a line of causality can proceed in this direction: in a consensual community with no important diversity of policy preferences, the selection of individual candidates can prevail over the choice of party; then, loose partisan groupings can adopt ballot forms favouring personal representation, as would have been the case in traditional local level elections. The other way around, the prevalence of party representation, as with closed lists, may make the parties more rigid and favour adversarial strategies and political confrontation. But in a well-established democracy, the introduction of institutional opportunities for the voters to choose individual candidates can move political parties to adopt more open procedures for the selection of candidates, and both the profusion of voters' personal choices and the parties' openness may promote the adoption of moderate policy positions in the electoral competition. In a future research agenda, this kind of significant relationships should be submitted to broad empirical tests and discussion.

As shown in several of the contributions to this book, weaker although perceptible correlations are found between ballot forms and other aspects of the political process such as electoral turnout, number of parties in the system, the degree of proportionality between party votes and party seats, women's representation, the turnover of members of parliament, the propensity of legislators to keep or shift party allegiances and coalitions, officers' corruption, and so on. Some of the just mentioned elements can depend on ballot forms only indirectly, through parties' strategies and voters' behaviour, or derive more closely from other regulations of the system, other institutional elements of the political system and even non-political variables. This also suggests that the two main dimensions of the electoral systems discussed here are largely independent and no significant trade-off among them is faced at the time of institutional choice.

It is interesting to note, nevertheless, that, according to some tentative hypotheses discussed in this book, relatively open procedures to select candidates can keep party members together, as they can feel free to promote their candidacies under relatively fair procedures, and indirectly maintain a low number of parties in the system. The United States is a clear example of the correlation between primary elections and a system of two parties which are inclusive tents. In contrast, closed party lists and similar devices not permitting personal representation can foster internal party tensions among party members and encourage party splits, as in some relatively recent European democracies.

Likewise, the possibility to vote for individual candidates can make the voters more faithful to their preferred political parties than if they have to choose between the party political label and the personal quality of the individual candidates, which may not always coincide. Open or semi-open systems for personal representation can thus indirectly favour lower electoral volatility in successive elections and higher stability of party representation.

Much more research is needed on this important and neglected subject. Regarding explanatory analyses, we should take into account that relations between different variables such as ballot forms and other aspects of the political process cannot be clarified with only statistical correlations of appropriate data, but they also require the specification of the mechanisms by which they may exist. Regarding the normative discussion about 'the best' electoral system mentioned at the beginning of this introduction, potential answers should bear in mind that a representative democratic government requires both fair party representation and efficient personal representation. In the final analysis, new contributions should help to understand how, by direct and indirect means, different types of ballot forms for party representation and personal representation can contribute to different levels of quality of democratic regimes.

THE BOOK

This book offers analyses of different ballot forms and procedures of voting for political parties and for individual candidates, their origins and consequences. They develop detailed analytic narratives for countries that innovatively introduced some of the procedures, as well as comparative data and discussion for some of the most common ballot forms permitting relatively high degrees of personal representation. We start with different procedures of candidate selection, which are displayed and discussed by Nir Atmor, Reuven Hazan and Gideon Rahat. Then, two significant examples of closed ballots are addressed: the single-seat system in Great Britain, which is critically reviewed by Helen Margetts, and the closed party list system in Spain, which is innovatively studied by Pedro Riera. A variety of 'semi-open' systems are put under scrutiny: primary elections, as they have been recently used in the United States and Latin America, by John M. Carey and Harry J. Enten; all the variants of mixed systems giving voters the opportunity to vote for both a party and some candidates, by Louis Massicotte; and the several forms of preferential vote for individual candidates within a party list, thoroughly analysed by Lauri Karvonen. Finally, two egregious examples of open ballot strongly promoting personal representation are well documented: the ordinal rank in Ireland, by Michael Marsh, and the open ballot in Switzerland, by George Lutz.

Most although not all the authors of this book joined this project at the Second Workshop on the Political Economy of Democracy, which was held at the Institute for Economic Analysis (of the Higher Council for Scientific Research, CSIC), in Barcelona, on 17–19 June 2009. We also want to thank the contributions of other participants in the workshop whose papers have not been collected in this book, but some of whose findings are explicitly or sometimes implicitly used in the Introduction and some chapters: Enriqueta Aragonès, Steven Brams, Paulo

T. Pereira, Joao A. Silva, Henk Van der Kolk, Dimitros Xefteris, as well as the encouragement and support of the Institute director, Clara Ponsatí, and the Institute's administrative staff, the assistance of Joan Ricart-Huguet, and the questions, reactions and interest of two dozen attendants who also helped us to think more and better.

From the very beginning, all the participants in this project have shared the feeling to be opening a gate to an unjustly understudied subject with paramount consequences on the quality of democratic regimes, as well as potentially fruitful new venues for future research. Rather than becoming a final treatise on the subject, the success of this book would be in inducing further discussions and revisions, collections of empirical data, and practical applications of the ideas we dare to present.

chapter two | candidate selection
Nir Atmor, Reuven Y. Hazan and Gideon Rahat

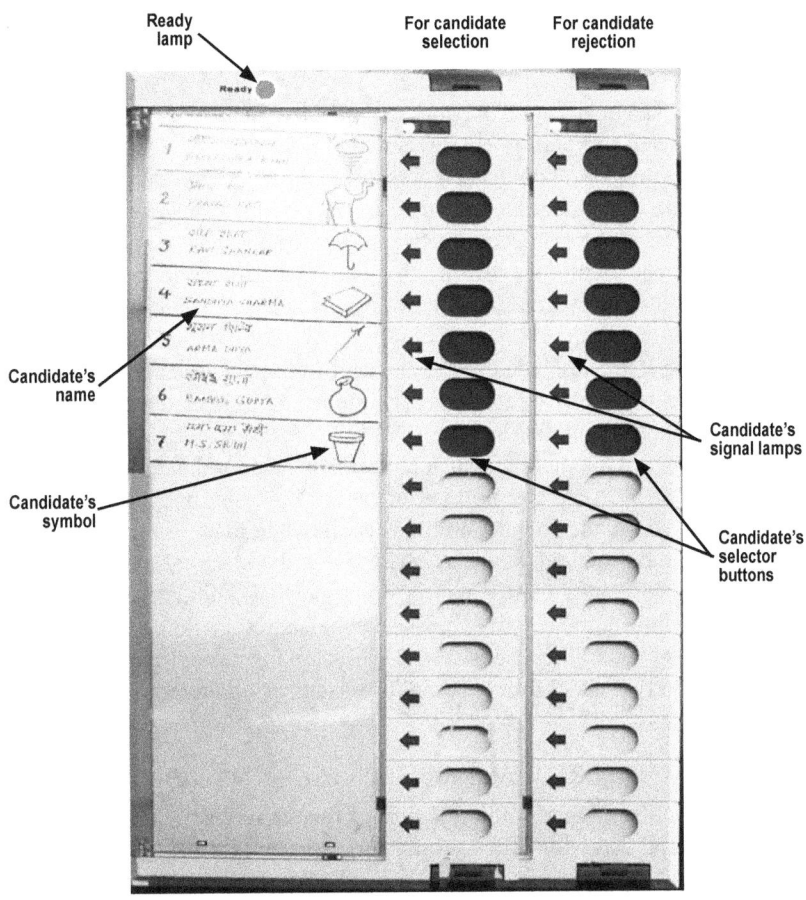

Electoral systems can be viewed as an important factor affecting the incentive to cultivate a personal vote, and thus as decisive for personal or party representation. But, the inter-party arena is not completely responsible for this outcome. Other arenas may also have a significant influence on the kind of representation, and may either support or undermine the impact of the electoral system. Candidate selection is such an arena. After all, almost any political aspirant, in any country, must pass two barriers in order to be elected to public office: being chosen by a selectorate and being elected by the voters. These two barriers vary in nature and relevance, they can be personal in nature or under the control of the party, but they are both significant and present everywhere. In this chapter we focus on the influence that the intra-party realm has on personal and party representation.

The study of candidate selection methods has recently been growing, although few have addressed the connection between candidate selection and the electoral system. The main attempt we identify in the literature to integrate both the inter-party and the intra-party vote in indices of personal versus party representation is Shugart (2001), who, in one of his three indices for candidate-centred versus party-centred systems, included the element of intra-party selection.[1] This paper clarifies the connection between electoral systems, intra-party selection and party versus personal representation.

First, we present the main dimensions that delineate candidate selection methods and connect them to the notions of personal versus party representation. Second, we illustrate the connection between the main dimensions that delineate candidate selection methods and the attributes of the electoral systems that enhance personal over party representation. We argue that candidate selection methods can play a crucial role in party versus personal representation, as demonstrated in the analysis of the political consequences of adopting more personal intra-party selection methods – which has become increasingly popular across both parties and countries.

PARTY AND PERSONAL REPRESENTATION WITHIN PARTIES

Candidate selection methods are the specific processes by which political parties choose their candidates for office prior to an election (Ranney 1981; Gallagher 1988a). On the one hand, since candidate selection methods are in most cases unregulated intra-party processes, they are less stable mechanisms than state institutional instruments such as electoral systems, and are relatively more prone to change. As such, they should be seen as reflecting politics. On the other hand, these changes are not frequent enough to justify an inclusive treatment of them as only a mirror. Thus, candidate selection methods should be treated as institutional mechanisms that both reflect the representative nature of the parties and can also affect personal and party representation.

---

1. De Esteban and López Guerra (1985) and Hazan and Voerman (2006) are rare exceptions, as is Strøm, Müller and Bergman (2003). Other authors mention the connection between these two levels of (s)election only in passing (for example: Duverger 1954; Gallagher 1988a; Lundell 2004). Carey and Shugart's (1995) assessment of the ballot already mentioned the ability of integrating both candidate selection and the electoral system, but this was significantly developed by Shugart (2001).

Our unit of analysis is a single party in a particular country at a specific time – which, we must emphasise, is quite different from the unit of analysis utilised when we focus on electoral systems. Many times, parties in a particular country use similar candidate selection methods, which may reflect constraints emanating from their specific traditions and institutional framework, as well as from the tendency of parties to imitate each other. Yet, the variance is still usually large enough within countries and across time to allow, in most cases, generalisations at the national level. The problem encountered in the study of candidate selection is that sometimes even focusing on a single party at a specific time is not sufficient, because different methods can be used by the same party in different districts. Moreover, many parties use systems that allow a significant role for more than one selectorate.

The procedure elaborated here for classifying candidate selection methods and their influence on personal and party representation is based on four criteria: candidacy, the selectorate, voting versus appointment, and decentralisation (Rahat and Hazan 2001; Hazan and Rahat 2006).[2]

Candidacy

Who can present himself or herself as a candidate of a particular party? Some parties are inclusive, as they grant the opportunity to compete to every eligible voter. Other parties impose requirements, such as long-time party membership, a pledge of loyalty, affiliation with certain organisations and additional restrictions. The number and degree of these requirements allows us to classify candidacy on a continuum according to the level of inclusiveness or exclusiveness.

At one end, the inclusive pole, where every voter can stand and there are no requirements from candidates, the party may have little to no influence as a gatekeeper. In other words, aspirants for office could practically impose themselves on the party, which must accept their candidacy, reluctantly or otherwise. Inclusivity may be the result of legal regulations, as is the case in the USA, but it can also be the trait of a party whose main interest is electoral success and is therefore open to any candidate who could help increase the party's share of the vote. Inclusiveness increases the potential candidate pool, and as the number of potential candidates grows, the personal qualifications of each of the candidates are emphasised.

At the other end, the exclusive pole, we encounter parties that impose a series of limitations upon aspirants.[3] This may be due to an attempt by the party to con-

---

2. Our arguments concerning the four dimensions of candidate selection could be seen as hypotheses. However, since we base our arguments on the available empirical data, they are more than mere hypotheses that must still be tested. Nonetheless, we make our arguments with caution, and hope to generate a healthy debate on this under-researched topic.

3. Probably the most exclusive example of candidacy requirements was in the Belgian Socialist Party in the 1960s. Beyond five years of party membership and membership in the Socialist trade union and health insurance fund also for at least five years, the party required membership and minimal purchases at the socialist co-op, a subscription to the party's newspaper and the holding of some party office. All of these pertained mainly to the potential candidate, but there were requirements placed on the candidate's family as well: his wife had to be a party member in the

trol the supply side of potential candidates, so that those who fulfil the enhanced eligibility requirements, and are subsequently both selected and elected, will behave according to the party line. In other words, specific restrictions may help not only to reduce the number of competitors, but also to assure certain behavioural patterns once in office and thus promote party representation. A party with strict candidacy requirements can arrive in office as a cohesive unit, manifesting a patent party culture, in so doing removing the need to utilise disciplinary measures in order to keep their elected representatives in line (Hazan 2003). Moreover, the party leadership can use the more exclusive candidacy requirements to reward loyalists and long-time activists, thereby creating a structure of selective party-focused incentives for potential candidates. In short, we argue that there is a linear relationship between inclusiveness in candidacy requirements and party versus personal representation.

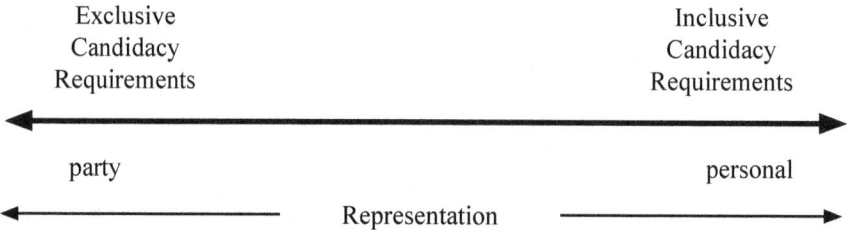

Figure 2.1: Candidacy requirements and party/personal representation

Selectorate

The selectorate is the body (or bodies) that selects the candidates. The selectorate can be composed of one person, or several or many people – up to the entire electorate of a given nation. The selectorate can also be placed on a continuum flanked by the most exclusive and the most inclusive. Between these two extremes we can classify different selectorates according to their extent of inclusion. One of the most familiar examples of a highly inclusive selectorate is the candidate-centred US non-partisan and blanket primaries in which every registered voter can vote for candidates from any party. The more inclusive selectorates, where a large number of participants take part in the selection process, tend to promote personal representation, while the more exclusive selectorates, such as a selected party agency or small elite, tend to favour party representation.

In exclusive selectorates, candidate selection is an intra-party matter, decided by a few leaders and senior apparatchiks behind closed doors. When a more inclusive selectorate is involved, candidate selection becomes a public contest in which candidates explicitly compete with their fellow partisans through personal campaigns. As Rahat and Sheafer (2007: 68–9) put it:

Selection through nominating committees symbolizes the cohesion of the

---

relevant organisation, enrolled in the trade union and insurance fund, while his children had to go to state schools and be members in the party youth organisation (Obler 1970; De Winter 1988).

group: It is about producing a balanced list of candidates through deliberation; usually, a selected party agency ratifies this list en-bloc. Selection by party agency and party members means that the aggregation of individual votes decides the composition of the list. The relatively small size of selected party agencies, as well as the deep involvement of their members in intrapartisan politics, enables selection coordination for the sake of producing a somewhat balanced candidate list, a team. Selection by the less informed, less committed, unstable, and atomistic crowd of party members transforms the process into a purely personal matter.

The connection between more inclusive participation in candidate selection and personal representation can be explained by the following. First, one of the consequences of widening participation to include party members or supporters is the massive registration drives by the candidates. These produce 'instant' members or supporters who join the party only to select a specific candidate, and not necessarily to promote the party as whole nor to stay affiliated for any extended time (Carty and Cross 2006; Rahat and Hazan 2006). Second, it is expected that candidates who are selected by an inclusive selectorate will be exposed to various pressures (including non-partisan ones), which could be both quite different from, and even contradictory to, that of the party programme, and the candidates will have to be responsive to them (Rahat 2008b).

When the selectorate is exclusive (i.e. a nominating committee) the incentives tend to favour party representation. The relationship between exclusive selectorates and party representation can be explained by the following. First, the more exclusive selectorates are based on a loyal group of activists operating on the grounds of promoting the party as whole. Second, legislators who are selected by an exclusive selectorate will be exposed to fewer pressures to deviate from the party programme, so their range of values and interests will be largely limited to those that the party claims to represent.

Kitschelt (1988: 130) encapsulated the major points of our argument when he claimed that, 'The very emphasis on individualist, participatory norms and ideologies is likely to create unexpected perverse effects in the parties' behaviour, such as a lack of activists' commitment to party work, high turnover, and the rise of informal party elites.' Candidate selection in an inclusive selectorate may thus become a personal enterprise rather than a partisan matter, an enterprise of instant members recruited by individual politicians and not one of active members loyal to the party.

In short, we argue that here too, as in candidacy, there is a linear relationship between the inclusiveness of the selectorate, and party versus personal representation. However, this is not so for the most exclusive end of the relationship – the single party leader. When we reach this end of the selectorate dimension, we once again encounter aspects of personal representation – loyalty is to the leader, who might or might not adhere to the party programme, which could in turn be based on the party leader. In other words, the peak of party representation could be the exclusive party elite, rather than the polar end of the continuum exhibited by a single party leader.

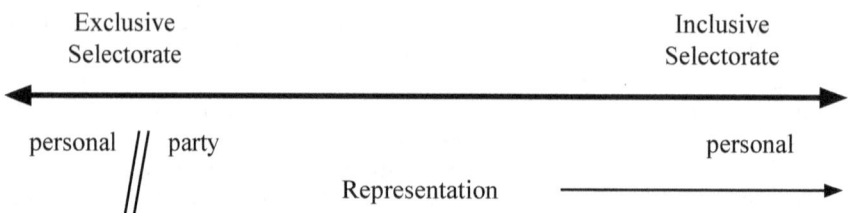

Figure 2.2: The selectorate and party/personal representation

Integrating the first two dimensions of candidacy and the selectorate, according to the levels of inclusiveness or exclusiveness, can demonstrate the connection between candidate selection methods and party-personal representation. In the US case, when candidacy and the selectorate are inclusive, the party has hardly a say when it comes to candidacies, and personal representation is maximised.[4] On the other hand, a high level of inclusiveness on one dimension combined with a high level of exclusiveness in the other would mean that the party leadership, or the party apparatus, retains control over the process, and thus the personal ramifications associated with inclusiveness can be offset. For example, the Italian Communist Party (PCI) included non-members as candidates, but this was done under the supervision of an exclusive selectorate (Wertman 1988). In a similar way, the Israeli ultra-religious parties have no formal rules regarding candidacy, yet the highly exclusive selectorates ensure that all selected candidates will be ultra-religious men. The Belgian Socialist Party acted in an opposite manner when it allowed an inclusive selectorate of party members to select among candidates who were screened using highly exclusive terms of candidacy (Obler 1970). If both candidacy and the selectorate are exclusive, party representation is maximised.

Voting versus Appointment
The third criterion, voting versus appointment, also has implications on party and personal representation. A voting procedure is one in which the aggregation of votes alone determines whether a specific person is to be the party's candidate in the general elections, or his position on the party list. In a pure voting system, all candidates are selected through a voting procedure, and no other selectorate can change the composition of the list. In a pure appointment system, candidates are appointed with no need for approval by any party agency except the nominating organ itself. Cases located between these extremes are called appointment-voting systems. Since the literature almost ignores this issue, we have to base the discussion in this section on theoretical considerations.

The connection between voting and personal representation is rather apparent – only voting procedures allow explicit competition among contestants; and where

---

4. Scarrow (2005: 9) describes one of the more well-known cases. 'A notorious instance of what happens in a party without such a safeguard occurred in the U.S. state of Louisiana in 1991, when voters in a Republican primary nominated David Duke as the party's gubernatorial candidate. Party leaders could personally repudiate the candidate, an outspoken white supremacist and former Ku Klux Klan member, but they had no way of denying him the use of the party label.'

candidates compete with one another in intra-party elections for the party nomination, it is not surprising that they will emphasise the personal over the party. To paraphrase Carey and Shugart (1995): voting procedures that differentiate candidates from their parties may induce politicians to cultivate a 'personal intra-party vote', thus emphasising personal over party representation.

Voting systems can be further distinguished on the basis of two elements. First, the position allocation formula according to their potential level of proportionality from proportional representation to various majoritarian systems. Second, the distinction between single-round (where all the candidates are selected at one and the same time) and multi-round (where candidates are selected gradually) selection methods.

Within this context, the proportional voting systems are usually less personalised while majoritarian systems are more personalised. In turn, the multi-round systems are usually less personal because they allow the party some control over the composition of candidates – if there is a problem, for example there are not enough women/minorities/labourers among the party's candidates, the multi-round system provides an opportunity for the party to fix this and create a more balanced team. Single-round voting systems are, in contrast, more personalised because they produce individual winners rather than an overall team.

An appointment procedure means that the power of selection is concentrated in the hands of a small group. However, this group is frequently composed of representatives of the major rivalling interests within the party, thus allowing for compromises rather than for a majoritarian takeover. The resulting candidate list can express the balance that the party organs think is appropriate in response to both inter-party (electoral image, personal popularity) and intra-party (loyalty, factional, social representatives) pressures and demands. Personal representation takes a back seat in appointment systems, and party representation is best served.[5]

In short, we argue that there is a largely dichotomous relationship between voting/appointment candidate selection methods and personal/party representation. While the extent of one kind of representation as opposed to the other can be affected by the actual voting system or by the scope of appointments.

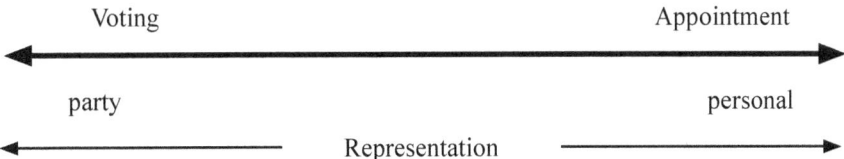

Figure 2.3: Voting vs appointment and party/personal representation

---

5. Indeed, there is a possibility that an exclusive selectorate would appoint, out of electoral considerations, those candidates who have a strong personal appeal, disregarding their loyalty record. Nonetheless, the national party leaders maintain the *potential* for punishing disloyal candidates, and thus such a case still supplies incentives for higher party unity.

Decentralisation
Candidate selection methods may be seen as decentralised when local party selectorates – such as a local leader, a local party agency, all party members or voters in an electoral district – nominate party candidates. Purely decentralised candidate selection methods – where every region selects a single local representative (either for candidacy in a SMD or for a list) – encourage personal representation. This may lead to pork-barrel politics and high responsiveness to local or regional level interests, which weaken the (national) party's influence. Decentralisation can also enhance the power of local selectorates to the point that it impairs the ability of the party to work cohesively in promoting national party programmes and policies. It must be stressed that a decentralised system can be highly exclusive – in other words, decentralisation and democratisation of candidate selection do not go hand in hand, the latter is more a result of an inclusive selectorate rather than decentralisation. For example, if a small nominating committee is the sole selector of candidates in each single member constituency, with no say for the party's central office, the candidate selection method would be highly decentralised and highly exclusive at the same time.

On the other hand, the selection of candidates based on purely centralised methods promotes the principle of party representation. When no sub-national party organisations have influence on the selection of candidates, the national party headquarters control the nomination process. This power over selection allows the party to choose loyal candidates, or to remove any disloyal ones. As a consequence, by controlling the nomination procedures the party can create incentives for candidates to behave like team players rather than as a collection of individuals.

In short, we can see a somewhat linear relationship between decentralisation of candidate selection and party/personal representation. A more centralised selection method will likely be more party-focused, and the decentralised processes will be more personal. However, this also depends on the extent of the first two dimensions – the level of inclusiveness of candidacy and the selectorate – in order to assess the extent of personal representation. Centralisation can offset some of the personal aspects of more inclusive candidacy or a more inclusive selectorate, or they can be advanced even further by decentralisation; whereas the personal aspects of decentralisation can be countered by more exclusive candidacy requirements or a more exclusive selectorate.

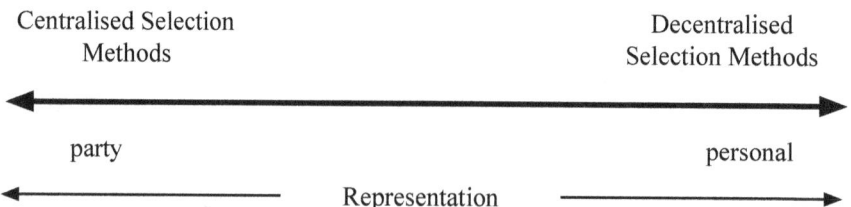

Figure 2.4: Decentralisation and party/personal representation

Figure 2.5 summarises our delineation of the four main dimensions of candidate selection and their connection to party and personal representation. Two important dimensions, candidacy and the selectorate, are both measured according to the degree of inclusiveness and both show a linear relationship with representation (albeit with a slight variation at the peak of exclusivity in the selectorate, the single leader). The other two dimensions show either a linear or even a dichotomous relationship with representation.

We can combine our estimation of the personalised/party nature of each dimension to provide a general picture of each party tendency towards party or personal representation. The significance of these differences is apparent when comparing the USA to the UK. Both countries use similar electoral systems, but when looking at candidate selection we witness a clear expression of the more personalised politics of the USA. The primaries used in the USA are highly inclusive in terms of both candidacy and the selectorate, they are also highly decentralised and are based solely on voting. In the UK, even after the democratisation of the last decades, the selection method is less inclusive. Moreover, exclusive and central appointing bodies still play an important role in the screening of candidates. This comparison also shows that the use of highly personalised candidate selection methods – like those in the USA – can counter the influence of the party-centred single member district elections.

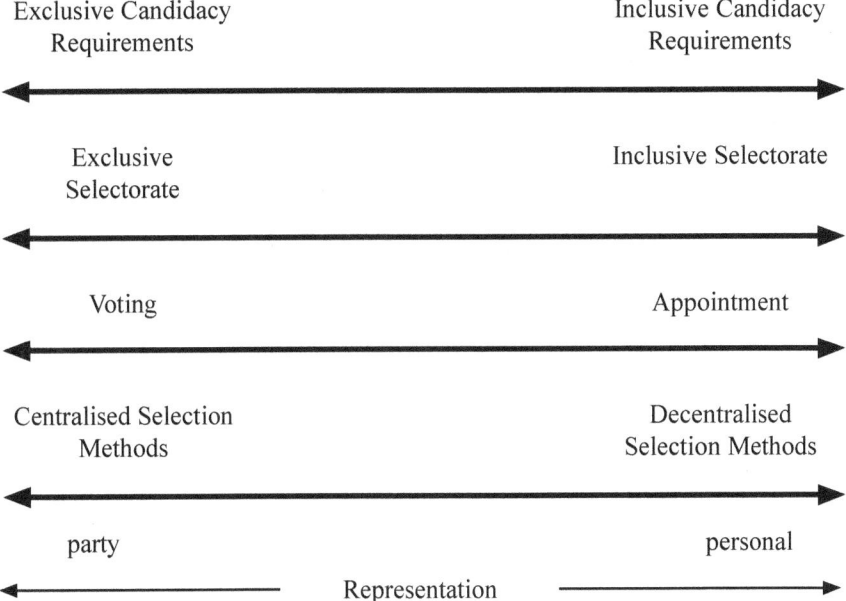

Figure 2.5: Dimensions of candidate selection and party/personal representation

THE CONNECTION BETWEEN CANDIDATE SELECTION AND ELECTORAL SYSTEMS

There is a general consensus among electoral studies experts that the three most important dimensions of electoral systems are the ballot structure, the district magnitude and the electoral formula, and that each of these includes a long list of subtypes (Rae 1967; Blais 1988; Taagepera and Shugart 1989; Blais and Massicotte 1996; Farrell 2001; Reynolds, Reilly and Ellis 2005).

This section examines the similarities between the dimensions of candidate selection methods that were presented in the previous section and the three main dimensions that delineate electoral systems: ballot structure, district magnitude and electoral formula as the most significant criteria of party versus personal representation. All three of these are relevant for the intra-party level as well, albeit after being adapted properly.

District magnitude is incorporated within the (third) dimension of decentralisation in the research on candidate selection. While it is likely that a decentralised electoral system will go hand-in-hand with a decentralised candidate selection method (the USA), and vice-versa (the Netherlands), this is not necessarily the case. These two criteria may co-vary independently – a party in a country with single-member districts can have a rather centralised candidate selection process (the Indian National Congress party in the 1950s and 1960s), and vice-versa (Labor in Israel in the 1990s). As much as district magnitude is an important criterion in order to assess party or personal representation, we address it based on the extent of decentralisation when we evaluate the political consequences of candidate selection on representation.

The electoral formula is integrated into the (fourth) dimension of voting versus appointments in the assessment of candidate selection. Once again, while there might be an intuitive connection between these two criteria, this is not necessarily so. A country with a proportional electoral system can have parties that use majoritarian voting systems to select their candidates (Likud in Israel in the 1990s, Fianna Fail in Ireland until recently), not to mention the possibility that under any national electoral formula parties can use appointment rather than voting as the system by which their candidates are chosen. Thus, once more, electoral systems research contributes an important criterion in order to assess party or personal representation in candidate selection, but it must be adapted in order to be operationalised properly at the intra-party level.

Ballot structure is also integrated into the dimension of voting and appointments. When we assess the number of votes given to each selector, or the ability to rank candidates, we do this within the parties by looking at their candidate selection voting system. However, there are two main caveats here. The first is that almost by definition, candidate selection is a personal race within the party, and only in extremely rare occasions will we see teams of candidates competing against each other inside a particular party.[6] The second caveat is that while it is possible

---

6. In the primaries conducted in Argentina's two large parties, the party members (and sometimes also 'party supporters') vote for competing lists of candidates (De Luca, Jones and Tula 2002).

to address and analyse ballot structure at the national level, this becomes increasingly difficult to do within parties for the following reasons. First, as difficult as it is to gather empirical data on candidate selection (as opposed to the wealth of data available on elections and electoral systems), it is even more difficult to obtain information about the ballots used by any particular party for a specific selection in (if they exist) the various districts. So, while we acknowledge the relevance of this criterion from the study of electoral systems, the ability to adopt it in a wholesale manner for the study of candidate selection is significantly circumscribed. Second, other dimensions already in the candidate selection framework will have a substantially more important influence on party and personal representation. For example, the inclusiveness of the selectorate has tremendous consequences for representation, above and beyond those of the ballot structure. Moreover, while inclusiveness at the national inter-party level does not vary – universal participation is both a norm and a defining element of democratic states – and thus cannot be assessed, it does shift considerably within parties. It is only here, at the intra-party level, that we can assess the ramifications of the inclusiveness of the selectorate, which exceed those of the ballot structure (Rahat, Hazan and Katz 2008).

When Does Selection Equal Election?
The consequences of candidate selection can be more or less significant as a result of a particular country's electoral system. For example, in countries with single-member districts, if the number of safe seats is either large or growing then the selection process of the major parties could be more decisive than the election itself. In both the USA and UK, more than one-half of the constituencies are safe for one party or the other, with majorities greater than 10 per cent, which means that the effective choice of who will become a legislator is made not by the voters in the general election but by the candidate selection process. Indeed, primaries were seen as an alternative to party competition in safe seats (Turner 1953). As Rush (1969: 4) stated about safe seats in Britain, 'selection is tantamount to election.' Moreover, in countries using proportional systems, the selection of candidates at the top of a party list can virtually guarantee election, particularly in the major parties, almost regardless of the results of the general election. In short, in the majority of democratic nations, in a majority of the parties, selection is equal to election. As Gallagher (1988a: 2) posited, 'It is clear that the values of the selectorate, often a small number of activists, frequently have more impact than those of the voters. This applies especially under electoral systems which do not permit any degree of choice between candidates of the same party; picking candidates often amounts to picking deputies.'

Comparing the levels of party cohesion – which, it can be argued, is a by-product of party representation, because more party-centred electoral systems should produce more cohesive legislators – in different countries illuminates the impact of candidate selection on the perceived effects of the electoral system, and on how one can offset the other. Members of the US Congress and the British House of Commons are both elected using the same electoral system, according to all three main components. However, the former are known for their low levels of party cohesion, while the latter exhibit quite contradictory behaviour. One possible explanation is the different candidate selection methods used in each country. US party candidates are selected through highly decentralised and inclusive primaries and solely through a voting system. British candidates are chosen in a multi-staged process, in which highly exclusive centralised selectorates are involved in appointing candidates for the short lists. Thus, while the electoral systems are similar, both the resulting behaviour of those elected and the process of choosing candidates are different.

It is, we argue, necessary to move beyond the inter-party arena if one truly wants to assess the difference between personal and party representation and its political consequences. That is, while electoral systems determine the distribution of power at the inter-party level, party and personal representation cannot be wholly explained by them if one does not take into consideration the intra-party arena as well. Studying the consequences of candidate selection could therefore be as important as studying electoral systems. Ranney (1987: 73) was correct when he argued, 'Candidate selection is as essential to realizing the ideal of free elections as free elections are to realizing the ideal of government by the consent of the governed.' The rationale for this claim becomes apparent when the chain of democratic delegation is perceived to start with candidate selection.

Adopting More Personal Intra-party Selection Methods
According to Mair (1997: 148),

> ... many parties are attempting to give their members more say rather than less, and that they are empowering rather than marginalizing them. Many parties now afford their ordinary members a greater voice in candidate selection than was once the case.' Indeed, parties in a number of democracies have democratised their candidate selection methods (Hazan and Pennings 2001; Hazan 2002). Moreover, more parties have made their candidate selection processes more inclusive in the last two decades than in the two decades that preceded them (Scarrow, Webb and Farrell 2000). A study of party rules versus party practice shows that even where the rules have hardly changed, many political parties have shown a trend toward democratising their candidate selection methods (Bille 2001).

In light of the fact that the democratisation of candidate selection methods constitutes a real trend, even if modest, it is important to assess the consequences of this phenomenon for party and personal representation. We posit that if party lists are assembled not by the party organs, but instead by more inclusive selectorates such as party members, the party's ability to aggregate policies and present a cohesive ideological image may be weakened. As Gallagher (1988a: 15) argued, 'Where nominations are controlled centrally, we might expect to find that deputies follow the party line faithfully in parliament, as disloyalty will mean deselection... If they do not depend on any organ of the party for reselection, one might expect to find low levels of party discipline in parliament... Party cohesion may be threatened unless control of selection procedures is maintained.' The ability of candidates to appeal directly to the party membership thus changes the loci of both representation and responsibility from the party to the personal. If the party does not function as a filtering mechanism, then the key actors in the process may become the candidates themselves, who will mobilise supporters directly.

Candidates who are chosen by an inclusive selectorate owe their loyalty to their voters in the candidate selection process, and not only to their party. Such candidates are no longer assured of a future in politics by being loyal team players; instead they must stand out and be recognised – not by the party leaders but by their now more inclusive selectorates. Democratising candidate selection thus produces dual sources of representation for candidates – party and personal. The immediate results include a tendency to disregard the party alongside a dramatic increase in individualist and populist politics; this is buttressed by a significant growth in the influence of the mass media, financial supporters and interest groups on politics in general, and on the candidate selection process in particular. In short, the narrow personal and special interests of candidates selected by more inclusive selectorates could overwhelm the more general party interests that legislators must take into account. As Epstein (1964: 55) claimed, '... it appears illogical to combine primaries, intended to make legislators independent of party, with a parliamentary system that requires cohesive legislative parties in order to provide stable government.'

Candidate selection methods are becoming more inclusive, more democratic, more personal, and this trend is taking place in countries where the electoral system remains unchanged for the most part. This means that in order to understand the ongoing developments in a country's politics, and to correctly assess personal and party representation, we must both add candidate selection to the electoral system in our analysis and we must also learn to distinguish between the inter-party and the intra-party levels. Movement on one does not have to coincide with a similar shift on the other. Moreover, due to the fact that electoral systems are based on national legislation, while in most countries candidate selection is at the discretion of the parties, we will see many more changes in the latter than in the former. Recently it has even been argued that democratisation of the selection process may serve as a bypass of the electoral system – if introducing more personal elements into the electoral system encounters too many barriers, the parties can alter their candidate selection methods and achieve somewhat similar outcomes (Hazan and Rahat 2006; Cross 2008; Rahat 2008a).

The Israeli case serves to make our point. Israel has an extremely party-centred electoral system – it uses a single nation-wide district and fixed party lists. In this context, Rahat and Sheafer's (2007: 77) study of political personalisation in Israel assigns an important role to the democratisation of candidate selection methods.[7] They see it as the change that led to personalisation in other aspects of Israeli politics,

---

7. Shomer (2009) adopts two of the four criteria used in this paper – selectorate and decentralisation – in constructing a scale of candidate selection methods according to their hypothesised incentive to generate a personal vote-seeking behaviour. Her findings concerning the Israeli case are somewhat different.

A political change (democratising candidate selection methods) initiates a change in the way the media cover politics, which then leads to a change in politicians' behaviour. The media adapt to the more personalised candidate selection methods by increasing their focus on politicians at the expense of covering political parties. Finally, recognising that the rules of the game have changed, and understanding that they need the media to communicate with their selectors and voters, politicians responded by increasing their personal activity.

We, therefore, present a two-dimensional diagram of party and personal representation in Figure 2.6. The unidimensional perspective is, as we elaborated, myopic in nature and eschews the intra-party level criteria which – especially in light of the fact that selecting candidates often amounts to picking legislators – can lead to a counter-intuitive or 'surprising' outcome if we focus only on the inter-party level.

Moreover, the need for a two-dimensional approach is demonstrated by the Israeli example of an electoral system on the extreme party end, but with parties situated along the entire candidate selection dimension covering both the extreme personal (Labour) and the extreme party ends (Shas).

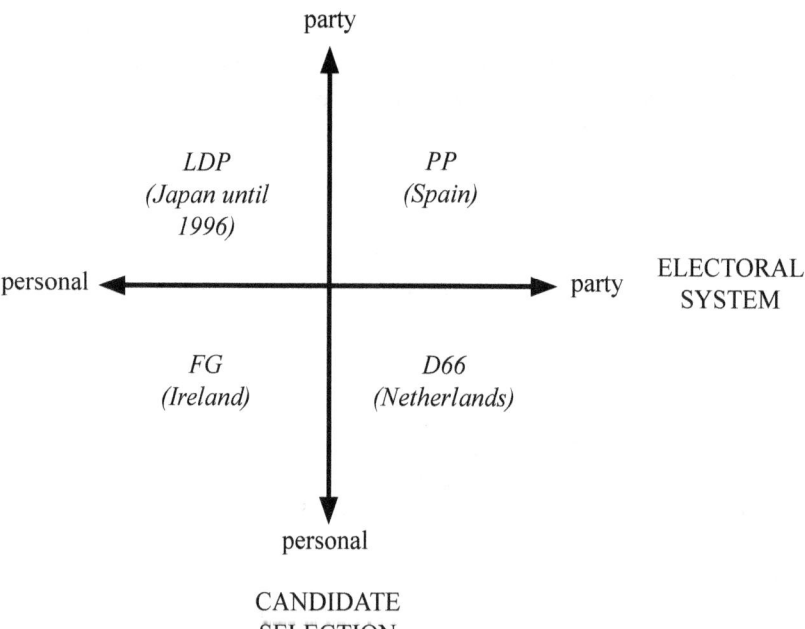

Figure 2.6: Personal and party representation between and within parties

CONCLUSION

It has been argued that candidate selection procedures within parties have important effects on politics in general, from the distribution of power (Schattschneider 1942; Ranney 1981) to the types of legislators elected and their behaviour (Gallagher and Marsh 1988; Narud, Pedersen and Valen 2002). For those reasons, among others, and since candidate selection processes play a large role determining who will be elected, it should be perceived as an inseparable part of the general election process. As such, this chapter has argued that candidate selection has dramatic and significant consequences on party and personal representation.

There are many directions which the research must now take in order to incorporate the study of candidate selection into the more developed field of electoral systems. For example, we need to ascertain if electoral systems characterised by party representation cultivate parties with greater flexibility in their choice of candidate selection methods, while electoral systems with significant personal representation are much more limiting in their menu of choices. Clearly, we need to look at both the inter-party and the intra-party levels if we are truly interested in understanding party and personal representation.

We have shown that party representation and personal representation do not necessarily have to reside in the electoral system, and we elaborated a possible 'division of labour' between the two levels of inter-party and intra-party (s)elections, each possibly focusing on only one aspect of representation. However, while on the one hand we see more examples of this combination, we still do not know if such a division of labour is compatible or dangerous. Only if we bring together the systematic study of electoral systems, together with the recently growing knowledge on candidate selection methods, can we advance the discussion about 'the best' electoral system.

chapter three | single seat
Helen Margetts

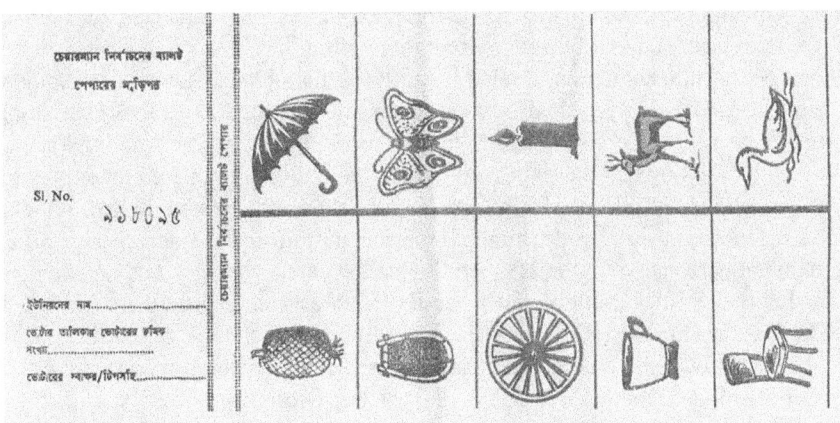

GREAT BRITAIN

INDIA

After two hundred years of using the first-past-the-post electoral system to elect members of the House of Commons, the United Kingdom with its system of elections in single-member districts by plurality rule has become a lonely outlier in Europe. Over the last centuries the system has been much heralded by its many supporters for its constituency link, its ability to form a 'strong government' and the simplicity with which voters cast their votes. Movements towards reform have been fragmented both across and within parties and unable to agree on which alternative system to support. Recommendations from a succession of commissions to examine the voting system have been kicked into the long grass and any proposal relating to general elections has failed to gather momentum or sustained support.

The years between the twentieth and twenty-first centuries brought dramatic change at other tiers of government with the introduction of mixed systems for the Scottish Parliament, the Welsh Assembly and the London Assembly, a proportional list system for European elections and Single Transferable Vote (STV) for local government in Scotland and Northern Ireland. Elections under this array of systems have fuelled support for the third largest party in the UK, the Liberal Democrats, which has remained significant and ultimately grown over the last century (in spite of various leadership battles, splits and mergers). The extent to which the party is under-represented by the electoral system in general elections has become increasingly visible, as the claim that the UK is a two-party system has steadily declined since its peak in the 1950s. There is also a trend in favour of smaller parties, the total of which has grown to around 10 per cent even in general elections. These developments culminated in the 2010 general election, when finally the electoral system returned a hung parliament and after five days of intensive negotiation, a Conservative-Liberal coalition. As a consequence, reform of the voting system seems more likely than it has been for many years.

In this chapter the single-seat system in the United Kingdom is examined for its qualities regarding party representation and personal representation. First, there is a brief look at party representation, outlining the UK's poor record on this aspect, while noting the developments at sub-national level that have brought change to the UK party system. Second, personal representation is looked at from two perspectives. The constituency link, so prized in UK political culture, is examined by looking at what representatives actually do, in terms of responding to citizens, and the extent to which it may be regarded as 'personal' representation. This is followed by a consideration of representation from the voters' perspective, looking at personal voting in UK conditions; the extent to which voters take personal characteristics into account when they cast a vote, such as the candidate's record on constituency work, rebelliousness from party control, or transgressions as highlighted in the members of parliament (MPs)' expenses scandal in 2009. It is found that the single seat electoral system performs very poorly in the UK regarding party representation, but also that, against some conventional wisdom, it scores lowly regarding personal representation. The chapter ends by considering the various possibilities for reform being considered by the new coalition government elected in 2010 and how they might affect the UK's performance on the matrix of party and personal representation presented in Chapter 1 (see Table 1.1).

PARTY REPRESENTATION AND DEVELOPMENTS IN THE UK PARTY SYSTEM

In terms of party representation, the performance of the UK electoral system is quite clear: it is notoriously disproportional. Deviation from proportionality has been about 20 per cent in all general elections since 1992. In terms of party representation, first-past-the-post can work reasonably well where there are two large parties attaining by far the majority of votes. However, over the last one hundred years, the UK party system has moved from being a three party system (in the 1920s), to a two party system (in the post-war period), to a three party system (from the 1980s) and the level of the third party vote is now back to the levels of the 1920s. The combined share of the vote attained by the two largest parties (Labour and Conservative) in 2010 was 65 per cent, lower than at any election since 1918. The Liberal Democrats' share of the vote was widely regarded as disappointing following the excitement of the campaign period, where it ran consistently over 25 per cent after the party leader, Nick Clegg, outperformed the other two major party leaders in the first televised debate. Even so, their share of the UK-wide vote was still their second highest score since 1929.

This poor performance of the single seat system by plurality rule with respect to party representation is exacerbated by the fact that the system does not treat the two largest parties equitably, but from the early 1990s has persistently favoured Labour over the Conservatives (Curtice 2010). This discrepancy is partly because Labour held constituencies containing fewer voters than those won by the Conservatives (something that would be addressed by the commitment of the new government to reduce the size of the House of Commons to 600 seats) and in part because turnout is lower in the average Labour constituency (by seven points in 2010).

In addition to increasingly poor party representation, developments in electoral reform at other tiers of government from the late 1990s have brought changes to the party system which have further worsened the extent to which the electoral system at national level represents parties, as well as greatly expanding the experience of some voters in terms of being able to choose between candidates and parties in elections. The key changes that have taken place since 1999 are:

- *Scotland:* 129 member parliament elected with Mixed System (73 single member constituencies, 56 seats or 43% in closed party lists in 8 regions).
- *Wales:* 60 member assembly elected with Mixed System (40 single member constituencies, 20 seats or 33 % in closed party lists in 5 regions).
- *London:* 25 member assembly elected with Mixed System (14 single member constituencies, 11 seats or 40% in closed party lists), Mayor elected with Supplementary Vote.
- *Europe:* 72 members elected by proportional representation with closed party list in 11 regions.
- *Local government*: elected with Plurality Rule (1/2/3 member districts), STV in Scotland and Northern Ireland.

The extent to which these systems have given voters experience of different electoral systems which allow them to choose between candidates and the possibility to vote for more than one party in the same election has undoubtedly fuelled an existent trend for support for smaller parties outside the biggest three. There is strong evidence that people split tickets in UK elections when they have the chance, for example in elections to devolved assemblies and when local and general elections are held on the same day (Dunleavy and Margetts 1997; Rallings and Thrasher 2003). In the 2010 election the two far-right parties, the United Kingdom Independence Party (UKIP) and the British National Party (BNP), both of whom have representation at the European level and in the London Assembly, ran candidates in the majority of seats (UKIP in virtually all seats) and between them polled 5 per cent of the national vote. The Green Party, although only attaining 1 per cent of the vote overall, won its first seat ever in the House of Commons.

Table 3.1: Seats, votes and disproportionality for Great Britain 2010

	Votes		Seats		Deviation
	No.	% v	No.	% s	(%s – %v)
Con	10,706,647	36.8	306	48.4	+11.6
Lab	8,604,358	29.6	258	40.8	+11.2
Lib Dem	6,827,938	23.5	57	9.0	-14.4
Scot Nat	491,386	1.7	6	0.9	-0.8
Plaid Cymru	165,394	0.6	3	0.5	-0.1
UKIP	917,832	3.2	0	0.0	-3.1
Green	285,616	1.0	1	0.2	-0.8
BNP	563,743	1.9	0	0.0	-1.9
Other	494,473	1.7	1	0.2	-1.0
Total	29,057,387	100.0	632	100.0	44.9

Deviation from proportionality = 22.5

The result, therefore, resulted in the UK's first hung parliament since 1974, an event long (and hitherto wrongly) predicted by UK political scientists. The result, achieved in the face of much scaremongering by the Conservative party during the campaign (including a party election broadcast on behalf of the 'Hung Parliament party', depicting a rope for the electorate to hang themselves by voting for a hung parliament i.e. Liberal Democrat), was vilified in some parts of the media, particularly the Conservative-leaning newspapers. However, the changes in the UK party system noted above make such a result highly possible in subsequent elections, as the first-past-the-post system fails to cope with an enlarged party system, the perceived electability of third party MPs, now part of the government, and the evident lack of equability in the way the party treats the two largest parties. As John

Curtice put it, 'first past the post is no longer a reliable instrument for producing majority government. In continuing to put their faith in first past the post, those who believe in the virtues of single party majority government are increasingly at risk of backing the wrong horse' (Curtice 2010).

PERSONAL REPRESENTATION IN THE UK

By its supporters, the UK electoral system is commended for its supposed personal representation. Under the first past the post system, voters choose one candidate from one party in 650 single member constituencies and it is this 'single member' characteristic (dating from the 1880s) that is often conflated with personalisation. The constituency link is prized greatly from all sides in political discussion, even when reform is under consideration. Take for example, this extract from a speech by Gordon Brown in 2009 in which electoral reform was being proposed for the House of Commons:

> Last year we published our review of the electoral system and there is a long-standing debate on this issue. I still believe the link between the MP and constituency is essential and that it is the constituency that is best able to hold MPs to account.

So how does this prized constituency link actually perform in practice; that is, what do MPs actually 'do' for their constituents? It is useful here to break down the role of a representative, borrowing from Eulau and Karps (1977) who analyse representation as responsiveness. These authors outlined four possible components of responsiveness: First, policy responsiveness, in providing a connection between constituents' policy views and the representative's participation in policy-making on important public issues. Second, service responsiveness, involving the efforts of the representative to secure particularised benefits for individuals or groups in his constituency. Third, allocation responsiveness, which refers to the representative's efforts to obtain benefits for his constituency through pork-barrel exchanges or through administrative interventions. Fourth, there is symbolic responsiveness which involves public gestures which create a sense of trust and support in the relationship between representative and represented.

Attempts to answer the question 'what do MPs do' face a lack of data on interactions between citizens and their representatives (as opposed to survey data based on citizens' or MPs' perceptions of the process). There is no systematic collection of letters or emails to MPs or visits at MP 'surgeries',[1] neither locally nor centrally. But available data suggest that relatively low levels of UK citizens actually interact with their national representatives. The Hansard Society (2008, 2010) found that only 17 per cent of the population had 'contacted or presented views to a local councillor or MP' in the last two or three years, a far lower figure than in Ireland (see Chapter 8) and slightly lower than in those UK nations where representatives are elected under different systems (the equivalent figures were 22

---

1. Surgeries are regular sessions in local offices in a constituency, where constituents may have a one-to-one meeting with their MP and seek their intervention on issues of local or individual concern.

per cent for Scotland, 19 per cent for Wales, 15 per cent for London). These figures remain unchanged on a similar audit carried out in 2008, in contrast with other forms of political engagement, some of which are rising, such as, for example, the 40 per cent who had signed a petition in the same time period, up 4 per cent on 2008, suggesting that the rise in electronic petition systems is having an effect on people's propensity to undertake this form of political participation.

Interaction with representatives for the 70 per cent of the UK electorate who use the internet should be facilitated by electronic applications such as www.writetothem.com (developed by the social enterprise MySociety). These applications use a postcode to automatically generate an email address to a user's representative, meaning that the user does not even need to know the name of their MP to send a communication. Such applications should also mean that there is more data available, but in fact there is little evidence about the extent to which online interaction has re-shaped the nature of citizen-representative communication overall (Williamson 2009: 6). Nearly all MPs now use email, and most accept emails from constituents in general and via MySociety in particular, but available data suggests that MPs are using the internet primarily to inform their constituents (via web sites, for example) rather than engage with them and that there has been no overall rise in communications (Williamson 2009). Only 53,527 messages were sent via the site to MPs in the House of Commons in 2008, 50 per cent of which were sent by people writing to an elected representative for the first time (www.writetothem.com/stats/2008/zeitgeist). The same data shows no evidence that the first past the post system generates particularly responsive representatives; 60 per cent of MPs responded in 2–3 weeks, compared to 67 per cent of Members of the Scottish Parliament and Welsh Assembly, both elected under proportional electoral systems.

When considering the significance in representation terms of these interactions between citizens and representatives, it is important to remember a distinctive feature of the UK political process as it has developed. That is, it is likely that the majority of such communications relate to personal matters –that is, issues relating to private goods– rather than policy or public good considerations. This 'social work' role of MPs appears to be distinctive to the UK and has developed over time. There is no 'official job description' for MPs, and the relationship between MPs and constituents are not subject to formal rules (Norton, 1994). In the early days of enfranchisement, local MPs played a prominent role as local dignitary and benefactor (what might be termed symbolic responsiveness) up until around 1910, but this beneficence declined in succeeding decades, as neither Labour nor Conservative MPs had many resources to provide support, particularly after the Second World War. Indeed at this time, many MPs focused their efforts on Westminster and their business interests and rarely visited their constituency: although there is no hard data, 'most MPs in the 1950s and 1960s did not live in their constituencies and …. received few letters from their constituents. In the 1959–64 Parliament, less than one third of MPs listed addresses that were within their constituencies' (Norton 1994: 710). A typical MP in the 1950s would have received between twelve and twenty letters a week; only two thirds of members held surgeries and with varying frequency (Dowse 1963). MPs would parade around their constituencies at important local events (being 'symbolically' responsive) and of course, at election time, but there were actually few interactions between constituents and representatives.

In the 1960s however, the local role of MPs increased significantly, and a survey in 1967 found that most estimated they received between twenty-five and seventy-five letters a week from constituency sources and a further one in 1986 found that the typical MP received between twenty and fifty letters a day, around half from constituents (Norton, 1994: 711). By the early 1980s, around 10,000 letters a month were being written to ministers, mostly in pursuit of constituency casework which had increased to 15,000 by the end of the decade (Norton 1994). Members spent increasingly more time in their constituencies and the amount of time spent by the average MP on constituency work increased from eleven hours a week in 1971 to sixteen hours in 1984 and has continued to rise ever since (Norton and Wood 1990). An analysis of the constituency casework of MPs in 1986 found that 90 per cent of the cases involved individuals rather than groups 'and were concerned overwhelmingly with the particular needs of the individual' (Rawlings 1990). These findings are in line with an analysis of his own casework by the Labour MP Tony Benn (who found that two-thirds of requests sought his intervention in a dispute with a public official) and a 1993 MORI survey of MPs (MORI, 1993). Certainly this aspect of MPs' work has increased in the last sixty years and although we lack hard data, research shows that in general, MPs are under greater pressure to devote time and energy to constituencies and generally adopt a responsive mode to dealing with these pressures, acting in order to meet demands rather than ignoring or dismissing them (Norton 1994: 714). Such interactions represent 'service responsiveness', in Eulau and Karps' (1977) terms.

Norton suggests that two obvious reasons for this increase are the growth in the electorate during the period and the growth of the welfare state; the greater the degree of public provision and the degree of contact between citizen and public agency, the greater the potential for problems and grievances. But another two reasons are cumulative. First, constituents are increasingly likely to know about the availability of their MP and how to go about making contact. Norton ascribed this increasing awareness to the growth of mass media and growing awareness of political issues. We might add the use of the internet as a readily available source of information about such matters from the 1990s. There is evidence that 50 per cent of the population would 'go to the internet first' to find out the name of their MP if they didn't know it (Dutton *et al.* 2009), and presumably their contact details and potential to help solve personal issues too. But Norton (1994: 715) points also to a cumulative effect; 'success breeding success', whereby where MPs have responded to constituent demands and achieved some response, there is a 'ripple effect – family and friends getting to know of the MPs action'. A 1978 survey reported a 'good' or 'very good' response in 75 per cent of cases and this majority of cases are likely to influence the propensity to approach their MP of those who hear about them.

Over time, the institution of the MP in the UK has become more like that of a social worker, albeit better paid and endowed with parliamentary authority.

Indeed, public perceptions suggest that voters themselves now accept the contemporary role of UK representatives as 'service providers' somehow 'right' and appropriate to democratic procedure. In a survey question regarding what people felt MPs should spend their time doing, 26 per cent felt that one of the three most important things was 'dealing with the problem of individual constituents' and 14 per cent that another was 'communicating with constituents on the doorstep or by telephone', and another 46 per cent chose 'representing the views of local people in the House of Commons'. These substantive figures do not come too far behind the 41 per cent who chose 'representing the UK's national interests' or the 37 per cent who chose 'debating important issues in the House of Commons' as one of the three most important activities (Hansard 2010: 101). This alignment of what MPs do and what constituents think they should do is indicative of a form of 'symbolic responsiveness'.

For allocation responsiveness, there is now some evidence that UK MPs undertake pork-barrel politics, but it is strictly limited to certain categories of politician, location and policy issue, and is widely regarded to be a far lesser phenomenon than in the USA or Ireland (see John *et al.* 2004).

Table 3.2: How MPs should and do spend time

- Which two or three, if any, do you feel are the most important ways that MPs should spend their time?
- Which two or three, if any, do you feel that most MPs spend their time doing?

	% Actually do	% Should do	Gap
Furthering personal and career interests	50	3	-47
Representing the views of their political party	37	11	-26
Presenting their views through the media	32	9	-23
Making laws	14	14	0
Participating in local public meetings and events	11	20	+9
Communicating with constituents on doorstep or telephone	3	14	+11
Dealing with the problems of individual constituents	13	26	+13
Debating important issues in the House of Commons	22	37	+15
Holding the government to account	8	31	+23
Representing the UK's national interests	9	41	+32
Representing the views of local people in House Commons	10	46	+36

Note: Base: 1756 GB adults 18+. Fieldwork dates: 18–19 November 2009.
Source: Hansard (2010) Audit of Political Engagement 7

The MP's role in practice looks like 'service' or 'symbolic' responsiveness rather than 'policy' or 'allocation' responsiveness. Any 'diary', blog or biography of a backbench MP will reveal a constant round of MPs surgeries, letters from constituents and local appearances, rather than discussion of policy issues with constituents. Of course, supporters of the constituency link and MPs themselves would argue that this work gives constituency MPs insight into the key policy problems and issues facing their constituents and, therefore, helps in the process of representing their constituencies. MPs' experience of interactions with constituents are frequently mentioned to support parliamentary interventions; for example, there were over 3,000 references to 'my constituents' recorded in Hansard (the UK parliamentary record) between June 2008 and June 2009' (www.theyworkforyou.com, 20 June 2010). However, such use of constituents' personal issues and problems tends to be selective (440 of these references were to 'one of my constituents') and is, arguably, a rather indirect way of achieving personal representation in 'policy responsiveness' terms.

There is a further way in which the single seat system pulls away from personal representation at the constituency level, deriving from the ways in which parties select their candidates to represent a constituency. In the nineteenth century, when parties were weak entities in British politics (that is, even weaker than now; they still have no legal basis) there was a tradition of local candidates putting themselves forward and choosing a party label *post hoc*. But there has been an increasing trend for party organisations to control and even mandate the selection process. In the Conservative party, the process is almost completely centralised; prospective candidates apply to Conservative central office to be included on the approved list of candidates; those whose CVs are approved attend a 'candidate's weekend' where they undergo an aptitude test and further scrutiny. Once they are approved on the official candidate's list, then they will receive details of local Conservative Associations looking for a candidate and can apply directly, after which they will be interviewed and, eventually, between three and five will attend a local meeting at which all members are entitled to vote. There is some scope for local autonomy in this largely centralised process, but only at the level of the local constituency association executive. A Conservative MP can only be deselected at a special general meeting of the local Conservative association, which can be organised if it is backed by a petition signed by more than fifty members.[2]

Labour MPs at one time were relatively safe once they had a seat, but in 1981 the rules were changed to require all Labour MPs to go through full-scale re-selection procedures in every Parliament; the reputation of being a 'good constituency MP' was some measure of protection against de-selection, one reason perhaps for MPs' responsiveness to increased demands from their constituencies

---

2. Allegations of sexism abound, particularly after a number of high-profile deselections of women candidates and a Conservative Party association chairman responded to David Cameron's call to put more women in parliament "If they are attractive, yeah, I would go for it" (*The Times*, 16 November 2009). Allegations that the process was also inherently racist were made when an eminent Asian barrister with a long-standing record in party politics was not asked for interview in any of the thirteen seats for which he applied (*The Independent*, 2 April 2000).

(Norton 1994: 717). The procedure changed again in 2001. Until then, constituency Labour parties would choose candidates from an approved list. Constituency wards and affiliates, such as trade unions, could nominate two candidates (a man and a woman) and the general council of the constituency would make a shortlist which was circulated to the local membership, who could then vote. But after 2001, a 'quicker' and also more centralised system came into force, allowing a constituency Labour party that needed a candidate to get one quickly by voting on a centrally approved Labour party shortlist, compiled by the National Executive Committee of the Labour Party.

The Liberal Democrats have a similar process, with a central list of approved candidates, to which prospective candidates apply. When constituencies have a vacancy it is advertised and approved candidates can apply to the constituency. Under the party's standing orders, the Liberal Democrat leadership can withdraw the whip from an MP, which effectively stops him or her operating as an MP in the Commons. If the whip is permanently withdrawn, then the MP's party membership would be suspended, meaning that the MP was automatically ineligible for re-selection to stand for the party at the next general election.

Personal Vote in the UK
It has been argued in the previous section that in spite of its reputation, the UK electoral system actually does a poor job in terms of engendering personal representation. Rather it pressurises MPs into being glorified and overpaid social workers, dealing more with private goods than public good issues, while centralised party selection procedures leave little possibility for personal choices in terms of candidate selection. So how do voters behave under these conditions, in terms of the limited extent the system provides to reward or punish representatives for their responsiveness or lack thereof? That is, when voters mark their 'X' against a party or candidate, are they prioritising the candidate, or the party?

This section does not provide a full analysis of personal voting but rather considers three possibilities for personal voting that might both indicate and encourage personal rather than party representation. First is the question of whether voters reward representatives for the constituency efforts outlined above. Second, do voters reward representatives for 'breaking free' from party control, for rebelliousness? And third, do they punish representatives for transgressions, which would suggest that they are responding to individual representatives rather than parties in general; this last hypothesis was tested to the hilt during the MPs' expenses scandal of 2009, which is discussed below. These three questions would seem to be the ones to answer, in terms of indicators of personal representation. Each would also seem to have a cumulative effect, in terms of encouraging a certain type of behaviour from representatives.

Although it was not until the 1970s that ballot papers even exhibited the party names, reflecting the weak status of parties (and indeed, continuing lack of legal basis), the conventional wisdom is that local candidates are 'lobby fodder', 'the mere bearers of party labels, the anonymous foot-soldiers in a battle waged far away in television studios' (Butler and Kavanagh 1988: 191). Even in free votes where there is no party whip, there is evidence that British MPs vote along party lines (Baughman 2004). Likewise, it is generally perceived that such behaviour is rational; that British voters have low levels of knowledge about their MPs in comparison with other countries and pay little attention to their voting record and, therefore, parliamentary representatives have little incentive to build a personal reputation (Pattie and Johnston 2004; Vivyan and Wagner 2010). Developments in the party system discussed above have challenged any lingering notions of partisan alignment, but a decline in voting along single party lines has not necessarily been replaced by a rise in personal voting.

So to what extent, if any, are representatives rewarded for their admirable constituency work discussed above? Quantitative evidence on this issue is sparse, but what is available suggests that their rewards are somewhat limited. Although, as noted above, it seems as if candidates are motivated to 'be a good constituency MP' to avoid deselection (that is, to get rewarded by the party), there is little evidence that they are rewarded for so being by the electorate. Evidence that they were rewarded in this manner would come from data on the electoral advantage of incumbent representatives. But incumbency advantage is relatively weak in the UK, particularly compared with the USA. Williams (1967) compared the performance of Labour and Conservative newcomers and incumbents in fifty-one seats and found that familiarity was worth between 1.5 per cent and 3.5 per cent of the vote for MPs. The retirement slump accounted for around 1.5 per cent of the vote (Gaines 1998).

Gaines (1998) subjected incumbency to systematic scrutiny by analysing its effect in all general elections between the 1950s and 1990s, addressing the question of whether the increased constituency service discussed in the last section actually increased the personal vote and testing the hypothesis that it would increase the incumbency effect. He found that incumbency advantage for Conservative and Labour members was relatively small (consistently lower than 2 per cent), and stable even over the period when descriptive accounts such as Norton (1994) suggest that the constituency role was dramatically increasing, implying that the role shift has not led to a rise in personal voting. For Liberal and later Liberal Democrat MPs the incumbency advantage was considerably higher, but even harder to ascertain due to the far smaller numbers of incumbent MPs or candidates and the far greater likelihood of tactical voting for Liberal candidates. He concluded that incumbency 'confers a unique, massive advantage on a Liberal candidate, the appearance of electability and insulation from tactical-vote loss' (Gaines 1998: 185).

> Overall, however, he found no evidence for a large and growing incumbency advantage, as would have been predicted by the personal-vote school: 'the British example could illustrate that the mere presence of the most basic incumbency advantage – the slight gain from visibility that comes from being in power – does not necessarily indicate that there is also scope to expand one's popularity base and augment the incumbent's edge in the process. British MPs may be in the process of demonstrating that, whatever their home styles, in the final analysis few of their constituents give a "monkey's left goolie" who the local candidates are' (Gaines 1998: 187–8).

There is more evidence that representatives are held accountable for their legislative behaviour, in terms of stepping outside party lines. Cowley and Stuart (2005) have argued that there has been a steady rise in the rebelliousness of MPs in the last decade and that the Labour leadership in the House of Commons faced forty-seven 'major rebellions' between 2001 and 2005 and a number of (normally non-rebellious) Labour MPs regularly voted against the party line (Cowley 2005). Vivyan and Wagner (2010) examined whether the rebellion of MPs in the 2001–5 Parliament, including over the UK's entry into the war in Iraq, had an impact on constituency voting in the 2005 general election, for example on the probability of voting for Labour for those constituents who disagreed with Britain's involvement in the war. Their findings found limited evidence that MP rebellion did indeed act as a signal to voters that their MP disagreed with party leadership and that constituents condition their response to this signal depending on whether they disliked the party leadership. However, voters appeared to take into account only the general rebelliousness of their MP, rather than their vote on any one issue –the accountability of MPs to their voters, in so far as the study provided evidence, was general rather than issue-specific. This finding does suggest a personal representation of sorts, in that voters are rewarding a kind of disposition towards rebelliousness, rather than a stance on a given policy issue –but would not encourage 'policy responsiveness' on the part of representatives.

In 2009 there was a dramatic development in UK politics that might have been expected to result in increased personal voting and provides an opportunity to test the extent to which voters punish representatives for individual transgressions. As with the other two elements of personal voting discussed, evidence of individual punishment would support the long-held thesis that the single seat system works against corruption.

In July, MPs' expenses were due to be made public under Freedom of Information. *The Telegraph* newspaper obtained them early and published them from 7th May in a (fantastically successful) bid to increase circulation, they disseminated them in a daily 'drip feed' fashion which gained massive public and press attention (500 articles on the BBC news, for example, and a massive peak in Google trends for MPs' expenses as a search term, see Figure 3.1). The most systematic issue was that many MPs had spent their £24,000 'second home' allowance, intended to allow them to maintain accommodation in London as well as their constituency, to the full, sometimes on extravagant purchases for second homes, sometimes on mortgages on houses neither in London nor in the constituency, and sometimes by 'flipping' between homes to maximise claims and to avoid tax. These events evoked massive public disapproval and became by far the most discussed issue in British politics, with 71 per cent of people saying that they had discussed the issue with family and friends in the last year or so (Hansard Society, 2010: 80), compared with 40 per cent who said they had discussed the leadership of the main political parties (a key issue in British politics during the period) and 37 per cent who had discussed the European Union.

So how did this event affect voters' perceptions of parties in general and individual representatives in particular? The Hansard Society (2010) found that pub-

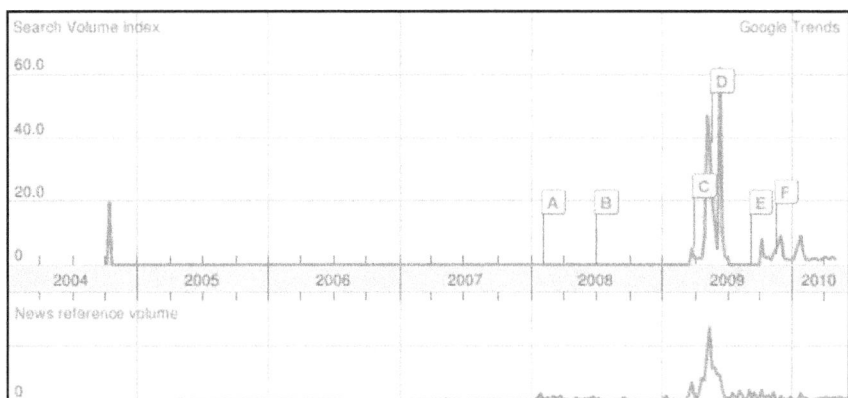

Note: Graph shows use of 'MPs' Expenses' as a search term on Google from 2008 to 2010, compared with the volume of news mentioning the issue over the same period.

The labels represent key newspaper revelations of the issue, as follows:

A. 'Spot-checks plan for MPs' expenses' Telegraph.co.uk – Feb 5 2008

B. 'MPs' expenses vote "harms trust"' BBC News – Jul 4 2008

C. 'MPs' expenses long overdue for review' *Scotsman* – Mar 31 2009

D. 'MPs' expenses: Michael Martin 'to stand down' Telegraph.co.uk – May 19 2009

E. 'Alan Duncan latest victim of MPs' expenses' Telegraph.co.uk – Sep 8 2009

F. 'MPs' expenses: fraud charges for six MPs and lords' Telegraph.co.uk – Nov 19 2009

Source: Googletrends

Figure 3.1: Relative use of 'MPs' expenses' as a search term 2009–2010

lic satisfaction with how Parliament works and how MPs generally do their job, which had been stable across three previous audits of political engagement, had fallen. In 2010, 38 per cent of respondents reported being dissatisfied with how Parliament works (up 5 per cent on 2008) and 44 per cent were dissatisfied with how MPs in general do their jobs, up 8 per cent from the previous audit.

Surprisingly, however, public dissatisfaction with individual constituency MPs had risen only slightly and 38 per cent of the public remained satisfied with how their own MP was doing their job. Even more surprisingly, perhaps, these events do not appear to have effected the reputation of MPs for being trustworthy, possibly because this has always been low in the UK in comparison with other professions and perhaps it has bottomed out. In 2007, for example, a comparison of professions found that only 18 per cent of survey respondents said that they would 'generally trust them to tell the truth', in contrast with 90 per cent for doctors, 86 per cent for teachers, 44 per cent for civil servants (Ipsos MORI, 2007). The most recent Hansard audit of political engagement (Hansard Society, 2010) found figures for trust in politicians almost unchanged from the last audit (in 2007), with 25 per cent of respondents saying that they would trust politicians 'a fair amount', 48 per cent saying 'not very much' and 25 per cent 'not at all', and the percentage of the public reporting 'not very much' trust in politicians actually declined from 51 per cent in 2004 to 48 per cent in 2010, suggesting that the MPs' expenses affair had not affected the already low trust levels (Hansard Society 2010: 89).

The MPs' expenses scandal was widely predicted to herald a crisis in British politics, including falling turnout and falling support for all three of the largest political parties (across which the misdemeanours of individual MPs were spread reasonably evenly, but particularly Conservative and Labour). However, the general election of 2010 provided no such clear evidence. Incumbents did relatively well (although note that over 100 MPs stood down at the election, many connected with the crisis, so there may be a selection bias). Conservative and Liberal Democrat incumbents caught in the crisis clearly did less well, but this was not the case for Labour (Fisher 2010). Turnout in the election was up from 61 per cent to 65 per cent, but was still lower than any election between 1922 and 1997, which was strange considering the closeness of the election result, and some commentators suggested that this might be due to the expenses crisis. But the turnout in the affected constituencies was no worse than others (Fisher, 2010). Indeed, Figure 3.1 suggests that in 2010 the issue has almost sunk without trace, not even re-emerging during the general election campaign.

PROSPECTS FOR CHANGE IN THE UK ELECTORAL SYSTEM

Electoral reform figured highly in the negotiations that led to the formation of a coalition government in 2010. The Liberal Democrats have long supported proportional representation, for obvious reasons, with a major chunk of the disproportionality of the UK electoral system relating to their under-representation. The Conservative party are equally strongly opposed to any change to the electoral system, and indeed a vicious attack on the viability of a hung parliament was a central theme of their campaign, once it looked as if Liberal Democrat support was growing. At one point during the discussions over the formation of the coalition, when the Liberal Democrats turned from the Conservatives to see what Labour were offering, the country witnessed the strange sight of the two largest parties battling to play a better reform hand, with the Conservatives offering a referendum on the Alternative Vote(AV) and Labour offering the AV with no referendum, and a referendum on some version of AV+. However, it became clear in the short, sharp negotiations with Labour MPs that the huge resistance to electoral reform (and, indeed to a coalition with the Liberal Democrats) within the parliamentary Labour party made the Liberal Democrats suspicious of the deal they were supposedly being offered. The Liberal Democrats' preferred system is the Single Transferable Vote, but they accepted the Conservative offer when the coalition deal was agreed and have spun it positively ever afterwards, combined with fixed term parliaments and a re-evaluation of districts to even out the number of voters per constituency. The leader of the Liberal Democrats, Nick Clegg, who became Deputy Prime Minister in the coalition, was placed in charge of political reform.

A referendum on the AV took place in May 2011. Although the Conservative Prime Minister, David Cameron, stood firm to his commitment to call the referendum, he campaigned against reform, after initially stating that he would not. The Labour Party leader, Ed Miliband, campaigned in favour of reform, but many senior figures and frontbench MPs campaigned against and the party was clearly split on the issue. The reform proposal was comprehensively defeated, with 68 per cent voting 'No', although turnout was higher than expected at 42 per cent.

If the AV were to be implemented, the UK would move up the vertical axis reflecting 'personal representation' in Table 1.1 in Chapter 1. Voters under the AV can rank candidates according to preference, allowing them to select more than one party and to support the candidate they prefer as well as the party they support, with the knowledge that if one of their preferences is not satisfied the other may well be. Party representation, on the other hand, will not be particularly improved. In the UK, the conventional wisdom is that AV would regularly offer an increase in the fit between parties and seats, albeit modest. But the AV is not a proportional system, and indeed under some conditions can even deliver a more disproportional result. Simulations of the UK elections in 1992 and 1997 showed that in 1992 there would have been a slight transfer of seats (election outcomes would have changed in only twenty-eight constituencies) which would have deprived the Conservatives of an overall majority, but in 1997 the system would have been markedly less proportional than plurality rule, giving the Labour party seventeen more seats than they actually won, the Liberal Democrats thirty-eight more and the Conservatives fifty-five less, producing a deviation from proportionality of 23.5, rather than that attained under FPTP which was 21 (Dunleavy, Margetts and Weir 1997).

In fact, the way that AV performs depends upon the breakdown of second preferences, particularly for the Liberal Democrats. In 1992, the majority of second preferences went to the Conservatives rather than Labour, in all regions apart from London and the North of England. In 1997 however, this position was reversed; 49 per cent of Liberal Democrat second preferences went to Labour, and only 18 per cent to the Conservatives. Provisional data from the British Election Study for the 2010 election suggests that the break down of second preferences was more similar to 1997 than 1992. It seems that 48 per cent of Liberal Democrats would have given their second preference to the Labour party, and only 12 per cent to the Conservatives, only one more point than to the Greens. Meanwhile, Conservative voters gave strong support to the far-right with their second preference; 41 per cent chose the UK Independence Party, and 10 per cent chose the British National Party, while 21 per cent chose the Liberal Democrats (British Election Study 2010 Campaign Panel, quoted in Norris 2010). Such data clearly sheds some doubt over the perceptions of Liberal Democrat voters, and to some extent Conservative voters, of the legitimacy of the coalition, but also suggests that an AV election in the forthcoming election in 2015 could produce a more disproportional result than plurality rule.

Advocates of preferential voting would argue, however, that it is not party representation that matters so much here, because the key point is that voters have the chance to support more than one party, and second preferences may be as important as first preferences. Advocates of proportional representation remain divided on the subject of AV, with some seeing it as a small but significant stepping stone on the way to a proportional system (with multi-member constituencies, for example, it would morph into STV) and others rejecting the proposed referendum and change.

A quite separate reform that has been discussed in recent years is that of primary elections for candidate selection. The Conservatives introduced primaries in 2008 for the selection of the mayoral candidate for London and have piloted primaries for MP selection (Gay and Jones 2009). Their leader promised it on a widespread basis (*Daily Telegraph*, 25 May 2009) as a response to the MPs' expenses crisis and the 2010 election included the election of the first MP to have been selected in this way, chosen by a postal ballot of all voters in a constituency in Devon in August 2009. David Miliband, at the time the front runner for the leadership of the Labour party, has also spoken in favour of 'US-style primaries' (*Daily Telegraph*, 7 August 2009) and in November 2010, his brother Ed Miliband, the newly elected leader of the party, announced that primary elections would be introduced for the next Labour leadership election (*Daily Telegraph*, 2 December 2010). Although some commentators have criticised European experience of 'primaries' for allowing party leaders to retain ultimate control over candidate selection and that it is has led to a more formal than real democratisation of the process (Hopkin 2001), if other parties followed suit it would draw a wider selection of people into the process than happens at present and release the UK system a little from party control of personal representation.

CONCLUSION: PERSONAL REPRESENTATION IN THE UK

The argument has been put forward in this chapter that as well as scoring lowly for party representation, the single seat system as used in the UK also scores lowly for personal representation, placing the UK firmly in the lower left quadrant on the matrix of representation shown in Chapter 1.

The evidence presented here suggests that in personal representation terms, the UK system and particularly the constituency link prioritise the notion of service responsiveness, with MPs focusing on constituency work in the pursuit of private redress rather than representing the views of their constituents on policy issues. Although the UK electorate has come to see this as an important part of MPs' work, they seem to do so rather symbolically. They do not reward their representatives for this constituency work in terms of personal voting, nor do they punish them for perceived transgression and wrong doing. Traditionally low levels of trust have changed little. The main evidence of personal choice in the election of representatives comes from limited evidence that voters reward representatives for breaking out of party control, although some commentators have argued that the time period for which this evidence exists is non-representative (Hattersley 2010). Overall therefore, the system does not encourage representatives to represent their constituents' views in policy terms, nor to keep themselves clear of financial transgression (something the UK electoral system was supposed to be particularly good at).

The single seat, plurality system has become increasingly incapable of reflecting the contemporary party system. After the 2010 election, prospects for reform look brighter than they have for many years. Indeed, the electoral reform movement, so long awaited and famously weak and splintered through its support for multiple systems and inability to coalesce around any one system, has co-ordinated sufficiently to organise a number of public demonstrations across the country, clear evidence that *something* has changed. In terms of personal representation, the most likely reform option, the AV, would certainly be an improvement, in terms of citizens being able to express more choices on the ballot paper and to vote both for their preferred candidate and the one that has more chance of winning. But as long as single constituencies, service-oriented MPs and rigorous party procedures for choosing candidates are maintained, it seems that an equally good bet for improved personal representation may lie in the introduction of primary elections for candidate selection.

chapter four | closed party list
Pedro Riera

SPAIN   PORTUGAL

One of the most widely-accepted statements in political science is that personal vote does not exist in closed-list proportional representation systems (CLPR). Under this sort of electoral rules, parties present ranked ballots and voters simply select one list over another. The electoral risk associated with nominating lesser-known candidates is attenuated by the fact that citizens tend to vote for the party list, not for the individuals on it (Jones et al. 2002). According to this conventional wisdom, it would make no difference whether the candidates are nominated before an election or simply appointed by parties once they know how many candidates for whom they have slots. In addition, there would be no point for candidates in CLPR systems cultivating a personal vote. In this sense, legislators' behaviour would be heavily constrained by the renomination rules but essentially unconstrained by the electoral process (Strom 1997). In fact, most seats in CLPR systems are 'safe', and, as remarked by Atmor et al. in their contribution to this book, 'selection is equal to election'.

By using data from the ten general elections that have taken place in Spain since the democratic transition, I aim to evaluate the merits and shortcomings of this conventional wisdom. In this chapter, I shall see whether citizens pay attention to candidates' attributes in elections conducted under CLPR rules, and, as a result, whether a sort of personal vote emerges in this type of contest.[1] To be more specific, my results will show that the vote shares of the two main Spanish parties slightly increase in those districts where the candidates on the top of the list are high-quality politicians. By this concept, I mean those candidates that have performed representative tasks in the past either at the national, the regional or the local level. In summary, Spanish voters choose a party rather than a candidate, although the quality of the candidates influences to some extent this kind of choice. I shall first discuss very briefly how incumbents (and challengers) recruit and allocate personnel to electoral positions. Or to put it differently, what are the factors that determine the districts in which high-quality candidates will run? Are party leaders trying to benefit from personal reputations of their most well-known colleagues? Are they just randomly allocating them to the top slots of the lists? I shall then tackle the consequences of the recruitment and allocation of personnel to electoral positions. Are incumbents stronger because they have at their disposal the ministers that are currently serving in the cabinet? Do these strategies make a difference to electoral results and in the survival in office of prime ministers? That is, are such strategies relevant for the outcomes of accountability? To sum up, do citizens in CLPR countries only pay attention to the quality of the party label? Or on the contrary, does this type of electoral rules also allow the existence of a sort of personal representation?

Several examples could serve to illustrate the different conditions under which the composition of the lists matter in Spain. However, the clearest anecdotal evidence for a certain amount of personal vote to be found is when the party in office allocates the ministers that currently serve in the government to the top positions

---

1. Following Swindle (2002), I shall distinguish between personalism, that is a characteristic of public policy, and personal voting, that is an aspect of electoral choice.

on the lists of some districts (Hopkin 1999: 96–7; Linz 1986: 648; Montero and Gunther 1994: 53). It is undeniable that officials of the party in power may see an electoral benefit in following this kind of vote-maximising strategies, apart from ensuring the election of some of the most important party notables. For example, this was the situation of the UCD (*Unión de Centro Democrático*, Union of Democratic Centre) government of Adolfo Suárez in 1979. Over two years, he had led the country from dictatorship to democracy; passed a Constitution with overwhelming parliamentary and popular support; and negotiated a socio-economic pact (the *Pactos de la Moncloa*) with the opposition and the unions that had brought down inflation. For all these reasons, Suárez hoped to achieve a substantial victory when he anticipated the elections by more than two years, and allocated the most popular ministers serving in his government to the top slots on the lists of several crucial districts. Fernando Abril Martorell was one of these cases. Born in Valencia, Abril Martorell had been appointed Second Vice President and Minister of Economy in 1978. Some months later, he was heading the UCD list from the district of Valencia in the upcoming general election. Although UCD ran slightly short of an absolute majority in the national Parliament, the party increased its vote ratio in Valencia by almost three percentage points (from 31 per cent to 33.8 per cent), and, even more important, obtained an extra seat from that district.[2]

Obviously, other Spanish prime ministers heading minority governments were less successful when they developed this kind of strategy. An example is José Luis Rodríguez Zapatero in March 2008. After forty-eight months in office, the constitutional inter-election period expired and the Socialist Prime Minister (from the *Partido Socialista Obrero Español* [PSOE]) was forced to call elections. As had happened in previous contests, party leaders decided that most of the members of the cabinet would head the Socialist lists in several districts. One of these districts was Valencia, where Abril Martorell had gained one additional seat for the UCD three decades ago. In the 2008 general election, the government official in charge of improving the performance of the Socialist Party in that district was María Teresa Fernández de la Vega. Appointed First Vice President and Minister of Presidency in 2004, she had survived all the cabinet reshuffles that had lasted the previous legislative term. Despite the fact she was originally from Valencia, 2008 was the first time Fernández de la Vega ran as a candidate there;[3] and electoral results seem to indicate that voters punished the Socialist Party for this reason. The elections of March 2008 produced a repetition of the 2004 results, and the continuation of Rodríguez Zapatero's minority government. However, the Socialists performed particularly badly in Valencia, where they lost votes (2 percentage points),

---

2. The performance of Suárez's party in Valencia also improved in relative terms. In 1977, when the list in that district was headed by a non-quality candidate, the vote share of the provincial list was more than 3 points lower than in the rest of the country (31 per cent against 34.4 per cent). In contrast, the performance of UCD in Valencia fell only 1 point below the average mean in 1979 (33.8 per cent against 34.8 per cent).

3. In 1996, 2000 and 2004, she had been elected in representation of Jaén, Segovia and Madrid, respectively.

and were not able to capture a new available seat.[4]

To sum up, some reconciliation between candidate selection and electoral performance literatures is certainly possible in the puzzle over whether the quality of the candidates determines the electoral fortune of the parties in CLPR systems. On the one hand, if the composition of the lists does indeed affect the ability of parties to win elections, then presumably politicians will seek to 'manipulate' them to their own advantage. On the other hand, the claim that parties tinker with the electoral lists in order to ensure their survival, or increase their vote totals, presupposes a belief on their part in personal vote. There would be no point in strategically allocating notables to the top slots of the lists if personal vote-earning attributes (PVEA) did not matter.

There are at least four substantive reasons that justify research on personal representation in CLPR systems. First, we know relatively a lot about the consequences of electoral systems on what Shugart calls the interparty dimension, that is, 'how electoral systems affect the translation of votes into seats for competing political parties, and how electoral systems affect the overall nature of the party system' (Shugart 2008: 29–30). In contrast, one of the most overlooked areas in the field of comparative electoral systems is the effects of electoral rules on what Shugart calls the 'intraparty dimension' (Shugart 2008: 36). In other words, we are not that familiar with the issue of how variations in electoral rules affect the internal organisation of parties and the ways in which individual candidates relate to constituents. Second, there have been numerous studies of the social backgrounds, occupations, and other attributes of legislators (e.g. Linz *et al.* 2000 on Spain). However, this literature has rarely linked candidates' variation in such attributes to the electoral performance of political parties.

Third, this lack of knowledge is particularly acute with regard to CLPR systems. Although some significant findings have emerged in the areas of geographical representation (Latner and McGann 2005) and female representation (Iversen and Rosenbluth 2008), the literature on personal vote under this sub-type of proportional rules is not very rich. And fourth, this oversight is particularly troublesome if we take into account the fact that CLPR systems are far from rare. According to Norris' classification, lists are closed in more than 50 per cent of the cases (35 out of 64) where a proportional formula is used in order to allocate seats to parties (2004: 41). In the same vein, Johnson and Wallack (2008) show that almost one fifth of the electoral systems in use in the world in 2005 combined closed lists with proportional representation. Yet, there is no literature that I am aware of that ties candidate' features to parties' electoral performance under CLPR rules; this is a major gap because of the ubiquity of this particular electoral system.

The rest of the chapter proceeds as follows. The second section presents the theoretical arguments in the literature on personal vote and the intra-party dimension of electoral systems. The third section discusses the hypotheses I seek to test.

---

4. This performance can be also considered disappointing if we take into account the fact that the vote share of the Socialist Party in Valencia was 3.7 per cent points lower than in the whole country (40.2 per cent against 43.9 per cent).

The fourth section describes the data and the methods I plan to use in order to do it. The fifth section summarises the main results provided by the econometric models and finally, the sixth section concludes.

THEORETICAL FRAMEWORK

In 1985, Arend Lijphart concluded that research on comparative electoral systems was considerably underdeveloped. By contrast, when Shugart updated Lijphart's survey of this literature twenty years later, he believed that we could speak of a mature field. Obviously, I do not seek to close this debate in this chapter. On the contrary, my goals are more modest here and I plan to examine whether personal representation really exists in CLPR electoral systems. Following Shugart (2008), I shall divide the empirical research on the intraparty dimension of electoral systems into two big topics (socio-demographic representation and the personal vote), and I shall focus on the latter. The personal vote has been typically defined as 'that portion of a candidate's electoral support which originates in his or her personal qualities, qualifications, activities, and record' (Cain *et al.* 1987: 9). The idea of the personal vote stands in contrast to a vote cast strictly for a political party, with little or no regard to, or evaluation of, the individual(s) representing that party in electoral contests. The implication of the personal vote for political representation is that in more personalised electoral systems, the agent of legislative representation is considered to be the individual politician, whereas in more party-centred electoral systems the agent of representation is the collective party (Carey 2009).

The seminal paper written by Carey and Shugart in 1995 provides the dominant theoretical framework to analyse the candidates' incentives to cultivate a personal vote. In these scholars' view, the incentives to cultivate a vote of this type depend upon three particular features of the electoral institutions: (1) the degree of party leadership's control over access to and rank in ballots, (2) the degree to which candidates are elected on individual votes independent of co-partisans, and (3) the fact that voters cast a single intra-party vote instead of multiple votes or a party-level vote. Needless to say, this index places Spain in the bottom of a rank of electoral systems according to the amount of incentives they generate to cultivate a personal vote. In addition, Carey and Shugart note that district magnitude has a modifying effect on the personal vote depending on the nature of the electoral system. On the one hand, as magnitude increases in electoral systems that foster personal vote-seeking behaviours, so also does the importance of this kind of strategies. On the other, increases in district magnitude decrease the value of the personal reputation of individual candidates in party-centred electoral systems.

One of the most important problems in empirical studies of the effect of electoral systems on the existence of personal vote is the lack of direct and straightforward measures of the dependent variable (Shugart 2008: 46). In this sense, some scholars have suggested the use of the frequency with which Members of Parliament (MPs) engage in constituency service. In fact, this is the strategy followed by Bowler and Farrell (1993) in their survey of the members of the European Parliament. In the same vein, Heithusen *et al.* (2005) also examine the constituency focus of MPs in six chambers that span a variety of electoral systems.

Needless to say, both studies find that electoral systems affect the priority that MPs place on constituency service.[5] Finally, André *et al.* (2009) propose a more direct test of Carey and Shugart's theory by using the legislators' perception of the relative value of personal and party reputations. Thanks to the survey data provided by the PARTIREP project,[6] they can cast some doubts upon the monotically positive relationship between personal vote and district magnitude that we expect to find in a country with flexible lists like Belgium. Unfortunately, this research design is not available for the Spanish case: as Montero and Gunther (1994: 53) point out, personal contacts of the legislators with their constituents are relatively infrequent in this country (see also Hopkin 2008: 387). In addition, elites' surveys on Spanish legislators' behaviour are still rare.

Closely related to personal vote and constituency service is the issue of political corruption. Broadly speaking, there are two main alternative perspectives on which electoral system generates more opportunities for incumbents and is the most suitable to advance narrow over general interests, and extract political rents for incumbents. On the one hand, Persson and Tabellini (2003) argue that the freedom to choose individual candidates (rather than party lists) is associated with less corruption. On the other hand, Kunicová and Rose-Ackerman (2005) find quite the opposite by showing that an index of particularism based upon Carey and Shugart (1995) has a positive and statistically significant effect on the level of political corruption in a sample of more than ninety countries. Finally, Chang and Golden (2006) provide the last test to date on the relationship between electoral rules and corruption. Looking at a large sample of contemporary democratic nations, their study shows that political corruption gets more (less) severe as district magnitude increases in open-list (closed-list) settings.[7]

There are at least two other cross-national tests of the effects of preference voting (or its absence) and magnitude on the personal vote. First, Crisp *et al.* (2004) examine the type of bills that legislators initiate in six Latin American countries. The evidence that they provide fits perfectly well with the theory: the probability of initiating a local bill rises with magnitude in nominal-vote systems,

---

5. The contribution by Scully and Farrell (2003) on members of the European Parliament counterintuitively suggests that those elected from open lists place more emphasis on traditional parliamentary activities. This effect, however, tends to disappear as district magnitude increases.

6. The PARTIREP project on 'Participation and Representation in Modern Democracies' collects data among legislators in fifteen national parliaments and sixty-two regional parliaments. Hosted by the Vrije Universiteit in Brussels, the project brings together five partner universities (Vrije Universiteit in Brussels, Université libre de Bruxelles, Universiteit Antwerpen, KU Leuven, and Universiteit Leiden), as well as leading scholars in each country. For more information, see www.partirep.eu.

7. For space constraints, I have restricted my literature review of political economy works to those that examine the effect of electoral rules (and, consequently, the presence or absence of personal vote) on political corruption. Nevertheless, political economists are becoming increasingly interested on this topic, and link legislators' personal vote-seeking strategies to government expenditures (Edwards and Thames 2007), trade protection (Hankla 2006; Nielson 2003), budget discipline (Hallerberg and Marier 2004), and efficacy in education spending (Hicken and Simmons 2008).

but declines with magnitude in list-vote systems. Shugart *et al.*'s (2005) piece also provides evidence about how the interaction of the type of electoral systems (list versus nominal) and district magnitude affects the behaviour and characteristics of legislators. Using data from six European cases under proportional representation, they show that the probability that a legislator will exhibit PVEA–operationalised as local birthplace and lower-level electoral experience-declines with magnitude when lists are closed, but rises with magnitude when lists are open. Unfortunately, this is only preliminary evidence. In fact, Tronconi and Marangoni's (2009) results on the Italian case significantly depart from what the theory predicts: candidates' level of localness and previous experience in government decline (or remain constant) as the district magnitude increases when the lists are open. This last finding leaves open the question of how useful legislators' PVEA are to voters as magnitude increases under preferential-list allocation methods.

Another interesting avenue of research in the field in the recent past has been the analysis of the assignment of legislators to committees. To my knowledge, there are at least a couple of papers that consider the committee assignments according to the tier (nominal or list) by which a member was elected in Germany (Gschwend *et al.* 2009; Heinz 2008; Stratmann and Baur 2002). Pekkanen *et al.* (2006) also show that members of the Japanese Parliament elected from PR lists and single-member districts have different electoral incentives and, for this reason, they receive different types of posts. And, obviously, there are tons of papers that focus on the legislative organisation of the contemporary U.S. Congress (Gamm and Huber 2002). Unfortunately, it is yet untested how do voter interests match with the committee system in CLPR systems (Shugart 2008: 48). Jones *et al.* (2002) provide the only study on committee assignment under party-centred electoral rules that I am aware of, but they do not use district magnitude as explanatory factor.

Finally, the deputies' electoral connection to voters affects the internal party unity. Legislative factionalism is higher in countries where candidates compete against members of their own parties for personal votes (either in primaries or in the general election) than where nominations are controlled by party leaders and electoral lists are closed (Carey 2009; Hix 2004; Sieberer 2006). Evidence from the Spanish case confirms the validity of this last argument: where legislators have to please only one principal, that is, the party leader, defections do not exist in practice.

To sum up, the literature that examines the relationship between electoral systems and personal vote across countries, although showing an increasingly comparative scope, has long been hampered by variation in the numerous intervening variables that influence legislative behaviour. As a consequence of this, several scholars have examined whether personal vote exists (or not) in a large collection of single-country studies that focus on different electoral systems: single transferable vote (Marsh 2007) and non-transferable vote (Hirano 2006) , closed list (Crisp and Desposato 2004) and open list (Golden 2003) proportional representation, mixed-member proportional and majoritarian rules (Canache and Mondak 2000), and single-member districts with plurality rule (Gaines 1998). In addition, other political scientists have taken advantage of the recent proliferation of countries adopting mixed-member systems, or of the current existence of bicameral systems where members of each chamber are elected according to different rules (e.g. Desposato 2006; Kunicová and Remington 2008; Moser and Scheiner 2005; Nemoto *et al.* 2008). In spite of this large literature, Morgenstern and Swindle (2005) find, however, only limited evidence that electoral systems affect the personal vote.

WORKING HYPOTHESES

For a given magnitude, the information demand on the voter is higher under an open rather than a closed list (Shugart *et al.* 2005). In this chapter, I do not plan to contest this argument. However, I want to show that the voters' allegiance to a party in a particular district is higher, for a given value of the rest of the variables that traditionally explain electoral behaviour, if they find on the top of the list a candidate with appealing attributes. Features like local origins and previous representative experience may provide voters with substantive cues to politicians' knowledge of the needs of the locality, and the ways to get them satisfied. In other words, whereas candidates, who have local origins, can be viewed by voters as people that 'know what they want', experienced candidates seem to 'know how to get it' (Shugart *et al.* 2005: 441).

On the basis of the literature on the personal vote, the traits of the candidates on the top of the lists should have an impact on the vote share obtained by Spanish parties at the district-level. Testing this kind of effect in this country involves simultaneously opportunities and problems. With regard to the former, Spain presents one of the lowest levels of party identification (Montero and Gunther 1994: 49). In addition, partisan 'anchorages' to secondary associations are also significantly weak (Linz and Montero 1999: 80). These two features of the Spanish scenario should lead to an increase in the levels of personal vote. Nevertheless, at least three institutional and political characteristics of democracy in Spain contribute to decrease the expected electoral importance of personal vote.

First of all, as we already know and I will explain more carefully in the next section, Spaniards are only asked to place a list of candidates provided by a party in an envelope and insert it into the ballot box. No preferential vote or any kind of panachage is allowed by the electoral system of the Congress of Deputies. This institutional framework ('closed and blocked lists'*)* should drastically decrease the levels of personal vote observed in a democracy. Second, most Spaniards are not able to remember the name of the candidate who is on the top of the list they vote for (Montero and Gunther 1994: 50). In fact, fewer than one out of five voters outside Madrid, Catalonia and the Basque Country could correctly do it in the 1982 and the 1993 elections (Hopkin 2001: 123). The benefit politicians may see in signalling their local origins or previous experience in representation will only have an effect in a context in which voters can make use of such information (Shugart *et al.* 2005: 437). This does not seem to be the case in Spain. However, remembering the name of the candidate on the top of the list and knowing his/her local origins or political record can be two very different things. It may be the case that voters usually forget the name of the candidates, but keep track of their local origins or their record in office. They may not exactly know how they are called, but know where the candidates were born, and whether they have or have no previous political experience.

A third factor that could potentially diminish the role of personal vote in Spain is the structure of incentives generated by the electoral system. In this sense, it could be argued that there is no point for Spanish voters paying attention to the PVEA of the candidates placed on the top of the list because their seats are usually safe. As has been previously noted (Blais and Lago 2009; Grofman and Selb 2009), marginality in PR systems entails a completely different meaning than in single-member districts. Candidates of the main parties below the first slot are really the ones that are at stake (Méndez Lago 2000: 96–101). However, it could be the case that voters believe that local birthplace and record of representative service of the candidate on the top of the list correlate with the level of local rootedness and political experience of the rest of the candidates within the list. In addition, it is plausible to think that citizens who are not able to name the candidate on the top of the list they vote for will not be aware of which are the marginal seats in their constituency either. Having in mind these two *provisos*, the PVEA of the candidate on the top of the list could be 'heuristics' that rational voters use in order to make decisions in elections (Popkin 1991).

Finally, there is still a fourth factor that could bias downwards the positive impact of high-quality candidates on the electoral performance of a given party. In this sense, the positive externalities that bring about the placement of highly-experienced politicians on the top of a list can also be hampered by the placement on a lower slot of a candidate with non-existent or, even worse, negative PVEA. In this sense, Hopkin (2008: 386) reports the PSOE's (*Partido Socialista Obrero Español*, Socialist Party) decision to place the former Minister of the Interior José Barrionuevo, under investigation for his role in the 'dirty war' against Basque terrorism, in a prominent position on the party list for Madrid in the 1996 election, thus ensuring him election and, as a result, parliamentary immunity from prosecution.

Once I have tackled all these general considerations, the hypotheses are the following:

Hypothesis 1: The vote share of a party should be higher in those districts where a 'local' candidate is running on the top of the list than where he/she is a parachutist and does not have any personal connection with the constituency.

Hypothesis 2: The vote share of a party should be higher in those districts where a 'high-quality' candidate is running on the top of the list than where he/she lacks any kind of track political record in the past.

Hypothesis 3: The positive effect of high-quality candidates on the vote share of a party in a given district should decrease as the district magnitude increases.

Hypothesis 4: The positive effect of high-quality candidates on the vote share of a party in a given district should decrease as the number of elections that have already taken place increases.

The rationale behind Hypothesis 1 is straightforward. As Gallagher (1988b: 251) points out, in many countries an inexperienced candidate from the locality may be looked on more favourably than a party member whose record was established in another part of the country. In fact, Ranney (1981) uses the pejorative terms of 'carpetbagger' and 'parachutist' for those aspirants who seek to be elected in a part of the country with which they have no connections. As I previously noted, citizens should be theoretically less willing to vote for this kind of candidate. However, in recent times media figures have became more important than local notables (Manin 1997: 220); and Spain does not constitute an exception to this pattern (Hopkin 2008). This apparent confinement of the personalisation of electoral politics to the national level could be particularly resilient in Spain.[8] This last empirical fact could contradict this hypothesis.

Hypothesis 2 is concerned with the quality of local candidates. Why should it matter? There are at least three arguments that could justify the existence of a positive relationship between the quality of the candidates and the electoral performance of the parties at the district-level. First of all, the quality of the deputies elected determines the quality of the resultant parliament, often of the members of the government and, to some extent, of a country's politics (Gallagher 1988a: 1). In a related sense, Colomer, in the introductory chapter of this book, also associates the personal representation or the choice of individual representatives to the high quality of representation and the effective promotion of the preferences of the community once these are well defined. Obviously, it is not easy to define high-quality candidates. In this chapter, I shall use a very narrow definition, and I shall conceptualise them as those candidates with experience in politics (Gallagher 1988b: 248). Some findings in the literature suggest that previous record in office might not be a good indicator of the quality of candidates. In this sense, Gaines (1998) only finds a very small effect of incumbency on the electoral performance of parties in the United Kingdom. In addition, it could be argued that the internal unity of parties suffers when a non-local high-quality candidate is chosen to head an electoral list; and voters tend to punish those parties that are perceived as disunited (Maravall 2007). Nevertheless, I shall test the existence of a positive association between the political experience of the candidate on the top of the list and the electoral fortune of the party.

We can trace back the origins of Hypothesis 3 to Duverger (1954: 356–9). In this scholar's view, large constituencies and list systems increase the influence of the party relative to the candidate. Citizens in this type of constituencies are unlikely to have personal knowledge of the candidates and are more prone to rely on

---

8. Probably being aware of the prejudices that voters have against parachutists, and having reached La Rioja a couple of months before the 1979 election, the conservative politician José María Aznar declined to run as a candidate of Popular Alliance (*Alianza Popular* [AP]) that year (Aznar 2004: 53). In 1982, Aznar was initially going to run as a candidate of AP in Soria, but internal discontent within the local branch of the party led the then conservative leader, Manuel Fraga, to change his mind and offer Aznar the number one candidacy of Ávila (Palomo 1990: 56–7). In fact, Fraga, the leader of AP for many years, has described the process of candidate selection as one of the most painful experiences in his entire political life (Palomo 1993: 45).

party label or sub-group membership as a voting cue. However, data reported by Montero and Gunther (1994) on the Spanish case stands against this theory: more than 70 per cent of voters from Madrid (where the candidates for the presidency of the Government are running) knew the name of the candidate on the top of the list in the 1982 and the 1993 elections. In contrast, voters from smaller constituencies were less likely to remember the name of the candidate on the top of the list they voted for. In addition, the relationship between knowledge of the candidates and district magnitude appeared to be non-linear: the least-known candidates were those running in middle-sized districts. To sum up, the next hypothesis aims to establish a negative relationship between district magnitude and the amount of personal vote. In principle, voters from smaller districts should be more prone to cast this kind of vote. However, the nationalisation of electoral campaigns decreases the role played by candidates from peripheral districts and, subsequently, could reduce their ability to successfully create a niche of loyal personal-oriented voters.

Finally, expectations on the role of time are also far from clear. On the one hand, it could be argued that candidates' personal attributes are increasingly important. According to Dalton and Wattenberg's data (2000), decline in party identification is more than evident in advanced democracies in recent times (Mair 2005: 14). In the same vein, Manin (1997: 219) argues that voters tend to increasingly vote for a person. Parties or platforms are no longer the crucial factor in order to explain voting behaviour. The predominant role of party labels in elections is characteristic of a particular type of representation, namely party democracy, which is progressively disappearing. In the same vein, the crisis of the party government model requires legislators to rely more on their own resources when it comes to re-election and the continuation of their political careers (Mezey 1994: 437). Other results from time-series are, however, less conclusive and show fluctuations rather than continuous growth in the impact of candidates' evaluations on vote choice (Bengtsson and Wass 2009). In addition, Manin (1997: 220) states that the growing importance of personal traits is more perceptible at the national level (on Spain see also Montero and Gunther 1994: 56). Hence, it is at best dubious that we should expect a positive effect of the passage of time on the impact of personal attributes.

DATA AND METHODS. WHY SPAIN?

For my empirical tests, I have assembled an original data set that is based on the biographies of the 1,000 politicians that have been placed on the top of the district-level lists[9] of the two main parties[10] in the ten general elections that have taken place in Spain since the transition to democracy.[11] There are at least two method-

---

9. I exclude Ceuta and Melilla from the sample.
10. These parties are UCD (*Unión de Centro Democrático*, Union of Democratic Centre) for the 1977 and 1979 elections, AP-PP (*Partido Popular*, Popular Party) for the elections from 1986 to 2008, and PSOE for all of them. According to Montero and Riera (2009), these parties have held at least 80 per cent of the seats in the Spanish Parliament during the whole democratic period.
11. The sources of information are the Ministry of the Interior for the electoral results (www.mir.es),

ological and one substantive reason that justify the election of Spain as my case of study. First, developing a single country study allows me to control the confounding effect of other institutional and political variables that might also explain the levels of personal vote observed in a given CLPR system. In every Spanish election during the current democratic period, the allocation of seats to parties has been proportional to the votes obtained by each party at the district-level following the D'Hondt method. Even more important for my purposes here, Spanish voters are not allowed to disrupt the ranked ballots presented by parties (Hopkin 2008: 378). Hence, analysing general elections in Spain is an excellent strategy to determine whether personal vote exists when the lists are closed.

Second, the variance in district magnitude in Spain is quite large in comparative terms (Monroe and Rose 2002). In this sense, all the seats, with the exception of Ceuta and Melilla, are allocated to parties in multi-member districts. However, magnitude varies a lot across districts by ranging from two to thirty-five. This implies that the effects of my key independent variables are tested in districts of low and high magnitude. I will take advantage of this fact and examine the existence of possible interactive effects between district magnitude and the quality of the candidates.

Finally, there is also a substantive reason to take Spain as the case study. Electoral reform has become an increasingly hot issue in this country over time. Fears of weak parties were behind the initial decision to adopt closed lists in a country with an important lack of democratic and electoral experience (Hopkin 2008: 377). However, in the nineties those worries were replaced by concerns with overly cohesive and centralised parties (Montero and Gunther 1994: 37–8; Montero 2000). This increasing internal monolithism of parties led some scholars to suggest the introduction of preference votes in order to grant voters more choice over the individual candidates they can elect to parliament (Montero 1997: 37–40). After the 2008 general election, a Parliamentary Commission was created in order to analyse the convenience of keeping the current electoral system; and in March 2009, the Council of State delivered a report in which the introduction of a sort of preferential vote was advocated (2009: 276). In fact, some analysts (e.g. Hopkin 2008: 391) argue that the most feasible electoral reform in Spain would involve the elimination of the closed lists since parties frequently advocate the partial opening of the lists in their electoral manifestos and this kind of reform would enhance voters' freedom of choice.[12]

In the econometric analyses, I shall take every Spanish district as an observation. The dependent variable (*Vote*) is continuous and takes the value of the vote share of UCD, AP (*Alianza Popular*, Popular Alliance), PP (*Partido Popular*, Popular Party) and PSOE in each election at the district-level. In recent times, the use of aggregate data at the subnational level in electoral studies on Spain has become relatively widespread.[13] The independent variables are:

---

and the Congress of Deputies for the candidates' biographies (www.congreso.es).

12. For a more detailed discussion of the parties' proposals, see Montero and Riera (2009).
13. As examples in the Spanish case, see de la Calle and Orriols (2010), Urquizu (2008), and Lago and Montero (2010).

1   a dummy variable, *Parachutist*, that takes value 1 if the candidate on the top of the list neither was born nor has developed his/her political career in the district where he/she is currently running, and 0 otherwise;

2   a vector of dummy variables (*Minister, National Minister, National Deputy, Regional Minister, Regional Deputy and Mayor*) that take value 1 if the candidate is a current or a former national minister, national deputy, regional minister, regional deputy, or the mayor of a locality in the district, respectively, and 0 otherwise;[14]

3   the decimal logarithm of the district magnitude minus 1 (*LogMagnitude*);[15]

4   a counter of the number of elections that have already taken place in each specific point of time (*Time*);

5   an interaction between the variable *Minister* and the decimal logarithm of the district magnitude minus 1; and

6   an interaction between the variable *Minister* and the counter of the number of elections. The coefficients of the independent variables using random effects models. This type of specification takes into consideration the limited unit-specific heterogeneity by partially pooling the data, and is recommended in this case because it allows control of unobservable differences both across districts and over time.[16]

---

14. In the 1977 elections, I have also considered previous political experience during the Francoist period. No Socialist candidate exhibits this kind of PVEA, but some UCD candidates performed representative tasks under the previous regime.

15. I subtract 1 from the district magnitude before calculating the decimal logarithm in order to get a final variable that has a minimum value of 0.

16. With regard to the estimation issues, I prefer to avoid the use of Panel Corrected Standard Errors (PCSE) for two main reasons (Beck and Katz 1995). First, by performing this latter kind of estimation we completely pool the panels and ignore all unit-specific variation. The cross-district variation in the average level of vote ratio by party reported in Table 4.1 suggests that, on the contrary, unit-specific heterogeneity can make a difference in the estimation. In addition, the asympotic behaviour of the generalised least squares estimators is a second technical reason to reject PCSE. Since the elements in the covariance matrix in the PCSE are estimated across panels for each point in time, they only become efficient as the number of repeated observations approaches infinity. Suffice it to remember on this issue that the number of elections held in Spain since the transition to democracy is still small (T = 10). In contrast, the estimators of the random effects models with maximum likelihood achieve their asymptotic behaviour as the number of panels (districts) approaches infinity (here, J = 50). Hence, this latter econometric technique outperforms PCSE with generalised least squares. In addition, the Breusch and Pagan Lagrangian multiplier test for random effects indicates that this type of effects have to be included (chi-squared(1) = 1050.64; p = 0.0000). This is the value of the chi-squared test from model 4 in Table 4.5. The rest of the values are analogous, and available upon request. Finally, according to the Hausman test for the fixed and random effects regressions, I use a random effects models instead of a fixed-effects model. For example, the differences in coefficients between the consistent (fixed effects) and the efficient (random effects) estimators are not statistically significant (chi-squared = 1.82; p = 0.9351) in model 4 of Table 4.7, and this fact leads me to use the latter.

Table 4.1: Electoral performance by district, UCD (1977–1979), AP (1982–1986), PP (1989–2008) and PSOE (1977–2008)

District	PSOE (%)	UCD/AP/PP (%)
Álava	29.06	24.46
Albacete	45.1	39.76
Alicante	42.35	40.3
Almería	45.5	38.68
Asturias (Ppdo. de)	40.88	36.1
Ávila	27.37	52.18
Badajoz	47.93	37.94
Baleares (Islas)	35.08	44.87
Barcelona	38.98	15.91
Burgos	32.72	49.16
Cáceres	46.9	39.38
Cádiz	47.79	28.9
Cantabria	37.57	43.96
Castellón	40.63	41.97
Ciudad Real	46.1	40.36
Córdoba	45.91	29.62
Coruña (A)	32.53	43.36
Cuenca	40.77	46.81
Girona	31.13	13.89
Granada	47.03	34.91
Guadalajara	35.01	47.03
Guipúzcoa	24.17	13.88
Huelva	51.97	31.46
Huesca	40.49	36.82
Jaén	50.65	32.13
León	38.86	43.53
Lugo	28.49	49.94
Lleida	28.87	18.86
Madrid (Com. De)	37.46	40.34
Málaga	47.53	31.26
Murcia (Región de)	39.65	45.33
Navarra	30.81	35.03
Ourense	29.53	48.67
Palencia	36.98	47.93
Palmas (Las)	27.12	41.41
Pontevedra	29.92	45.79
Rioja (La)	37.92	45.74
Salamanca	35.29	48.79
Segovia	31.89	49.87

District	PSOE (%)	UCD/AP/PP (%)
Sevilla	51.29	27.42
Soria	33.2	50.8
Sta. Cruz de Tenerife	33	32.58
Tarragona	35.06	20.1
Teruel	36.78	42.05
Toledo	41.99	42.73
Valencia	40.31	34.82
Valladolid	38.34	42.52
Vizcaya	25.65	16.32
Zamora	34.57	48.37
Zaragoza	36.53	35.2
Total	37.81	37.78

Source: Ministerio del Interior (www.mir.es).

Finally, I would like to address the fundamental problem of causality that it could be argued that exists when high-quality candidates run in districts where the party traditionally performs well; and not the other way round, as I try to show here. I think that this is not very problematic because the top slots are basically safe seats for both major parties in every district. The expected electoral fortune of a party in a given district does not determine the strategic allocation of a candidate with high PVEA to that district because, whenever he/she runs, he/she will get elected.

Table 4.2: Descriptive statistics – candidates in Spain

Variable	Observations	Mean	Std. Dev.	Min.	Max.
Vote	1000	37.80	11.51	5.59	68.15
Socialist	500	37.81	9.98	12.39	63.67
Conservative	500	37.78	12.87	5.59	68.15
Parachutist	889	0.30	0.46	0	1
National Minister	992	0.15	0.36	0	1
National Deputy	992	0.62	0.48	0	1
Regional Minister	992	0.15	0.36	0	1
Regional Deputy	992	0.21	0.41	0	1
Mayor	992	0.09	0.28	0	1
District Magnitude (Logged)	1000	1.53	0.63	0	3.52
Time	1000	4.5	2.87	0	9

Source: Own dataset based on data available from the Ministerio del Interior (www.mir.es) and the Congreso de los Diputados (www.congreso.es).

70 | personal representation

RESULTS

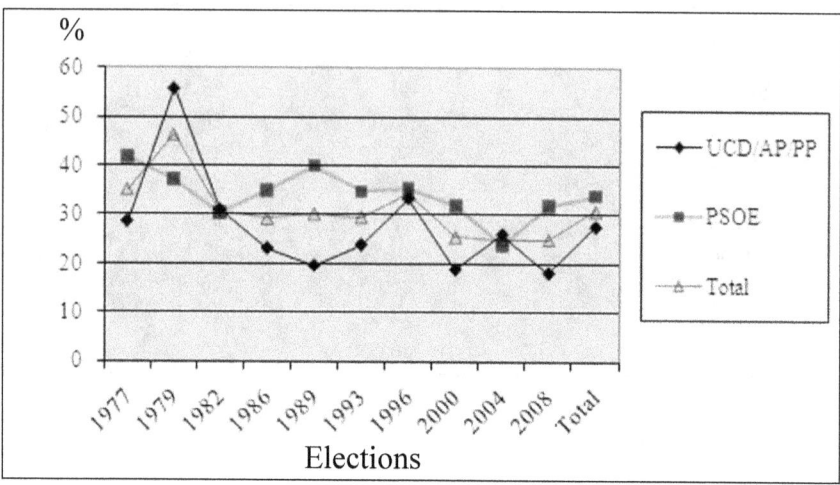

Note: Data show the percentage of candidates on the top of the lists that neither were born nor have been elected in previous local contests within the district where they are currently running. Data on the PSOE has been collected for all the elections; data on the conservative parties depends on the year under study: UCD for 1977 and 1979, AP for 1982 and 1986, and PP from 1989 to 2008.

Figure 4.1: Ratios of parachutists by party and election

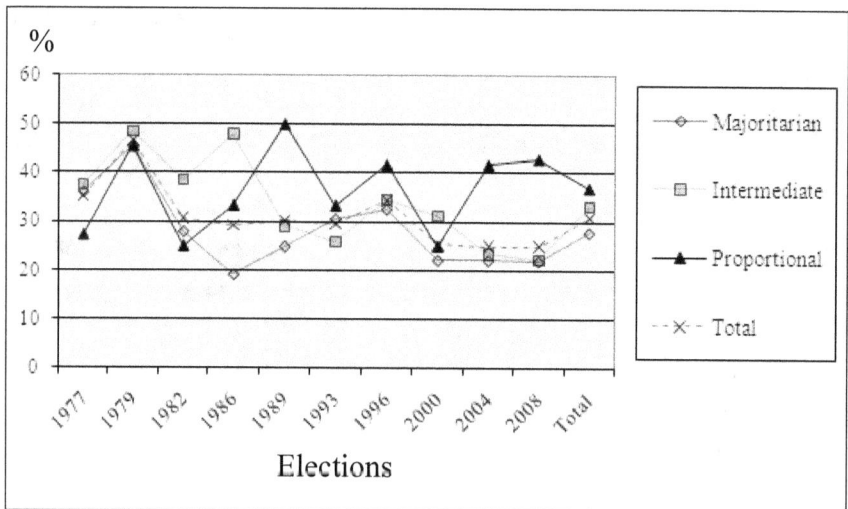

Note: Data show the percentage of candidates on the top of the lists that neither were born nor have been elected in previous local contests within the same district where they are currently running. The districts have been divided into three types according to their magnitude: majoritarian districts are those with magnitudes from 2 to 5; intermediate districts are those with magnitudes from 6 to 9; and proportional districts are those with magnitudes above 10.

Figure 4.2: Ratios of parachutists by district magnitude and election

Figures 4.1 to 4.4 display some preliminary evidence on how widespread is the placement of candidates with high PVEA on the top of the lists.[17] First of all, I offer the ratios of parachutists on the top of the lists across parties (Figure 4.1), district magnitudes (Figure 4.2) and elections (both). As can be seen, there is a slight temporal trend with regard to parachutists since candidates without any kind of local connection seem to have become more frequent in recent elections. In addition, the Socialist Party appears to be more prone to place carpetbaggers on the top of the lists than its conservative opponents, though the differences are probably non-statistically significant. Finally, the effect of district magnitude on the likelihood of observing a parachutist on the top of the lists fits what we could expect according to the literature on personal vote: non-local candidates become slightly more frequent as district magnitude increases.

In Figures 4.3 and 4.4, I present some similar evidence about the placement on the top of the lists of candidates that serve as ministers at the time of the election.[18] As can be seen, this strategy has been far from unusual during the current democratic period in Spain. Figure 4.3 shows that almost two thirds of the members of the cabinet at the time of the election (65.69 per cent) run on the top of a list.[19] In fact, almost 90 per cent of the then current UCD ministers were placed on the top of a list in the 1979 election. After the period of the mid-nineties, when the highly discredited incumbent Socialists tended to rely on other types of strategies in order to get re-elected, the placement of ministers on the top of the lists became again widely used both by the PP (2000 and 2004 elections) and the PSOE (2008 election). How important is district magnitude as a predictor of the districts where the ministers were running? In Figure 4.4, I divide districts into three groups according to their magnitude,[20] and display the percentage of candidates on the top of the lists of the incumbent party that are current ministers. As can be seen, it is substantially more likely to find a member of the cabinet on the top of the lists in the so-called proportional districts (those where ten or more seats are allocated). This finding runs against what we would expect according to Carey and Shugart's theory. However, it could be the case that parties allocate ministers to larger districts with the aim of obtaining more than one extra seat.

---

17. The descriptive statistics of all the variables used in this chapter are presented in Table 4.2.

18. In this part of the analysis, as in Tables 4.5 to 4.7, I rely on data about Ministers because I assume that they are the candidates with the highest level of PVEA.

19. There are two basic destinations for those members of the cabinet that do not run on the top of a list. On the one hand, some of them simply withdraw from politics, like the Prime Minister Aznar in 2004, or abstain from running as a candidate, like the Vice President Gutiérrez Mellado in 1979. On the other, most of them strengthen the lists of the biggest districts. For example, Ernest Lluch (Minister of Health) and Javier Solana (Minister of Education) were included in the Socialist lists of Madrid and Barcelona in the 1986 and 1989 elections, respectively.

20. Majoritarian districts are those with magnitudes from 2 to 5; intermediate districts are those with magnitudes from 6 to 9; and proportional districts are those with magnitudes above 10.

| personal representation

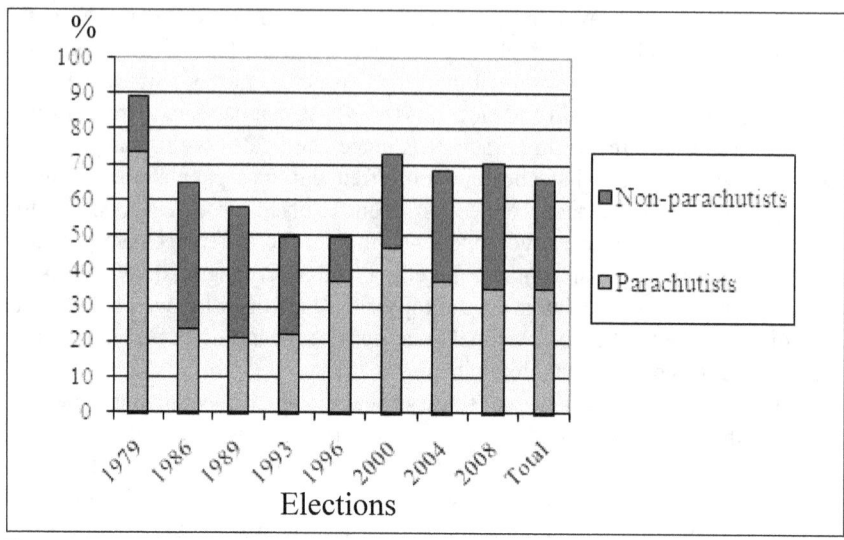

Note: Data show the percentage of ministers at the time of the election who are placed on the top of a list. Parachutists are those ministers who were heading a list in a district where they were neither born nor have been elected in previous local contests. UCD was in power after the 1977 and 1979 elections; the OPSOE was in power after the 1982, 1986, 1989, 1993, 2004 and 2008 elections, and the PP was in power after the 1996 and 2000 elections.

Figure 4.3: Ratios of ministers strategically allocated by birthplace and election

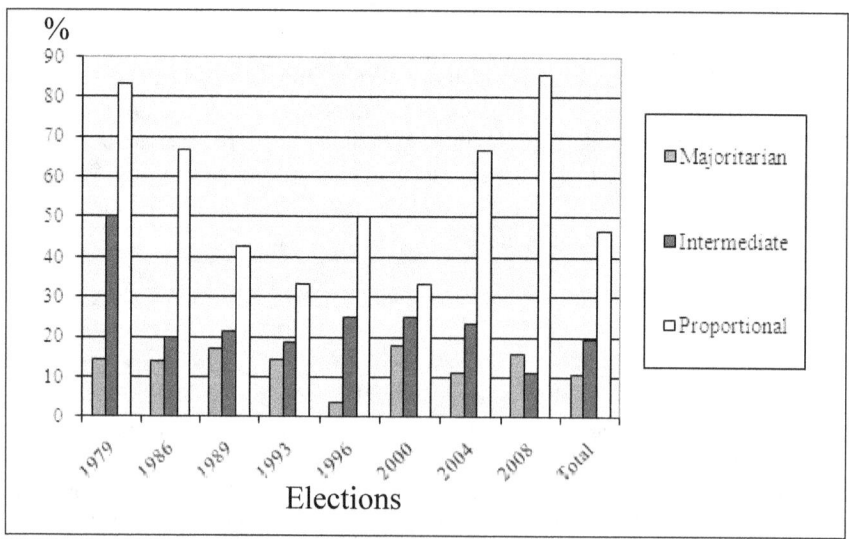

Note: Data show the percentage of ministers at the time of the election who are placed on the top of a list. The districts have been divided into three types according to their magnitude: majoritarian districts are those with magnitudes from 2 to 5; intermediate districts are those with magnitudes from 6 to 9; and proportional districts are those with magnitudes above 10.

Figure 4.4: Ratios of ministers strategically allocated by district magnitude and election

Table 4.3: Mean comparison tests by birthplace

	All the districts	**PSOE**	**UCD/PP**
Observations	884	457	427
Non-Parachutists	37.78 (11.49)	37.20 (9.64)	38.39 (13.17)
Parachutists	39.74 (10.90)	40.17 (10.10)	39.27 (11.73)
Difference	-1.95	-2.96	-0.88
t	-2.51	-3.14	-0.70
$p > t$	0.01**	0.001***	0.482

Note: Standard deviations in parentheses; ***$p<0.01$, **$p<0.05$.

Table 4.4: Mean comparison tests by membership of the national government

	All the districts	**PSOE**	**UCD/PP**
Observations	992	500	492
Ministers	41.39 (10.01)	40.81 (8.17)	42.04 (11.81)
Non-Ministers	37.60 (11.37)	37.41 (10.14)	37.78 (12.41)
Difference	3.79 (1.13)	3.40 (1.37)	4.25 (1.82)
t	3.35	2.47	2.33
$p > t$	0.0008***	0.013**	0.019**

Note: Standard deviations in parentheses; ***$p<0.01$, **$p<0.05$.

In Tables 4.3 and 4.4, I present evidence that bears on the first two hypotheses sketched out in the previous section. To be more specific, I have estimated whether the differences in the vote share of the parties at the district level between those districts where the candidate on the top of the list is either native or a (current or former) minister, and those where these are not the cases, are statistically significant. First of all, parties' performance seems to be better if the candidate on the top of the list is a parachutist rather than a 'local'. This result stands against my hypothesis about the negative effect of parachutists on the electoral performance of a list, and holds for the overall sample (p<0.05), and the Socialist candidates (p<0.01). In contrast, the electoral fortune of the conservative parties seems to be uncorrelated with the level of localism that exhibit the candidates on the top of the lists. With regard to Hypothesis 2, the vote share of a party is 3.79 percentage points higher in those districts where a minister is running on the top of the list (compared to those in which the top-candidate is not neither a current nor a former member of the cabinet). This difference is statistically significant at the 0.01 level. This result also holds for both parties separately ($p<0.05$).

In order to avoid establishing spurious relationships and take into account the particular characteristics of a given district and election that could bias my results, in the last part of the chapter I have performed some multi-variable analyses. The results of all the models are displayed in Tables 4.5 to 4.7. In particular, I have run six specifications: a pure 'native' model, where the only regressor is the dummy variable *parachutist*; a pure 'expert' model, with only the dummy variable *minister* as a regressor; an additive model in which both previous variables are included; a full additive model in which the rest of the explanatory factors about the quality of the candidates are included; a first interactive model in which an interaction between *minister* and the decimal logarithm of the transformed district magnitude is added to the third specification; and a final model in which an interaction between *minister* and the counter of the number of elections held at each point of time is added to the third specification.

Table 4.5 includes the results of the econometric models for the whole sample.[21] In the first model, the coefficient of *parachutist* is, according to my expectations, negative, but statistically insignificant at the traditional levels of confidence. This pattern is repeated in the rest of the models. If the whole theory I have set in the chapter were right, voters would care about the quality (or, in this case, the lack of quality) of the candidates on the top of the lists and should punish parties for placing parachutists there. However, this does not seem to be the case and the coefficient does not reach statistical significance. Hence, either parties are able to successfully hide the lack of localness of some of their candidates, or voters simply do not care about this issue. In contrast, model 2 shows that the presence of a national minister on the top of a list fosters the vote share of a party at the district-level by almost 4 points ($p<0.01$). This result holds in model 3, where the two previous regressors are combined. In the 'full' additive specification (model 4), *parachutist* is positive but also non-statistically significant. In addition, top-candidates that have served as regional ministers do not improve the electoral fortune of a party at the district-level. In contrast, the rest of the variables about the previous political experience of the candidate on the top of the list (*national deputy*, *national minister*, *regional deputy* and *mayor*) have, as expected, a positive and statistically significant effect on the vote share of a party in a given constituency. The size of the effects are about 3.5 percentage points for all of them but *regional deputy*, whose positive impact is below 2. Hence, *ceteris paribus*, that is, once we take into account variation across units and over time, parties perform better in those districts where high-quality candidates are placed at the top of the list.

Results do not fit my expectations about how the level of personal vote changes across districts with different magnitudes. In this sense, the interaction in model 5 between minister and district magnitude is negative, but it is far from statistical significance. This result leads us to think that the amount of personal vote can

---

21. The same models have been replicated introducing the evolution of the GDP in the year before the election at the district-level. The results do not change at all, and are available upon request.

Table 4.5: Determinants of personal vote in Spain, PSOE (1977–2008), UCD (1977 and 1979), AP (1982 and 1986) and PP (1989–2008)

Independent Variables	Models					
	1	2	3	4	5	6
Parachutist	-0.085 (0.669)		-0.710 (0.671)	0.266 (0.675)	-0.085 (0.671)	0.058 (0.641)
National Minister		3.829*** (0.747)	3.830*** (0.750)	3.395*** (0.737)	4.538** (1.988)	5.048*** (1.483)
National Deputy				3.184*** (0.554)		
Regional Minister				0.143 (0.859)		
Regional Deputy				1.811** (0.741)		
Mayor				3.603*** (0.989)		
Magnitude (Logged)					-3.802*** 1.250)	
Minister*Magnitude (Logged)					-0.293 (1.036)	
Time						0.943*** (0.094)
Minister*Time						-0.471* (0.243)
Constant	38.27*** (0.897)	37.27*** (0.879)	37.81*** (0.903)	34.71*** (0.992)	43.60*** (2.087)	33.26*** (1.008)
Overall R-squared	0.0084	0.0184	0.0110	0.0364	0.0513	0.0541
Observations	889	992	889	889	889	889
Number of panels	100	100	100	100	100	100

Note: The dependent variable is the vote share of each party at the district-level; The models are estimated using a Random Effects Model; Standard errors are given in parentheses; *** $p<0.01$, ** $p<0.05$, * $p<0.1$.

Table 4.6: Determinants of personal vote in Spain, PSOE (1977–2008)

Independent Variables	Models					
	1	2	3	4	5	6
Parachutist	-0.358		-0.568	-0.771	-0.579	0.010
	(0.884)		(0.880)	(0.907)	(0.881)	(0.827)
National Minister		2.687***	2.639***	2.464**	4.610*	6.738***
		(1.000)	(0.975)	(0.969)	(2.716)	(2.381)
National Deputy				3.810***		
				(0.742)		
Regional Minister				-0.569		
				(1.198)		
Regional Deputy				2.355**		
				(1.176)		
Mayor				0.556		
				(1.447)		
Magnitude (Logged)					-0.730	
					(1.537)	
Minister*Magnitude (Logged)					-1.029	
					(1.375)	
Time						0.960***
						(0.119)
Minister*Time						-1.012***
						(0.382)
Constant	38.43***	37.38***	38.04***	35.26***	39.18***	33.56***
	(1.016)	(1.031)	(1.032)	(0.742)	(2.561)	(1.177)
Overall R-squared	0.0234	0.0151	0.0039	0.0102	0.0002	0.0653
Observations	457	500	457	457	457	457
Number of panels	50	50	50	50	50	50

Note: The dependent variable is the vote share of the Socialist Party at the district-level; The models are estimated using a Random Effects Model; Standard errors are given in parentheses; *** $p<0.01$, ** $p<0.05$, * $p<0.1$.

Table 4.7: Determinants of personal vote in Spain, UCD (1977 and 1979), AP (1982 and 1986) and PP (1989–2008)

	Models					
Independent Variables	1	2	3	4	5	6
Parachutist	0.367		-0.895	0.695	-0.676	0.244
	(1.004)		(1.022)	(1.057)	(1.030)	(0.997)
National Minister		4.980***	5.069***	4.440***	4.093	4.614**
		(1.106)	(1.160)	1.150)	(2.928)	(2.043)
National Deputy				2.431***		
				0.837)		
Regional Minister				0.540		
				(1.298)		
Regional Deputy				2.454**		
				(1.023)		
Mayor				5.956***		
				(1.447)		
Magnitude (Logged)					-6.561***	
					(1.889)	
Minister*Magnitude (Logged)					0.713	
					(1.575)	
Time						0.927***
						(0.150)
Minister*Time						-0.098
						(0.337)
Constant	38.08***	37.16***	37.57***	34.71***	47.57***	32.94***
	(1.495)	(1.444)	(1.505)	(0.799)	(3.154)	(1.642)
Overall R-squared	0.0017	0.0221	0.0192	0.0618	0.1866	0.0504
Observations	432	492	432	432	432	432
Number of panels	50	50	50	50	50	50

Note: The dependent variable is the vote share of UCD (1977 and 1979), AP (1982 and 1986) and PP (1989–2008) at the district-level; The models are estimated using a Random Effects Model; Standard errors are given in parentheses; *** $p<0.01$, ** $p<0.05$, * $p<0.1$.

also be modified by the importance that strategic voting has acquired in Spain. It is a commonplace in political science that small district magnitude increases the number of voters that tactically defect from their most preferred party, and choose a second option (Cox 1997). If the utility of the vote drives the citizen's decision, and this seems to be very often the case in the smallest Spanish districts, it make it more difficult for other kinds of considerations (e.g. the quality of the candidates on the top of the lists) to have an effect on the vote shares of the parties (Montero and Gunther 1994: 63).

Finally, time does seem to have an impact on how personal quality of the candidates influences the electoral performance of the parties. As I expected, local candidates lose importance as the number of elections held under democracy increases. This result implies that the positive effect of placing a minister on the top of a list has almost disappeared after ten democratic elections. The decreasing impact of the quality of candidates over time could be a consequence of the fact that the two larger parties present ministers and these two parallel strategies neutralise each other. However, empirical data seem to run against this idea: in only five out of fifty districts, both PSOE and PP presented ministers simultaneously in the 2008 election. In addition, as can be seen below, the decreasing impact over time is only observed in the case of Socialist ministers.

In Tables 4.6 and 4.7, I have split the sample in two halves: one for PSOE, and the other one for the main conservative party in each point of time. Results are in general according to what we have seen in the pooled sample. However, some of the coefficients are reduced to statistically insignificant values. For example, mayors are no longer a proper device to improve electoral performance of the Socialist Party (model 4, Table 4.6). In contrast, this factor keeps its explanatory power in the models where the vote share of the main centre-right party is endogenised. Hence, either the Socialist Party does not sufficiently highlight the record of political service at the local level of its candidates, or voters do not reward it. It is also important to note that the decrease in the positive effect of ministers placed on the top of the list that we observe in the pooled sample over time is exclusively driven by Socialist politicians. The size of the coefficients indicates that in the last two elections Rodríguez Zapatero did not get any benefit from placing his ministers on the top of a district-level list.

CONCLUSION: NORMATIVE AND EMPIRICAL IMPLICATIONS

One of the fundamental matters for democracy is the trade-off between local and national representation. It is undeniable that parties help to solve collective action problems and reduce transaction costs in the electoral arena, acting as *brand names* based on voters' party identification, the state of the economy, or the government's legislative record in office (Kiewiet and McCubbins 1991: 39); and closed-lists seem to reinforce the benefits that citizens extract from parties as the main agents of national and programmatic representation. Unfortunately, this kind of electoral rules forces us to pay the price of less local representation (Shugart *et al.* 2005), and even the election of unpopular candidates.

In this chapter, I have shown that voters in Spain are moderately able to judge the quality of the candidate on the top of a district-level list, and, as a consequence, vote accordingly. To be more specific, previous representative experience of these particular candidates is an informational shortcut that rational voters use in order to make electoral decisions. This kind of heuristics seems to have lost importance in recent elections, although we should be very careful about coming to a definitive conclusion on the role of time. In addition, not all my theoretical predictions are confirmed by the econometric models. In this sense, two of the empirical findings of the chapter run against what I expected. First, localness of the candidate on the top of the list does not determine the vote share of the party at the district-level. Second, the importance of personal vote-earning attributes does not decline when district magnitude increases. To sum up, we should avoid adopting a deterministic approach in the study of the effects of electoral systems. In spite of the large literature that establishes that candidates have no incentives to pursue a personal vote in a closed-list PR system, I have showed that some levels of this kind of vote exist in Spain.

These positive findings notwithstanding, any definitive answer to the question about the levels of personal vote that exist in countries with this sort of electoral rules should be postponed for at least two reasons. First of all, many voters cannot remember when they are asked the name of the candidate who heads the district-list of the party they vote for (Montero and Gunther 1994). This empirical fact leads me to think that an ideal extension of the chapter should introduce as explanatory factor how well-known are the top-candidates within the district. Unfortunately, this type of data is not available for many elections. Second, previous elections in Spain have shown that large parties are usually expected to win more than one seat per district, and, subsequently, marginal candidates are not placed on the top of the list. According to this view, and if we accept that candidates also obtain an electoral benefit in exhibiting the correct attributes under closed-list systems, voters should be specially prone to reward those parties whose marginal positions in the lists are occupied by high-quality candidates. In the meantime, and as long as we do not offer definitive evidence on this latter effect, we should retain the idea that Spaniards vote for parties more than for candidates.

chapter five | primary elections
John M. Carey and Harry J. Enten

UNITED STATES OF AMERICA

Primary elections open competition over the selection of candidates within parties beyond high party officials to voters. In this chapter the implications of competition in the selection of presidential candidates are evaluated from the perspective of parties and from that of voters. We draw on presidential elections throughout Latin America from 1978–2006 to compare the performance of candidates selected by primaries with those selected by other methods in general elections. We also present new data from the US primaries during the 2008 electoral cycle to estimate whether greater competition encourages turnout in primary elections. The data from Latin America show that primary-selected presidential candidates outperform those chosen by less open procedures. The data from the 2008 US presidential primaries show no consistent effects of competitiveness on turnout, and among Democratic contests turnout was actually higher as uncertainty over the outcome declined.

Allowing voters to determine the selection of candidates is increasingly common in recent decades, but it is still not the norm among presidential democracies. Primaries have played a role in candidate selection in the major parties of the United States of America for over a century and have determined these decisions for four decades. Since the late 1990s, Uruguay has required all presidential candidates to be selected by primary, and in 2009 Argentina adopted legislation mandating primaries for all subsequent elections. Panama required primaries for all parties in its 1999 election and Paraguay did the same in 2003. Beyond these cases, however, parties decide for themselves whether to open candidate selection to voters or to maintain more centralised control over these critical decisions.

Because these presidencies are all one-person (rather than collegial) executives, all the elections we examine are contests for a single seat, and none allows for the ordinal ranking of candidates in the general election. Thus, according to the classification of electoral systems advanced in the introductory chapter of this volume, the adoption of primaries in these cases is always a move from a closed to a semi-open single-seat election. As such, it increases voters' opportunities to seek personal representation. To the extent this opportunity appeals to voters, primaries should attract them. Yet the decision to select candidates by primary must be taken by parties – generally by party leaders and officials for whom a primary implies relinquishing control over the party's biggest prize, the presidential nomination. So primaries present a conundrum for party leaders: is there an electoral benefit – or potentially a cost – associated with allowing more personal representation in presidential elections?

This paper evaluates the implications of competition in the selection of presidential candidates from the perspective of parties and from that of voters. We assume that the fundamental electoral interest of parties is to win votes, so our benchmark for whether open competition in candidate selection benefits parties is the impact of selection by primary on vote shares. We assess voter gusto for competition by estimating whether greater uncertainty over which candidate will prevail prompts higher rates of turnout in primaries.

We draw on two separate sources of data. To assess the effects of primaries on candidate strength, we rely on data from general elections throughout Latin

America, which frequently pit primary-selected candidates against those designated by party organisations. Incomplete data on voter eligibility rules, and on primary turnout, across these elections present obstacles to relying on the Latin American data to estimate effects of primaries on participation. So we draw on new data from the USA, taking advantage of the unique sequential primary format, to evaluate whether the competitiveness of nomination contests at the national level affect turnout in state-level primaries.

PRIMARIES AND CANDIDATE STRENGTH[1]

The Primary Penalty Hypothesis

Primary elections have a longer and more extensive history in the USA than in any other country and, although primaries were initially advocated by progressive reformers early in the 20th Century as enhancing democracy, they have generally been regarded sceptically by observers whose primary concern was choosing the strongest candidate for the general election. The standard proposition is that primaries mobilise ideologically extremist electorates which, in turn, choose candidates unappealing to the general electorate (Key 1947; Ranney 1968; Polsby 1983; Crotty and Jackson 1985; McCann 1995; Colomer 2003). The counterfactual proposition is that the more savvy selectors, looking toward the general election, could identify stronger candidates than primary electorates. Let us call this the primary penalty hypothesis. An alternative reason to expect a primary penalty is that primary campaigns are inherently divisive, subjecting their participants – whatever their initial appeal – to public criticism and opening up internal divisions within parties (Hacker 1965; Kenney and Rice 1987; Lengle, Owen and Sonner 1995; Atkeson 1998).

Although logically compelling, the primary penalty hypothesis has found mixed support in studies of US elections. Moreover, neither rationale for the primary penalty – ideological extremism or battle scars from primary competition – is as compelling in environments outside the USA. The extremism argument depends on a political system in which parties are paired on alternative sides of a median voter, such that median primary voters are located away from the general election centre of gravity (Brady, Han and Pope 2005). The primary electorate of a party positioned at the median voter, by contrast, should not stray from the centre, nor should the activist bases of parties with competitors on their ideological flanks be expected to be ideologically extreme.

In short, in multi-party systems there is less reason to expect that political bosses should be able to pick stronger candidates than primaries would. Electoral competition outside the USA generally includes more than two parties. In presidential elections among Latin American democracies over the past three decades, more than eight parties or coalitions ran candidates on average, and the mean effective number of vote-winning candidates in those elections was greater than three.

---

1. The data and results in this section of the paper are drawn from previous research by Carey, partly in collaboration with John Polga-Hecimovich.

Concern that primaries should leave even their winners indelibly scarred are also less compelling outside the USA. The US presidential primary system is unique in that it is drawn out over half a year across a long sequence of state-level contest. In the latter half of this paper, we exploit the sequential format of US primaries in an effort to gain leverage on the effect of competitiveness on primary participation. For present purposes, however, the point is that the US primary calendar is unique. Presidential primaries elsewhere are one-shot, national affairs, less inclined to leave candidates depleted financially and politically.

An Alternative Hypothesis: Primary Bonus
Political reformers advocating the adoption of primary elections do so on grounds of openness, transparency, and more inclusive democracy (Latin America Data Base 2005; Reuters 2005). To the extent this claim rings true with voters, primaries may be general election assets rather than liabilities. There is good reason to expect that transparency in internal party decisions should appeal to voters in Latin America, for example, where cynicism toward political parties is widespread. Political parties are among the least trusted institutions in the Latinobarómetro opinion poll, with only 24 per cent of respondents, regionwide, expressing 'much' or 'substantial' confidence in parties in the 2009 survey (Latinobarometro 2009). In short, there is a lot of room for parties to improve their standing in the eyes of voters in presidential democracies, and the potential for personal representation to appeal over pure partisan representation. If voters value intra-party democracy, selection by primary might confer an electorally valuable stamp of democratic legitimacy.

Primaries might also be more effective than elite-driven search processes in identifying candidates with broad popular appeal, particularly those who are not already well entrenched among capitol-city elites. Carlos Menem's emergence in the 1988 *Partido Justicialista* (PJ) primary in Argentina is an example. As governer of tiny La Rioja Province in Western Argentina, relative unknown Menem faced Buenos Aires governor Antonio Francisco Cafiero in the race for the PJ nomination. Menem's flamboyant and hard-nosed style of campaigning proved effective. His unexpected victory over Cafiero attracted widespread media attention to his personal charisma and political canniness, and he went on to win the general election by 15 per cent of the popular vote (McGuire 1997; Latin America Data Base 1999).

Another potential advantage of primaries is in generating consensus – or at least mitigating dissent – within coalitions of parties that seek to endorse a joint candidate but lack an established selection procedure. By turning the decision on candidate selection over to voters, primaries relieve party leaders and coalition partners of the prickly task of choosing a common candidate, and may legitimise the anointed candidate in the eyes of those partners who do not get the nod. In 1999, for example, a bloc of Chilean Christian Democrats threatened to bolt from the *Concertación* coalition and support a candidacy by Senator Andrés Zaldívar, but were mollified by an agreement to hold an intra-coalition primary election. Zaldívar lost the contest to Socialist Ricardo Lagos, but the Christian Democrats remained on board, perhaps encouraged by Lagos' pledge during the primary campaign 'to be the third president of the *Concertación*, not the second Socialist president,' and Lagos won the ensuing general election (Notisur 1999).

Testing the Primary Bonus Hypothesis
Earlier work, the results from which are reviewed here, tests the primary penalty and primary bonus hypotheses against data from every democratic presidential election in Latin America from each country's most recent transition to democracy (or since 1978 for those countries that have experienced uninterrupted democratic elections since that time) through 2006 (Carey and Polga-Hecimovich 2006, 2008). The data include 821 presidential candidates across 95 elections in 18 countries, of which 60 candidates from 33 different parties and coalitions, across 37 elections in 15 countries were selected by primary. Each observation in the data is a candidate in a given election.

The regression analysis identifies the effect of holding a primary on the performance of presidential candidates by controlling for the baseline strength of each candidate's party and the strength of partisan tides running toward or against that party in order to estimate the marginal effect of having been selected by primary or not.

The dependent variable is the candidate's general election vote share. The independent variables include baseline party strength, measured by the percentage of vote won by the candidate's party in the previous election; whether the candidate's party currently holds the presidency; whether the candidate himself is the incumbent president; whether the candidate is endorsed by more than one party; average annual growth rate of GDP over the previous presidential term; and the interaction between economic growth and incumbent party status. Including the latter term allows the analysis to test for the differential effects of strong/weak economic performance on parties inside and outside of government. The intuition is that strong economies help governing parties at the next election, but not necessarily opposition parties, whereas weak economies hurt those in government.

The effects of all these control variables are as expected. The strongest predictor of a candidate's vote share is her or his party's share in the previous election. However, given that Latin American voters have tended to lose patience with incumbent parties (often with good reason), it is not surprising that, other things being equal, candidates from incumbent parties tend to lag behind the vote shares of their winning predecessors – by almost 8 per cent, for example, if the economy has been stagnant over the previous presidential term. Economic growth does nothing for opposition party candidates, but it helps those from incumbent parties – or rather, mitigates the general tendency of incumbent parties to lose vote share (see also Molina 2001). The break-even point for incumbent party candidates is around 6 per cent annual GDP growth over the previous term. Above this point, an incumbent party candidate can expect to increase on his predecessor's vote share, but that daunting threshold is eliminated entirely if the incumbent himself is allowed to run for consecutive re-election.[2] Finally, being endorsed by other parties besides

---

2. There is inevitably something of a selection effect driving this result, as the incumbent presidents

one's own also helps presidential candidates, with coalition candidates receiving an average boost of around 5 per cent above their party's expected vote share.

Having controlled for baseline party strength and current political context, it is straightforward to estimate the marginal effect on a party's vote share of nominating its candidate by primary. The regression analysis shows a stunning primary bonus of 5 per cent of the general election vote. This result is robust to alternative specifications of the statistical model – for example, dropping all minor party candidates (those who capture less than 3 per cent of the vote) from the analysis or controlling for whether a given primary-selected candidates faced any other competitors also selected by primaries. When the field contains more than one primary-selected candidate, the primary bonus is shared and the expected electoral diminishes slightly but the estimated net effect remains positive at over 4 per cent and statistically significant.

On the whole, the evidence from Latin American presidential elections refutes the primary penalty hypothesis and supports the idea of a primary bonus. Increasing personal representation in the form of primary competition within parties, it appears, appeals to voters and attracts them to the party in the general election over and above levels of support that would be expected based on incumbency, coalition participation, and economic performance. This result calls for closer examination of the nature of this apparent electoral advantage. For example, if the inclusiveness of intra-party decisions is the key selling point, then primaries that attract more participation might be expected to yield greater rewards than less inclusive contests. If transparency is the critical selling point, then primaries tainted by fraud might undercut any advantage. There is anecdotal support for these scenarios in the Latin American experience, but the data are not sufficiently detailed or complete to confirm them statistically (Carey and Polga-Hecimovich 2008). We have data on participation levels, for example, for only about a quarter of the primaries conducted since 1978, and coding primaries reliably for fraud is notoriously difficult. With time, as more parties in more countries select candidates by primary, our reservoir of information on these contests should expand, allowing for more precise estimates of the size and sources of whatever electoral advantage primaries confer.

---

included in the data who opted to run for re-election – Menem in Argentina in 1995, Cardoso in Brazil in 1998, Chavez in Venezuela in 2000 and 2006, and Uribe in Colombia in 2006 – all enjoyed considerable popularity at the time. (Fujimori's two re-elections in Peru, in 1995 and 2000, are not included in the analysis because the country's Polity IV score was below 5 in those years.) Recent constitutional reforms in many presidential democracies should increase the frequency with which incumbent presidents stand for re-election, allowing the incumbent-president effect to be estimated more precisely, and distinguished with greater accuracy from the incumbent-party effect.

COMPETITION AND PRIMARY PARTICIPATION

Although the Latin American data cannot yet decisively confirm that primary participation boosts candidate strength, there is a widespread belief among US candidates and campaigners that this is the case. A Democratic National Committee memo from the heat of the 2008 primary season, for instance, pointed to higher turnout in Democratic than Republican primaries as evidence of 'unprecedented enthusiasm for our candidates, [while] the news continues to be worrisome for John McCain' (Democratic National Committee 2008). *Prima facie*, this logic appears unimpeachable with respect to the 2008 presidential election, where the Democratic primary contests attracted voter participation well above that for any previous presidential primary contest and, of course, the Democrats eventual nominee, Barack Obama, won a convincing victory in the general election.

There is also evidence from other electoral environments that competitive elections attract higher turnout than non-competitive ones. Powell (1982), for instance, shows that elections in systems where small vote shifts can affect seat distributions on the margin generate higher turnout than systems, like that of the USA, where the vote share that must shift to affect outcomes tends to be larger. A review of related literature concludes that 'closeness has been found to increase turnout in twenty-seven of the thirty-two studies that have tested the relationship, in many different settings and diverse methodologies' (Blais 2000). Whether voters are motivated by the belief that their individual votes might be pivotal, or close competition simply compels voter attention, attracting them to the polls, the hypothesis that competition breeds participation finds some support in diverse environments. In this section of the paper, we examine whether variation in competitiveness within US primaries is correlated with variation in voter participation.

Comparative analysis of electoral participation is complicated by the myriad varying factors that might reasonably account for turnout. Voter registration and compulsory voting rules vary, as do parties, platforms, the stakes of elections, and the demographic composition of electorates. Even within a given polity, the inherent appeal of candidates varies from election to election in ways that ought to affect turnout but are difficult to measure to allow the analyst to isolate and estimate the marginal impact of competitiveness.

Why the US Configuration Offers Leverage

The unique configuration of US presidential primaries, with multiple contests spread across states and over an extended campaign period, offers potential analytical leverage on the effect of competitiveness. In 2008, both the Democratic and Republican parties conducted presidential primaries across forty-one states on sixteen different dates between January and June.

Across that range of contests, competitiveness varies in two important ways. First, at the state level, some primaries are dominated by a particular candidate, while others are more closely contested. John McCain won over 70 per cent of the Republican primary vote in Idaho and 80 per cent in Nebraska, whereas in Georgia, McCain, Mitt Romney, Mike Huckabee, and Ron Paul all had totals within 3 percentage points of each other. Among the Democrats, Barack Obama doubled Clinton's vote totals in South Carolina and nearly so in Virginia, whereas the two were within a few per cent of each other in Connecticut, Indiana, and Missouri. Second, the competitiveness of the national-level contests for the nominations varies over time as the primary season wears on. At the time of some primaries, each nomination was widely believed to be wide open, whereas at the time of others the outcomes were understood already to be effectively determined.

Our innovation in this study is to draw on a measure of competitiveness that precisely gauges the beliefs of voters at the time of each primary about how indeterminate was the national-level contest for each party's nomination. We use the Iowa Electronic Markets (IEM), which are real money prediction markets operated by faculty at University of Iowa Henry B. Tippie College of Business. The markets allow any person who pays a five US dollars registration fee to buy and sell contracts, worth a minimum of five US dollars to a maximum of five hundred US dollars, on the likelihood of an event happening (Henry B. Tippie College of Business 2008). The markets vary widely in type, but the political prediction markets, in which investors can buy or sell the chance of a candidate's chance of winning an election, are among the most popular. Prior research indicates that these markets are more stable and more accurate than polls in predicting the final results of elections (Berg, Forsythe, Nelson and Rietz, 2003; Berg, Nelson and Rietz 2003).

During the 2008 primary season, investors could buy and sell contracts on a candidate's chance of winning their party's nomination. For the Democratic primary, contracts were available for Hillary Clinton, Barack Obama, John Edwards, or none-of-the-above. For the Republican primary, investors could purchase contracts for Rudy Giuliani, Mike Huckabee, John McCain, Mitt Romney, Fred Thompson, or none-of-the-above. An investor could purchase contracts on multiple candidates and in both markets. The markets opened in March of 2007 and closed when each party officially nominated its ticket at its national conventions – the end of August 2008 for the Democrats and the beginning of September 2008 for the Republicans.

Figure 5.1 shows the IEM's closing price for the main Democratic candidates on the day before each primary. The markets reflect the relative chances for each candidate to win her or his party's nomination. Before the Iowa Caucus, the IEM regarded Clinton as the favourite for the Democratic nomination, but Obama's victory in Iowa provided a boost to his prospects. Clinton regained her edge following her unexpected victory in the New Hampshire primary, but Obama once again overtook her with his convincing victories on February 5th when twenty-five states held primaries. He maintained this lead through the rest of the primary season, despite slight declines in Iowa market value following losses in the Ohio and Texas primaries on March 4th and the Pennsylvania primary on April 22nd. Obama's victory in North Carolina and surprisingly close second place finish in Indiana on May 6th effectively wrapped up the competition for convention delegates, which registers in the IEM as the value of his contracts approach 1.00.

Figure 5.2 shows the analogous prices for the Republican contest, which was also uncertain at the beginning of the nominating process, but resolved itself much

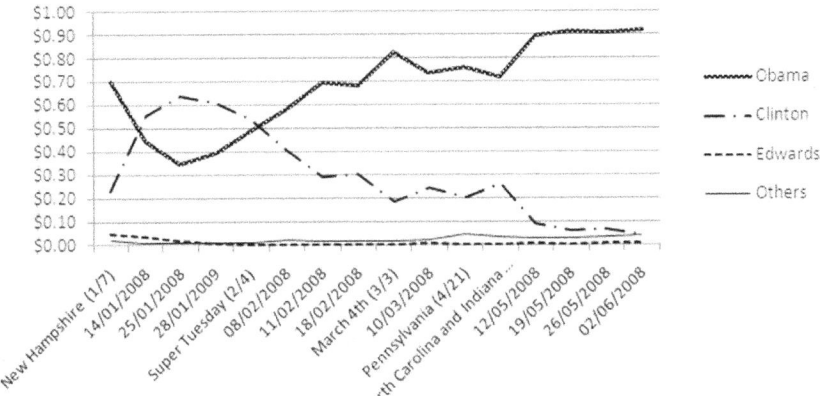

Figure 5.1: Closing prices for Democratic candidates on the Iowa Electronic Market as of the day before primary elections

more quickly. Although the ultimate winner, McCain, was the favourite even before the first primary, Giuliani also had substantial credibility in the markets, due in part to his name recognition from his actions after 9/11. Following losses in each of the first nominating contests – in Iowa, Wyoming, New Hampshire, Michigan, South Carolina, and Florida – Giuliani's IEM price plummeted. Romney, on the other hand, moved into second place with a victory in Michigan, and his contracts gained value on the expectation he would capitalise on this victory due to his moderate persona and large campaign war chest. McCain, however, began to pull away with victories in New Hampshire on January 8th and South Carolina on January 19th. The IEM put his chances of winning the nomination at close to 100 per cent after victories in Florida on January 29th and most of the February 5th primaries, which forced Romney from the race. McCain accumulated a majority of delegates, and thus locked up the nomination for all intents and purposes, after winning all of the March 4th primaries.

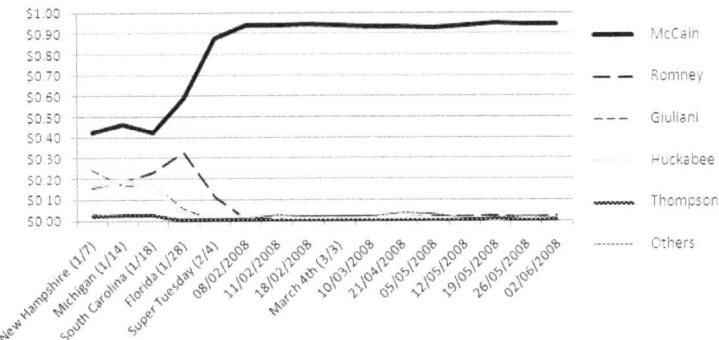

Figure 5.2: Closing prices for Republican candidates on the Iowa Electronic Market as of the day before primary elections

Models and Variables

Our strategy is to isolate any potential impacts of competitiveness at both the state and national level on turnout by comparing the various state primaries within each party against each other. The idea is that this holds the particular election year and the set of candidates constant while the sequence of many primaries provides variance in competitiveness at both levels and, thus, analytical leverage. Of course, not every other factor that might have driven variance in participation rates across the 2008 US primaries was constant across all the contests within each party. The fields of candidates contesting each primary – and critically, their resources – fluctuated on both sides as the electoral calendar drew on. John Edwards dropped from the Democratic field after the early primaries, as did Fred Thompson, Rudy Giuliani and, eventually, Mitt Romney from the Republican field. Nevertheless, the same core candidates – Barack Obama and Hillary Clinton on the Democratic side, John McCain and Mike Huckabee for the Republicans – contested most of them, providing much more continuity in the field of candidates than in studies that span different general elections or compare turnout across countries.

Our dependent variable is voter turnout. The rules of US primaries vary from state to state, however, in ways that directly affect which voters are eligible to participate and, therefore, what is the appropriate standard by which to measure turnout. Our analysis draws on data from forty-one primary elections for each major party.[3] Even among primary contests, however, there are important differences in rules that affect voter eligibility and, thus, how to measure turnout. We divide primaries into three types:

Open: Any voter, regardless of political affiliation, can vote in any party's primary.[4]

Semi-closed: Voters affiliated with a given party, or voters unaffiliated with any party, can vote in that given party's primary, but those previously affiliated with a different party cannot.

Closed: Only those voters previously associated with a party can vote in that party's primary (Blumenthal 2008; Runner 2009).

We analyse each type of primary separately with the dependent variable, turnout, measured as follows:

Open = Votes / Voting Eligible Population

Semi-Closed = Votes / (Registered Partisans + Independents)

Closed = Votes / Registered Partisans[5]

---

3. Nine US states do not hold primary elections.

4. We include here 'semi-open' primaries in which a voter affiliated with another party can sign a form establishing affiliation at the time of the primary in order to establish eligibility.

5. Data on the number of registered partisans for all states are from October 2008 (Winger 2008). This is, of course, after the 2008 primaries concluded, and raw registration numbers certainly

Separating primaries by type limits the number of observations in each analysis but it is necessary to maintain comparability across observations.

We focus on three key independent variables that reflect different dimensions of competitiveness. First, to estimate the degree to which the national-level contest for the party nomination was up for grabs, we use IEM closing prices from the day before each primary to calculate:
Uncertainty$_{PD}$ = 1 − Maximum(Price$_{PD-1}$), where:

P denotes a given party, and

D denotes a given date of a primary.[6]

We calculate the indeterminacy of primary competition at the state level similarly, but using proportions of the state-level vote rather than IEM share prices. Thus, National Uncertainty reflects how far short of a 'sure bet' was the leading candidate for a given party's nomination on a particular day, whereas State Uncertainy reflects the extent to which a given state's primary was not dominated by a single candidate.

Our third and last measure of competitiveness is whether any convention delegates were actually at stake in a given primary. This measure is necessary partly for reasons idiosyncratic to the Democratic nomination battle in 2008, when five states held primary elections that did not allocate delegates. The most notorious cases here were also the most important. In 2007, the Florida and Michigan state-level Democratic parties moved to reschedule their presidential primaries earlier in 2008 than national-level party rules allowed. Their motivation was to raise the prominence of their respective primaries by holding the contests before the nomination had been effectively decided. The Florida and Michigan moves triggered a showdown, however, with the national Democratic Party Chairman, Howard Dean, who sanctioned the states by stripping them of their convention delegates. In addition to Florida and Michigan, there were also no delegates at stake in the Democratic primaries held in Idaho, Nebraska, and Washington state, and in the Republican primary held in Montana, where delegate selection is determined in separate caucuses. As an indicator of the currency of competition in primary elections, then, we include a dummy variable, No Delegates, which takes a value of

---

increased between primary dates and October, with each candidate's voter registration efforts leading up to the general election. This implies that the denominators in our calculation of turnout are somewhat inflated, which will depress our estimates of turnout rates somewhat. This should not affect our ability to detect effects of competitiveness on primary turnout, however, unless rates of post-primary voter registrations across states varied with the national-level competitiveness of either nomination contest at the time primaries were held. We see no reason that this should be the case.

6. We also calculated an alternative measure of how even the top two candidates in a given party were, as follows:
Closeness$_{PD=1}$ − (ABS(Price$_{C1PD-1}$ − Price$_{C2PD-1}$)),
where C1 denotes the first-place candidate and C2 the second-place candidate. The two measures are highly correlated, and the none of the results reported here are affected by using one or the other.

one for these five Democratic contests, and zero otherwise.

We rely on ordinary least squares regression models as follows:

Turnout = a(Constant)

+ B1(National Close)

+ B2(State Close)

+ B3(No Delegates)

In separate analyses (not shown), we also controlled for some additional factors that are regarded to affect turnout. Among demographics, education and unionisation are widely recognised in US voting studies as driving turnout (Wolfinger and Rosenstone 1980; Nie, Junn and Stehlik-Berry 1996; Milligan, Moretti and Oreopoulos 2004; Uhlaner 1989; Leighley and Nagler 1992). We tested models that included state-level measures of the proportion of the population over age twenty-five with some post-secondary education, and the proportion of the workforce that is unionised.

Another factor that varies across US primaries, of course, is time. Although all the data in this paper are from the 2008 cycle, the cycle itself stretched over many months. If voter interest naturally flags over time, turnout could decline even if competitiveness does not. Alternatively, if voters' interest builds as they learn more about the candidates from national news stories, turnout could increase independently from competitiveness or other factors. Either way, we regarded it as worthwhile to test for the effects of how late a primary occurs in the cycle. We included in our models a day counter variable taking a value of 1 on January 1, 2008 (one week before the first primary, in New Hampshire) and running to 155 (the day of the last primaries, on June 3, in Montana, New Mexico, and South Dakota).

None of these control variables produced results indicating a consistent pattern of impact, and their inclusion did not alter the direction of the estimated effects of our competition variables. However, the demographics and time controls do consume statistical degrees of freedom that are precious given the very small number of observations in our models. Therefore, we present our results without including them.

RESULTS

Before turning to the statistical results, Figure 5.3 illustrates the relationships between time, national-level competitiveness, and turnout for open primaries.[7] The horizontal axis represents time, while competitiveness at the national level (solid lines) and turnout (dashed lines) are represented by the height of the lines – grey for the Democrats and black for Republicans. Note that uncertainty over the outcomes of the races, as estimated by the Iowa Electronic Markets, is at its peak early, then drops precipitously for the Republicans and much more gradually for the

---

7. Open primaries are the most numerous type and, of course, involve the most voters. Analogous graphs for semi-closed and closed primaries exhibit similar characteristics.

Democrats. Turnout, by contrast, is more stable in both parties, although it show a gradual increase over time on the Democratic side. In short, the graph shows no obvious connection between the degree to which the nominations are regarded as up in the air and patterns of voter turnout in open primaries.

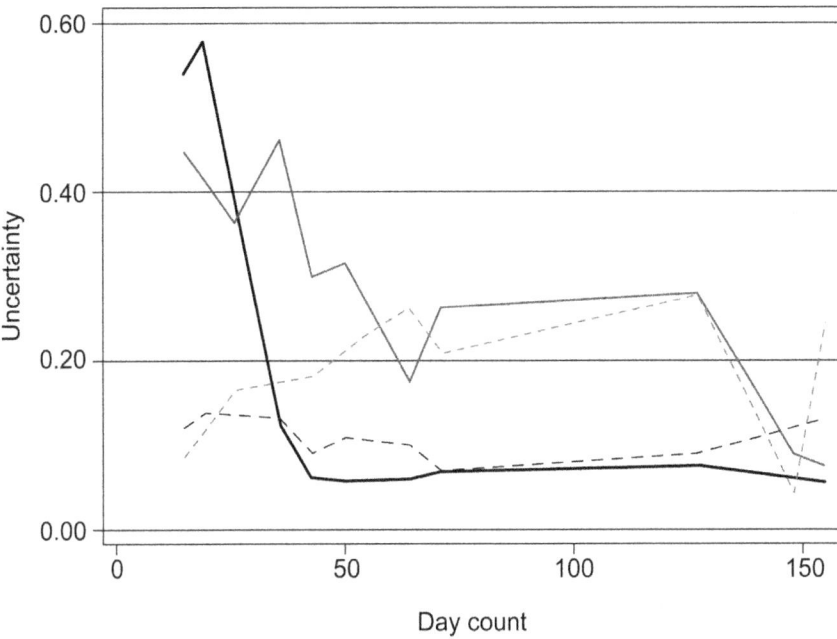

Note: Solid lines represent National-level Uncertainty. Dashed lines show turnout as a proportion of the voting-eligible population. Black for Republicans; Grey for Democrats. Day Count begins on January 1, 2008. On days where multiple primaries were held, the height of the dashed line represents the mean turnout for that party.

Figure 5.3: Uncertainty and turnout over time among open primaries in 2008

The results from our regression analysis, shown in Table 5.1, confirm this unanticipated result. Beginning with the Republicans, the coefficients on our competitiveness variables are inconsistent, both across national-level and state-level Uncertainty, and across the models for the three types of primaries. The coefficients on National Uncertainty are indistinguishable from zero for both open and closed Republican primaries. National Uncertainty is associated with higher turnout among semi-closed primaries, but this category includes only eight Republican primaries, so we are cautious about drawing inferences. Close state-level contests are associated with slightly higher Republican turnout in open primaries, but lower turnout in the semi-closed category, and there is no measurable effect in closed primaries. Overall, then, there is no clear pattern connecting competitiveness to turnout among the Republicans.

On the Democratic side, the story is more puzzling, as the estimated effect of national-level uncertainty on turnout leans towards negative, rising to conventional thresholds of statistical significance in two of the three types of primaries, and very nearly so in the third. The estimated effect of state-level Uncertainty, by contrast, is never statistically discernible from zero. Finally, when No Delegates are at stake in a given primary, turnout is depressed, as expected. In substantive terms, these results suggest that, other things being equal, if you move from the closed Democratic primary where National Uncertainty was lowest (South Dakota at .08) to one of those with the highest National Uncertainty (say, New Mexico at .46), there is an expected *drop* in turnout of 16 per cent. Less dramatically, even a drop of one standard deviation in National Uncertainty – for example, from Maryland at .30 to Louisiana at .42 – yields an expected drop in turnout of 5 per cent, which is substantial when mean turnout in closed primaries is 33 per cent. The results are similar for both open and semi-closed primaries on the Democratic side.

These patterns show up graphically in Figures 5.4a to 5.4c, which plot turnout against National Uncertainty for each of the three types of primaries. Within each panel of the figure, the Republican observations are indicated by state marker labels in standard up-and-down font, whereas Democratic observations are in the font tilted at a 45-degree angle, allowing us to juxtapose the patterns between parties. Those Democratic primaries that allocated no convention delegates are labelled in lower-case letters.

There is no apparent relationship between uncertainty and turnout in the Republican contests. The positive estimate on this variable in the semi-closed category was clearly produced by the high turnout in the New Hampshire primary,

Table 5.1: OLS regressions of turnout on measures of competitiveness, by party and type of primary.

	Republican			Democrat		
	Open	Semi-Closed	Closed	Open	Semi-Closed	Closed
National Uncertainty	-.00 (.03)	.64*** (.13)	.50 (.43)	-.17* (.10)	-.45 (.25)	-.42** (.20)
State-Level Uncertainty	.12*** (.04)	-.24* (.13)	.07 (.24)	.13 (.23)	.74 (.47)	-.17 (.44)
No Delegates	.04* (.02)			-.13*** (.03)	-.34** (.12)	-.01 (.12)
Constant	.06*** (.02)	.19*** (.04)	.25** (.09)	.21* (.11)	.17 (.20)	.63*** (.19)
Ajusted R^2	.41	.79	.06	.46	.40	.16
N	18	8	15	18	9	14

* $p \leq .10$, ** $p \leq .05$, *** $p \leq .0$

which was an outlier on National Uncertainty, occurring in January 2008 before the Republican field had thinned. Among the Democrats, however, the negative correlations between uncertainty and turnout is visible in these graphs. Note that the two main 'off-diagonal' observations, with low turnout along with low uncertainty, are Idaho (among open primaries) and Nebraska (in the semi-closed category) – neither of which allocated delegates by primary.

Our analyses show scant evidence to suggest that competitiveness in primary elections drew US voters to the polls in 2008, and some indication that Democrats turned out more when uncertainty over the outcome of the nomination was lower. We urge caution about drawing strong inferences from these data, given the very small number of observations at hand. Nevertheless, it is worth considering several potential explanations for the murkiness of our results. First, it may be that in US presidential primaries, competitiveness does not attract voters – particularly Democrats – to the polls. Even if that was the case in 2008, however, we suspect that the particularities of that year limit our ability to generalise from it.

The 2008 primary was a genuine watershed on the Democratic side in ways that affected turnout and may well have overwhelmed normal patterns of variance across states. In American history, there had never been a woman nor a minority candidate who had been a viable contender for the presidential nomination of one of the major parties. In 2008, the top rivals for the Democratic nomination were a woman and an African American. The Democratic contest captured the public's attention and mobilised voters at unprecedented levels. Overall, slightly over 37 million voters cast ballots in Democratic primaries in 2008, eclipsing the previous record of 23 million votes, from 1988 by 60 per cent (Cook 2007). Note from Figures 5.4a to 5.4c that Democratic turnout rates far outstripped those among Republicans in all three types of primaries – those open to all voters, those open to Independents along with registered Democrats, and those limited to registered partisans. In terms of overall turnout, 2008 was simply off the charts for the Democrats.

The Democratic primary contest in 2008 was unusual in the demographic characteristics of the main contenders, the high degree of competitiveness, and the unprecedented levels of participation. At the very least, 2008 suggests that participation in primaries is an electoral asset to parties in the general election. It is not necessarily the case that the larger factors at play in boosting overall turnout should overwhelm factors that drive variance among states, but the Democratic turnout tsunami of 2008 certainly presents that possibility. In order to determine whether competitiveness, *per se*, boosts turnout more generally among Democratic primary voters, it would be necessary to replicate the analysis conducted here for years prior to 2008 – a project that falls beyond the scope of this paper.

96 | personal representation

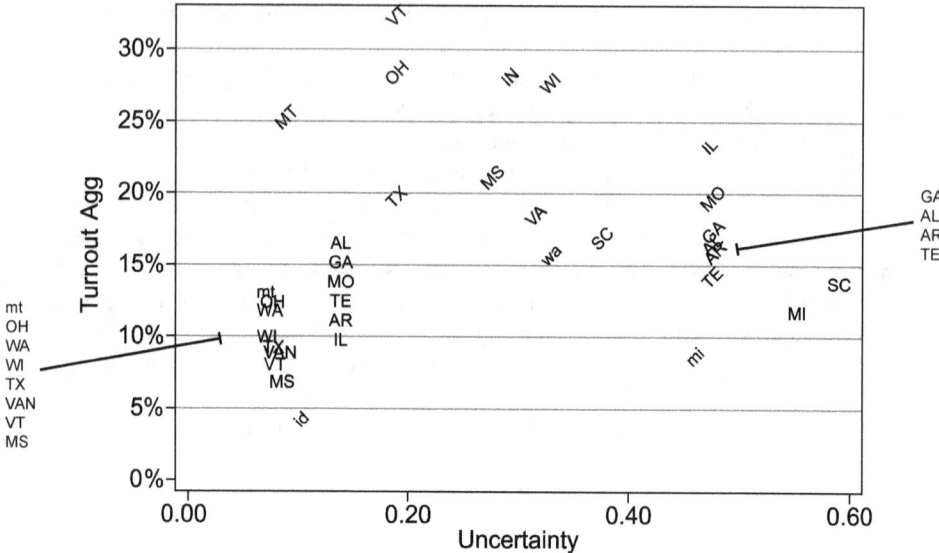

Figure 5.4a: Turnout vs national uncertainty – open primaries

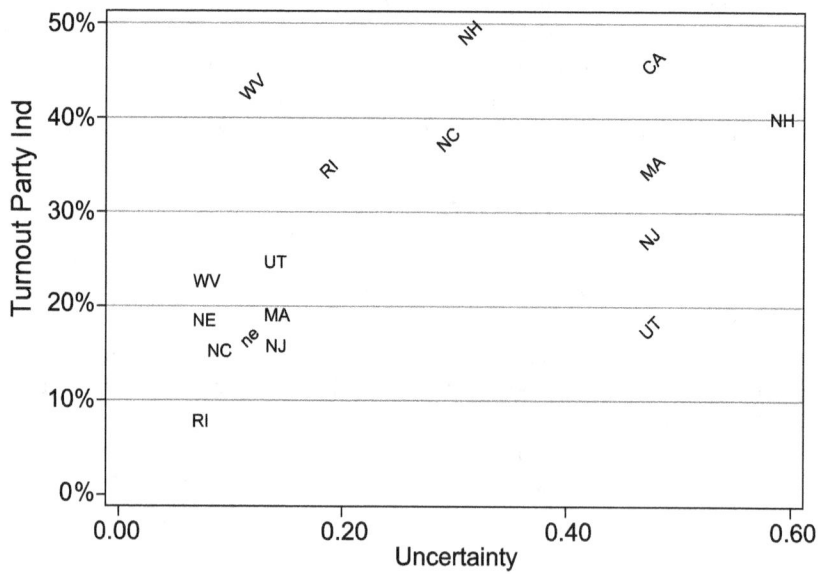

Figure 5.4b: Turnout vs national uncertainty – semi-closed primaries

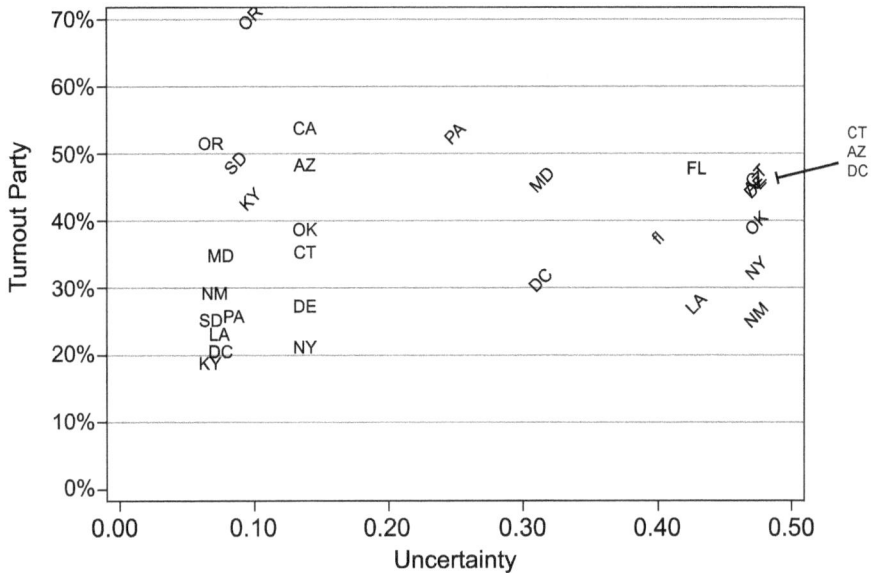

Figure 5.4c: Turnout vs national uncertainty – closed primaries

Note: Republican observations are represented in standard font. Democratic observations are in font tilted at 45 degrees. Primaries that allocated no national convention delegates are in lower-case font.

CONCLUSION

Primary elections open competition over party nominations to voters, tipping the balance between party representation and personal representation toward the latter. We asked in this paper what are the effects of this competition on the strength of candidates in the general election, and on voter participation?

First, although the conventional wisdom, based largely on US elections, has long been that primaries tend to produce weak candidates – battle-scarred and more ideologically extreme than the median voter in the general election – analysis of Latin American elections shows that candidates selected by primary win higher vote shares, other things being equal, than do candidates selected by less inclusive methods. Instead of a primary penalty, that is, there appears to be a substantial primary bonus for parties that open their nomination process to voters. In this sense, increasing personal representation appears to be complementary with the overall partisan goal of winning elections, not at odds with it.

Second, based on data from the 2008 presidential primaries in the USA, we found no evidence that greater levels of competitiveness generated higher voter turnout – and on the Democratic side, turnout was actually higher in states that conducted primaries when uncertainty over the fate of the nomination was lower.

The data provide us limited analytical traction to determine why this might have been so, but given the extraordinary characteristics of the Democratic contest and the unprecedented levels of turnout, we suspect that factors unique to 2008 account for the patterns of participation in that year.

chapter six | mixed systems
Louis Massicotte

GERMANY

Mixed electoral systems aim at reaching the best of both worlds by combining the plurality/majority principle with proportional representation (Shugart and Wattenberg 2001). In the 1990s, this type of electoral systems became more widespread, which in turn stimulated scholarly inquiry on systems that hitherto tended to be dismissed as eccentric (at best) or manipulative (at worst) undertakings (Cox and Schoppa 2002; Kostadinova 2002, 2006; Herron 2002; Nishikawa and Herron 2003; Moser and Scheiner 2004; Ferrara, Herron and Nishikawa 2005; Thames and Edwards 2006; Crisp 2007, Hainmueller and Lutz Kern 2008).

The idea behind the most successful mixed electoral system ever devised so far, the German system, was to mix the principle of proportionality with the presence of a sizeable contingent of directly elected members. This hybrid soon became known as 'personalised proportional representation' (*Personalisierte Verhältniswahl*). The formula did not acknowledge one of the claimed virtues of first-past-the-post, namely the manufacturing of legislative majorities, for it was otherwise a proportional representation (PR) system, but aimed at introducing another of its alleged virtues, the presence of legislators who nurtured a specific constituency. In this chapter the aim is to explore to what extent the PR tier in mixed electoral systems may also provide for personal representation.

MIXED ELECTORAL SYSTEMS TODAY

Electoral systems could be called mixed either because of their mechanics or because they result in outcomes that are halfway between majoritarian or proportional ones. A typical mechanical definition is offered by Massicotte and Blais (1999). A mixed system is one which combines plurality or majority with proportional representation, provided that either category includes more than 5 per cent of the total membership. This kind of definition acknowledges that some mixed systems result in almost perfectly proportional outcomes, while others produce disproportional outcomes. This approach is not universally accepted (Shugart and Wattenberg 2001), but the trend among scholars has been to consider mixed systems as a distinct category of their own, with the proviso that different ways of combining PR with majority or plurality will admittedly result in very different kinds of outcomes.

Based on Massicotte and Blais (2000) and other sources (Hicken and Kasuya 2003; Birch 2006), there were at the turn of the millenium thirty-nine mixed electoral systems governing nationwide elections in thirty-four countries scattered on all continents, to which could be added the mixed systems existing in thirteen of the sixteen German Länder and those introduced in Scotland, Wales and London. This was a marked increase compared with the 1980s, and led some to speak of mixed systems as 'the wave of the future'.

Looking at the present situation (late 2010), we find twenty-nine mixed systems existing in twenty-six countries, while the list of mixed systems at the regional or local level has stayed the same (see Appendices 6.1 and 6.2). The mixed systems existing in Albania, Azerbaidjan, Croatia, Ecuador, Guinea-Conakry, Italy (for both houses of Parliament), Kazakhstan, Kyrgyzstan, Russia and Ukraine have been repealed, while the life of Taiwan's second house (the National Assembly) has been terminated. The systems existing in Armenia, France (for Senate elections), Georgia, Senegal, Taiwan (for the Legislative Yuan), while staying mixed, underwent major reforms. Venezuela moved from a corrective (MMP) system to a superposition (parallel) system in August 2009. Lithuania substituted plurality for majority run-off for the elections in single-member districts in 1999, but made the reverse move after the 2000 election. The changes brought in Bolivia, Germany, New Zealand, Japan (for both houses of Parliament), Panama, the Philippines, South Korea, Thailand and Tunisia may be dismissed as cosmetic, as the number of members returned from each tier was slightly altered. Only in Andorra, Cameroon, Chad, France (municipal elections), Hungary, Mexico (for both houses of Parliament), and the Seychelles have the electoral systems seemingly remained unaltered throughout the decade.

The only countries that introduced mixed electoral systems during the decade appear to be Lesotho (2001) and Monaco (2002). MMP systems devised in the Canadian provinces of Ontario, Quebec, New Brunswick and Prince Edward Island have all been rejected either by politicians or at referendums, while in Scotland and Wales, Additional member-system (partly compensatory) became under attack for blurring within constituencies the distinction between constituency and list members, leading the British Parliament to abolish dual candidacies for Welsh National Assembly elections. In Germany, citizen groups aiming at 'personalising' the strict PR list system existing in the city-state of Hamburg secured in 2004 the rejection of an Mixed member-proportional system and the adoption instead of a two-tier PR list system allowing voters to influence the selection of legislators through cumulative voting and panachage (Massicotte 2009).

While the heyday of mixed electoral systems seems to be over for now, they remain an important family of electoral systems worth scrutinising due to their ability to secure some dose of personal representation, not only within their majoritarian tier, but within their PR tier as well.

FORMS OF PERSONAL REPRESENTATION IN MIXED SYSTEMS

In all but nine of the existing mixed systems, elections for the majoritarian tier are held in single-member districts. A single multi-member district is used in Monaco, but panachage is allowed. In Japan, the survival of Single Non-Transferable Vote for the majoritarian component of the second chamber also ensures a strong element of personal choice.

In the proportional tier in mixed systems, closed party lists tend to predominate.[1] The sole exceptions we found (six) were Japan, Lithuania, Monaco, Panama and, at the regional level, the German Länder of Baden-Württemberg and Bavaria. However, there are some jurisdictions where the election of proportional representation members is not entirely determined by their position on the party list, but permit some personal choice. There are various ways for the rankings determined

---

1. This is true even for local elections held in the two Länder (North Rhine – Westphalia and Schleswig-Holstein) where MMP (mixed-member proportional, or corrective mixed system) is used for that purpose. In all other Länder, local elections are held under PR with open lists.

by each party to be altered in one way or the other. Here is a summary of the procedures used.

Japan

In 1996 Japan introduced a mixed system that provides for the election of 300 members in single-member constituencies, plus 180 (until 2000: 200) members returned from 11 multi-member districts. Electors have two votes, one to be cast for a candidate in a single-member constituency, the other for a political party in a multi-member district. In the latter, members are returned on the basis of closed party lists. However, depending on what the party prefers, a party list may indicate a single name for each spot on the list (as in standard closed party lists) or assign a specific spot to many candidates who happen to be standing in a constituency as well. In the latter case, should the party be entitled to a seat corresponding to this spot, the seat will go to the candidate who did best in the single-member constituency where he or she was running.[2] Both approaches are not mutually exclusive, as a party may assign a few spots specifically while assigning other spots to many candidates simultaneously. Over previous elections, the Komei and Communist parties have chosen to spurn dual candidacy, which means that their lists are fully closed, while the Liberal Democratic, Democratic and Social Democratic parties allowed dual candidacies.[3] Professor Ryosuke Imai has computed that constituency losers who were elected thanks to the party list numbered 84 in 1996, 79 in 2000, 120 in 2003 and 117 in 2005.[4] In 2009, according to Professor Airo Hino, the number fell to 97.[5]

Lithuania

Seventy of the 141 Members of the Lithuanian *Seimas* are elected in a single nationwide constituency, in parallel with the 71 Members who are returned from single-member districts. Voters have a distinct ballot for the national tier. The election law used for the 1992 election provided for closed lists, but starting with the 1996 elections, voters are now allowed to express in addition up to five individual preferences within the party list they voted for. Such preferences are indicated by marking the candidate electoral number in the space provided for that purpose

---

2. Which candidate will fill the seat assigned to a multi-candidate spot on a party list is decided by each candidate's *sekihairitsu*, i.e. his or her ratio of closeness to the winner. The ratio is computed by dividing the losing candidate's votes by the winning candidate's votes in the single-member constituency. A candidate who lost on a 52 per cent-48 per cent outcome will fare less well than a losing candidate who obtained 35.1 per cent of the vote while the winning candidate won 35.2 per cent. In other words, seats go to defeated constituency candidates who lost by the smallest margins, not to those who lost with the highest *number* of votes (as in Baden-Württemberg) or the highest *percentage* of the vote (as in West Berlin before 1975). Whether the candidate was running in a large or a small constituency does not matter.

3. Email from Professor Airo Hino to the author, July 7, 2009. See also Reed and Thies (2001) p. 400.

4. Email from Professor Airo Hino to the author, July 9, 2009.

5. Email from Professor Airo Hino to the author, September 18, 2009.

(see Appendix 6.3 for a sample of the Lithuanian ballot paper). No more than one preference may be expressed for any candidate.

Seats are first allotted to parties based on their nationwide share of the party vote, provided they were able to cross the 5 per cent-threshold. Second, the preferences expressed for individual candidates on each list are summed up and then weighed according to a complex formula whereby the total number of individual preferences cast for each candidate (his or her ' electoral rating ') is multiplied by his or her 'party rating', a figure based on the relative position of the candidate within the list. For example, in the party list of the Social Democratic Coalition at the 2000 election, the first candidate on the list got a party rating of 2780, while the 140th and last candidate on the list got, as required by the law, a party rating 20 times lower, i.e. 139. All other candidates on the list got a party rating lower than 2780 and higher than 139, depending on their position on the list. On the basis of the figures arrived at by multiplying electoral and party ratings, a new post-election rating is determined for each candidate. Seats won by each party go to the candidates who have the best post-election rating within their party list.

The impact of individual preferences is reduced somewhat by the provision that party candidates who simultaneously ran successfully in a single-member constituency must be deleted from the party list. If few voters bother to express individual preferences, or if most voters cast their preferences for the first five on the list, the party ratings will be decisive. Should however voters use their preferences in a discriminating way, the order determined by the party may be altered beyond recognition.

Monaco

The procedure for electing Members of Monaco's National Council is simpler, and empowers voters to express genuine personal preferences for both tiers. There is a single national constituency of twenty-four seats, a reasonable choice in this tiny principality. Each party nominates a list of candidates ranked in alphabetical order, which reduces to nil the effect of the ranking on the list. Each elector votes only once, by inserting one of the party lists in the envelope provided, but the voter may amend this list by crossing out some names and writing the names of candidates from other lists. There is no limit to the number of changes an elector may make on a list. Each name on a ballot paper so submitted is counted as a vote for the individuals supported by the voter. Hence in 2008, the 4,650 valid ballot papers cast resulted into 95,526 individual votes. Sixteen seats go to the candidates who secured the highest number of personal votes. The eight remaining seats are allotted to parties depending on their vote share, and the seats so won by each party go to its unelected candidates who obtained the highest number of personal votes.

Panama

The mixed system used for electing Panama's unicameral Parliament is based on the territorial coexistence of the plurality and PR principles. In the 26 single-member districts, Members are returned by plurality. In the remaining 13 multi-member districts (returning between 2 and 7 Members for a total of 45), seats are first distributed among parties according to a variant of LR-Hare. Electors either vote for a party list or express preferences for candidates within a list, and seats won by each list go to the candidates who won the highest number of personal preferences.

Baden-Württemberg

The Landtag of this south-western German state includes 120 Members, of whom 70 are elected by plurality in single-member constituencies, with 50 corrective seats (a MMP system). Voters cast a single (constituency) vote, that is also used for allocating seats among parties, a now unique feature among German jurisdictions.

A distinctive, and indeed unique, feature of the Baden-Württemberg system is that no party lists are used. Instead, the compensatory seats (as they have to be called) allotted to each party go to its 'best losers', i.e. to the defeated constituency candidates of that party who obtained the highest *number* (not the highest percentage) of votes within the region. A Member so elected is referred to as having a second seat *(Zweitsmandat)* for the constituency, the first seat *(Erstmandat)* going of course to the candidate who came first in the popular vote. Whenever more than two parties are represented in the Landtag, it is quite possible that the same constituency ends up with a third or even a fourth *Zweitsmandat*. As a consequence, one needs to be nominated in a constituency in order to get a compensatory seat. Dual candidacy is implicit under that procedure.

At first sight, this is a welcome answer to two criticisms often heard against closed party land lists: that there is no formal connection between a Land list Member and a specific constituency, and that voters have nothing to say about the composition of the list. Members filling compensatory seats must campaign in a specific constituency and once elected, remain connected with it instead of sitting for the region or for the Land as a whole. Further, the party brass cannot control as tightly the allocation of compensatory seats, unless they are in a position to impose their own favourites in constituency nominations. One may even say that voters to some extent determine collectively themselves the rank-ordering of candidates for compensatory seats by supporting one individual more than another, although the political complexion of the constituency probably has more to do with the rank-ordering than the popularity of individual candidates.

Bavaria

The Bavarian Landtag has 180 Members, including 91 elected by plurality in single-member constituencies, with the remaining seats being compensatory within each of the seven regions. The distinctive feature of the Bavarian system is that unlike what happens elsewhere in Germany, the 'second' (party) vote is not cast for a party list, but for one specific candidate within a party list. For that purpose, two distinct ballots are printed for each constituency. The first one, used for electing the constituency member, is small and includes only the name and party affiliation of each constituency candidate. The second one is much larger (about the size of an unfolded broadsheet newspaper) and includes the names of all list candidates fielded by each party in the region. In the largest region, this meant in 2008 no less than 569 names.

When marking the name of one list candidate on the second ballot paper, voters express support not only for the candidate's party, but also their desire that this specific candidate be elected. The ballot paper does not offer the possibility of voting for a party list without specifying a candidate. Should a voter, mistakenly or not, mark on the ballot the names of *many candidates of the same party*, the ballot will be counted as one vote for the party when seats will be distributed among parties, but will not be considered for the allocation of seats to candidates.[6] A further refinement, which requires the printing of slightly different party ballot papers for each constituency, is that in each constituency, the party ballot paper *omits* the names of party candidates who are running in this constituency. Because voters can choose only a list candidate who is not running in their constituency, preferences become a measure of the popularity of candidates outside their constituencies. To enable each constituency candidate to secure the highest possible support, the law requires that all constituency candidates fielded by a party must be also on that party's list. Of course, other candidates may be added on the party list as well.

Seats are distributed based *not* on party votes, as is normally done in Germany, but on the sum (*Gesamtstimmen*) of constituency and list votes cast in the region for each party. Once we know how many seats each party will get, then comes the determination of who will fill the list seats won by each party. The votes received by each candidate on the party list, first as a constituency candidate (if standing), and as a party list candidate in the constituencies of the same region, are totalled. For example, in 2003, Minister-President Edmund Stoiber received 54,068 votes in his constituency (*Stimmkreis* No. 110) plus 698,425 in the other constituencies of the region of Upper Bavaria, hence a total of 752,493 that made him the most preferred candidate on the Social-Christian Union (CSU) regional list. Less prominent candidates usually receive more votes in their constituency than from outside, and the percentage of the latter within a candidate's total vote is a good index of their own name recognition (or lack of it). The order in which candidates have been entered on the ballot paper is then altered based on the total number of votes received by each candidate. List seats go to the candidates who got the highest number of personal votes, provided of course that they have not already been elected in a constituency. Counting the votes is a somewhat cumbersome operation. In 2008, the names of constituency candidates elected, as well as the total number of votes cast for each party, were known by the end of election night, while the names of list candidates elected were disclosed at 2pm two days later.

DO PERSONAL PREFERENCES MATTER?
THE SNAKES AND LADDERS GAME

Open party lists may not be popular with legislators, judging from the small number of jurisdictions where they exist. Yet, based on the number of people who care to express preferences when they are allowed to do so, and on the magnitude of the

---

6. The number of ballot papers marked for no specific candidate (*ohne Kennzeichnung eines Bewerbers*) is actually very low: 0.8 per cent of second votes in 1994, 1.5 per cent in 1998, 1.2 per cent in 2003 and 1.4 per cent in 2008.

changes these preferences wrought, they seemingly matter very much, transforming what could have been a quiet ratification of the selection made by the party brass into a deadly game of snakes and ladders. We examined recent election results in jurisdictions where voters are allowed to express personal preferences for candidates in order to assess to what extent these preferences altered the outcome. This kind of analysis cannot be conducted for Japan and Baden-Württemberg, because it is impossible to know the standing of the candidates who obtained compensatory seats within their respective parties.

Lithuania

In order to gauge what effect individual preferences had on the composition of the legislature, we examined the detailed results all four elections where voters were empowered to express preferences. For each party or coalition, we examined the party ranking of candidates on their national list, we deleted the names of the candidates who won election in a constituency, and we assumed that the remaining candidates would have been elected as list candidates according to their respective party ranking. Then we compared these names with the list of Members who were actually elected, based on the post election rating devised as described above.

Some changes brought by preferences were quite spectacular. In 2008, for example, one candidate of the Liberal and Centre Union was downgraded from the 6th to the 17th position on the list. One Rising Nation candidate was promoted from 23rd to 4th position, while a candidate from the Liberal and Centre union went from 141st to 7th. Coefficients of correlation between pre- and post election ratings within each of the 16 party national lists ranged from 0.58 for the Lithuanian Poles' Electoral Coalition to 0.87 for the Party 'Order and Justice' (Liberal Democratic Party).[7]

To be promoted from 141st and last to the 7th position was certainly heartening for the candidate who accomplished this feat, yet she failed to get elected (though she stood an excellent chance of filling the next vacancy). Did these changes make any real difference in the end, apart from inflating (or deflating) some personal egos? The answer is yes, the effect of individual preferences was important.

In 1996 (see Table 6.1), preferences led to the demotion and defeat, as well as to the promotion and election, of 14 candidates on the national lists submitted by the parties winning seats in the national constituency. In both 2000 and 2004, 15 candidates owed their election to preferences. This amounts to about one-fifth of all list seats at stake.

Preferences had an even stronger effect in 2008 on the composition of the legislature. No less than 24 list Members (out of 70) owed their election to individual preferences, which is one-third of the total. Within each party list, the working of the preferences ensured the election of at least one candidate who would have otherwise been defeated. The changes were quite spectacular within the Homeland Uni

---

7. The author wishes to express his gratitude to André Blais, of the Université de Montréal, and Simon Labbé – St-Vincent, who computed the coefficients.

Table 6.1: The effect of individual preferences in Lithuanian legislative elections

Parties or Coalitions that won seats in Parliament	Candidates elected thanks to preferences	Total elected
1996		
Homeland Union (Lithuanian Conservatives)	9	33
Christian Democratic Party	3	11
Lithuanian Democratic Labour Party	0	10
Centre Union	2	9
Social Democratic Party	0	7
Total	14	70
2000		
A. Brazauskas Social-Democratic Coalition	5	28
The New Union (Social Liberals)	6	18
Lithuanian Liberal Union	3	16
Homeland Union – Lithuanian Conservatives	1	8
Total	15	70
2004		
Labour Party	4	22
Coalition Brazauskas/Paulauskas 'Working for Lithuania'	3	16
Homeland Union (Conservatives, Christian Democrats)	3	11
Coalition of Rolandas Paksas 'For the Order and Justice'	3	9
Liberal and Centre Union	1	7
Union of Farmers' Party list and New Democratic Party	1	5
Total	15	70
2008		
Homeland Union – Lithuanian Christian Democrats	8	18
Rising Nation Party	1	10
Party 'Order and Justice' (Liberal Democratic Party)	5	13
Lithuanian Social Democratic Party	5	11
The Coalition 'Labour Party + Youth'	1	8
Liberals Movement of the Republic of Lithuania	3	5
Liberal and Centre Union	1	5
Total	24	70

on (Christian Democrats), with 8 out of 18 securing their election thanks to individual preferences, within the Rising Nation Party (5 out of 13), the Party 'Order and Justice' (liberal democrats) (5 out of 11) and the Liberal Movement of the Republic of Lithuania (3 out of 5). They were far more modest within the Social Democratic Party (1 out of 10), the coalition 'Labour Party and Youth' (1 out of 8) and the Liberal and Centre Union (1 out of 5).

One may wonder whether preferences had an adverse or positive effect on women candidates. There is no evidence of that. In 2004, two women owed their defeat to preferences, but two other were elected thanks to them. In 2008, preferences had the effect of increasing female representation, as respectively four and six women candidates were defeated and elected.[8]

Judging from the literature on Lithuanian elections (Clark 1998, Fitzmaurice 2003, Jurkynas 2005, Krupavicius 1997), these changes went virtually unnoticed. Indeed, the very existence of preferential voting for candidates in the national lists is hardly mentioned.

Panama
Candidates in multi-member ('plurinominal') districts are ranked by parties, and the order in which candidates appear on the list presumably reflects whom parties would like to be returned. Yet voters have their own ideas about that, judging from the results of the 2009 legislative election. Out of 45 legislators returned from multi-member districts, 19 would not have been elected if the party rankings had not been altered by voters' preferences. In 2004, preferences were decisive in securing the election of 17 of the 51 legislators returned from multi-member seats. Again, such changes were ignored by the literature (Singer 2005).

Monaco
It is not possible to infer anything with regards to party rankings from the results of the most recent (2008) legislative election in Monaco, because candidates were ranked by alphabetical order on their respective part lists. Variations in candidate support within each list were not very wide. The least preferred candidate within the *Union pour Monaco* list got 2,042 votes, against 2,403 for the most preferred. For the *Rassemblement et Enjeux pour Monaco*, the range was 1,641 to 1,838. The range for the list *Monaco Ensemble* was wider (378 to 830).

Bavaria
Statistical reports on various Landtag elections, and the detailed results of the three most recent ones (1998, 2003, 2008), provide interesting clues as to how the Bavarian system works in practice. Our findings can be summarised as follows.

First, *not all parties compose their lists the same way*. Most parties rank candidates in the order in which they would like them to be elected, with the top spot

---

8. Data on candidates on the Election Commission's website for the 1996 and 2000 election were incomplete. Among demoted candidates in 2000, there were 6 men and 9 whose gender was unknown. Among promoted candidates, there were 12 men, 2 women and one whose gender was unknown.

invariably going to the party leader in the region. However, the CSU has a long-standing practice, seemingly confined to Upper Bavaria in the past, but spreading now to other regions as well, of allocating only the first dozen spots on the list this way, while the lower positions are allotted based on the alphabetical order of candidates. Hence, the rank-ordering in this case does not reflect the standing of the candidates within their own party. This of course minimises the political significance of the changes that preferences bring to the rank-ordering of candidates. Not too much should be made of a Mrs. Zeller being promoted or a Mr. Bayerstofer demoted. No major party so far has pushed this logic to the extreme by presenting a list where *all* names are arranged alphabetically.

Second, *most preferences usually go to the top candidate of parties in their own region* (Faas and Schoen 2006). In 2003, Minister-President Stoiber got ten times more votes than the second most favoured CSU candidate within the region of Upper Bavaria. The same was true for the Social-Democratic Party (SPD) leader Franz Magnet, with 229,585 votes, and 49,639 for the next preferred SPD candidate. In 2008, votes cast for Minister-President Beckstein amounted to a whopping 72 per cent of the individual preferences cast for all 24 CSU candidates in Middle Franconia.

Third, there is strong evidence that *voters feel free to promote or to demote candidates from the positions they were allotted on the list* (James 1999). For example, in 1998, the unpopular Minister Prof. Ursula Männle was demoted from the third to the 42nd spot on the list and lost the election. Conversely, there are instances of candidates being promoted from the 52nd and last spot on the list to the 14th.[9] This pattern of behaviour is not new. Over the three elections held in the 1950s, for example, it was found that on average only 14 per cent of the candidates kept the same rank on the list when preferences had been counted, while 41 per cent were promoted and 45 per cent were demoted. The Bavarian Office of Statistics at that time computed rank correlation coefficients illustrating the extent to which the preferences of the voters altered the rank-ordering among the seven leading candidates on a list. For the 1958 election, the figures were 0.65 for the CSU, 0.86 for the SPD, 0.62 for the Bavarian Party, 0.78 for the BHE (Refugees' Party) and 0.73 for the Free-Democratic Party (FDP). This suggests that SPD voters were at that time less inclined to question the rank-ordering decided by their party, while supporters of other parties were more inclined to do so.

Fourth, *voters' preferences do have an impact on individual careers*. At the most recent election (2008), 23 list members (out of 96) owed their election to the changes brought by preferences to the rank-ordering of candidates determined by the parties. In 2003, even leaving aside alphabetically-ordered candidates, whose promotion or demotion had little political significance, we found 22 list candidates (5 CSU, 12 SPD and 5 Greens) who were defeated through individual preferences, and an equal number who owed their election to them. As there were 88 list seats to be distributed, this is one-quarter of the total. In 1998, using the same method,

---

9. This happened to a Bavarian Party candidate at the 1958 election. The same year, a CSU candidate was promoted from 37th and last to 5th.

we found 17 candidates (5 CSU, 10 SPD and 2 Greens) who were defeated through individual preferences. There were then 100 list seats to be filled. Sketchy figures for previous elections suggest that in the largest region (Upper Bavaria), leaving aside the CSU because of the particular way they compose their lists, preferences were decisive in securing the election of at least 7 members in 1974, 3 in 1978, 2 in 1982, 5 in 1986, and 3 in 1994 (about 30 list seats were at stake in each case).

A disturbing feature is that *women candidates traditionally tended to suffer more than others from the changes brought by preferences.* In 2003, 8 women lost their election through preferences while only 4 owed their election to them, a net loss of 4. In 1998, the prejudice caused by preferences to women candidates was even more glaring, as 11 women owed their defeat to preferences while none was elected thanks to them. This squares with research on earlier elections. In 1990, preferences were fatal to 6 women candidates. In 1974, 1978 and 1982, more women candidates were downgraded than promoted.[10] However, in 2008, the number of women who secured their election through preferences was equal to the number of women who were defeated through them. Among the former was the former high-profile CSU rebel Dr. Gabriele Pauli, who ran for the Freie Wähler party in the region of Middle Franconia. The leaders of her newly adopted party had reservations about her candidacy and she was ranked only eighth on the party list. Nevertheless, she obtained 31,317 of the 69,259 second votes cast for the party's list candidates in the region, which made her by far the highest preferred candidate on the list, and she got one of the two list seats won by her party.

Given the impressive changes wrought by the preferences expressed by voters, one may wonder why their impact has not been even higher. In fact, demoted candidates may be elected in the end if they do not fall too low in the public's esteem, while candidates promoted often remain unable to reach electability level. Further, a substantial portion of preferences go to candidates who have already been elected in a constituency, and therefore serve little purpose except to illustrate how popular these candidates may be outside their own constituency. In 2003, no less than 92 per cent of all preferences expressed for CSU candidates in Upper Bavaria went to candidates who won a constituency, and therefore had no impact whatsoever on the allotment of the list seats won by that party. When no list candidate is elected for a party, as happened to the CSU in most regions in 2008, preferences have no impact at all. Preferences have a more significant impact for SPD, Greens, FDP and Freie Wähler legislators, as most are elected through the list.

---

10. See K. Heepe ' Bessere Wahlchancen für Frauen durch Personenwahlsysteme?', *Zeitschrift für Parlamentsfragen,* March 1986, 102–13; R.-O. Schultze and J. Ender, 'Bayerns Wahlsystem – verfassungs-politisch bedenklich?', *Zeitschrift für Parlamentsfragen,* March 1991, 150–60; B. Hoecker, 'The German Electoral System: A Barrier to Women?', 65–77 in W. Rule and J. F. Zimmermann (eds) (1994) *Electoral Systems in Comparative Perspective. Their Impact on Women and Minorities,* Westport Conn: Greenwood Press, 72–3.

CONCLUSION

We found that the popularity of mixed electoral systems seems to be waning, yet they remain an admittedly diverse but important group of electoral systems, and the various types we identified in 1999 (superposition or parallel, corrective or MMP, coexistence, fusion, 'supermixed') still remain in existence. The vast majority of mixed systems at the national and regional level do not allow voters to modify the order of election decided by the parties.

Within the few jurisdictions that allow personal voting, modalities vary widely. Monaco goes the farthest by allowing panachage, even for the majoritarian tier. Southern German States also go very far in allowing personal voting, in keeping with the traditional disdain in this region for closed party lists. The Bavarian system truly empowers voters, because the single vote cast for the list seats is cast for an individual, not for a party. It is impossible to vote for a party without indicating the candidate you prefer. In Panama, preferences are optional but when expressed, they are decisive. Lithuania is less liberal on that account, as preferences are also optional, but their impact is qualified by taking into account party rankings before the final allocation of seats is made.

In Baden-Württemberg, the ranking of the candidates who will get the compensatory seats is determined by the number of votes obtained by defeated party candidates, which in turn is heavily determined by party strength in constituencies, but to the extent that candidate selection at this level cannot be decided by central party elites, the latter have little control over who will fill these seats. Japanese party officials have a greater say. They may go for standard closed lists if they wish, and they determine who fill fit the multi-candidate spots (if any), while the decision as to which one of these individuals will fill the seat is left to the vagaries of local contests.

Yet, the main finding of this chapter is that wherever they have a chance to express individual preferences, voters seize the opportunity. The alterations in the ranking of candidates are sometimes important. They lead to the defeat of candidates who otherwise might have relied on prime spots on the party lists in order to get elected, and result into the election of candidates who did not enjoy this advantage. There is evidence that preferences had an adverse effect on women representation in Bavaria, but not in Lithuania. In mixed systems, preferences for individual candidates can rarely be expressed, but they definitively matter. The literature on such elections rarely, if ever, mentions the alterations brought by voters' preferences to the membership of the legislature. Which leaves scholars focusing on personal representation with an embarrassing question: whenever preferences matter, does it really matter? It may be that other scholars should give more attention to this dimension, instead of focusing entirely on party representation.

112 | personal representation

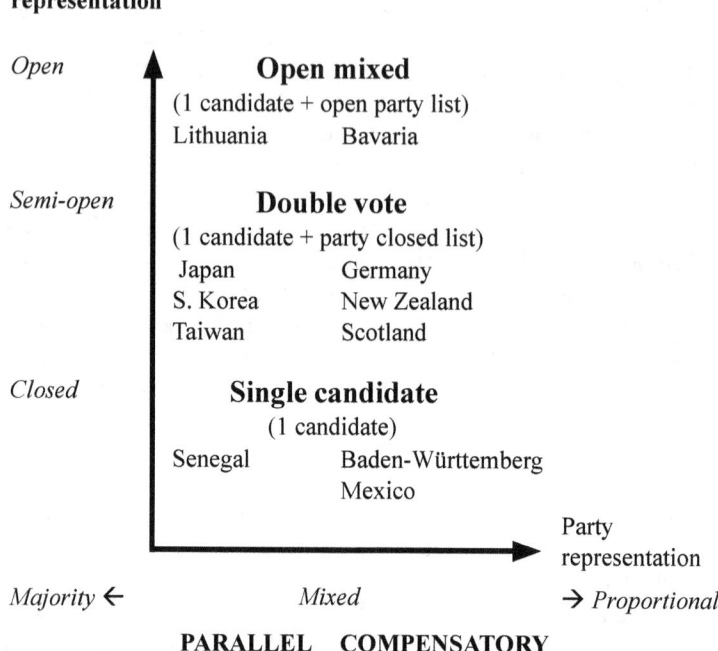

Figure 6.1: Party and personal representation in mixed electoral systems

APPENDIX 6.1: MIXED SYSTEMS AT STATE LEVEL (2009)

Country	Type	Number of votes	Party list
Andorra	Superposition	2	Closed
Armenia	Superposition	2	Closed
Bolivia	Correction	2	Closed
Cameroon	Supermixed	nd	Closed
Chad	Supermixed	nd	Closed
France Senate	Coexistence	1	Closed
Georgia	Superposition	2	Closed
Germany	Correction	2	Closed
Hungary	Supermixed	2	Closed
Japan Rep.	Superposition	2	Closed/Seats may go to best losers
Japan Council	Superposition	2	Closed
Lesotho	Correction	2	Closed
Lithuania	Superposition	2	Open
Mexico Deputies	Correction	1	Closed
Mexico Senate	Superposition	1	Closed
Monaco	Superposition	1	Open
New Zealand	Correction	2	Closed
Niger	Coexistence	1	Closed
Panama	Coexistence	nd	Open
Philippines	Superposition	2	Closed
Senegal	Superposition	1	Closed
Seychelles	Superposition	1	Closed
South Korea	Superposition	2	Closed
Taiwan	Superposition	2	Closed
Tajikistan	Superposition	2	Closed
Thailand	Superposition	2	Closed
Tunisia	Correction	1	Closed
Venezuela	Superposition	2	Closed

APPENDIX 6.2: MIXED SYSTEMS AT REGIONAL OR LOCAL LEVEL (2009)

Country	Type	Number of votes	Party list
France:			
Municipalities	Fusion	1	Closed
Germany:			
Baden-Württemberg	Correction	1	Seats go to best losers
Bavaria	Correction	2	Open
Berlin	Correction	2	Closed
Brandenburg	Correction	2	Closed
Hesse	Correction	2	Closed
Lower Saxony	Correction	2	Closed
Mecklenburg-Vor.	Correction	2	Closed
N.Rhine-Westphalia	Correction	2	Closed
Rhineland-Palatinate	Correction	2	Closed
Saxony	Correction	2	Closed
Saxony-Anhalt	Correction	2	Closed
Schleswig-Holstein	Correction	2	Closed
Thuringia	Correction	2	Closed
United Kingdom:			
Scotland	Correction	2	Closed
Wales	Correction	2	Closed
London	Correction	2	Closed

Note:
Superposition = Parallel
Correction = Compensatory

mixed systems | 115

APPENDIX 6.3: BALLOT PAPER USED FOR ELECTING THE NATIONAL LIST MEMBERS IN LITHUANIA

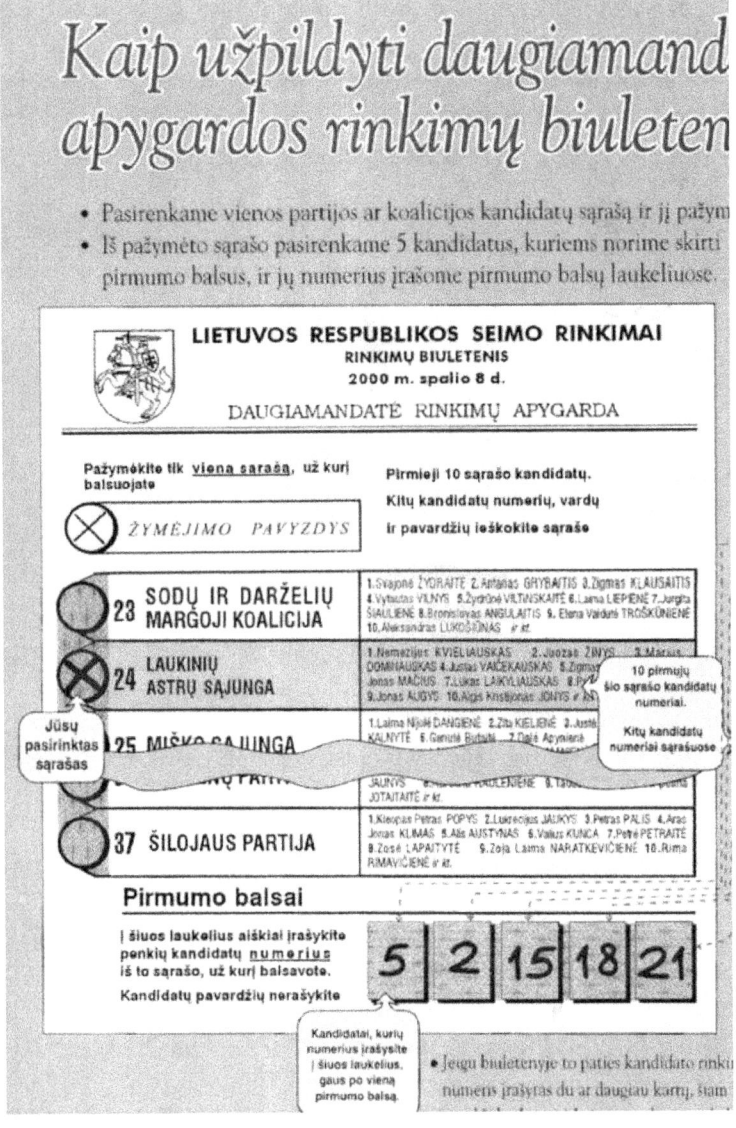

LITHUANIA

NOTES ON SOURCES

Websites consulted:
BAVARIA: Office of the Landeswahlleiter, www.statistik.bayern.de/wahlen/landtagswahlen/

LITHUANIA: Central Election Commission, www.vrk.lt/en/.

MONACO: www.elections.monaco.net/

PANAMA: Tribunal Electoral, www.tribunal-electoral.gob.pa/home.asp

Primary sources:
State election laws:
ALBANIA: Electoral Code, www.cec.org.al/2004/eng/legjislacion/kodizgjedhor/Electoral%20Code.pdf

ANDORRA: Election law, www.eleccions.ad/2009/Normativa/Lleis.html

ARMENIA: Electoral Code, www.venice.coe.int/docs/2007/CDL-EL(2007)010-e.pdf

BOLIVIA: Codigo Electoral, www.cne.org.bo/centro_doc/normas_virtual/codigo_electoral.pdf

CHAD: Code électoral, www.lexadin.nl/wlg/legis/nofr/oeur/arch/tch/Tchad_code_electoral.pdf

FRANCE: Code électoral, http://perlpot.net/cod/electoral.pdf

GEORGIA: Election Code, http://cec.gov.ge/uploads/attachments_old/262_2492_810535_ElectionCodeofGeorgia-updated%5B18%5B1%5D.12.2007%5D.pdf

GERMANY: Bundeswahlgesetz, www.bundeswahlleiter.de/de/bundestagswahlen/downloads/rechtsgrundlagen/bundeswahlgesetz.pdf

HUNGARY: Act C of 1997 on Electoral procedure, www.valasztas.hu

LESOTHO: National Assembly Elections (Amendment) Act 2001, http://aceproject.org

MEXICO, Codigo Federal de Instituciones y Procedimientos Electorales, http://normateca.ife.org.mx/internet/files_otros/COFIPE/COFIPE14Ene08yNotaArtInvalidados.pdf

LITHUANIA: Law on the elections to the Seimas, www3.lrs.lt/pls/inter2/dokpaieska.showdoc_l?p_id=324962

MONACO: Loi n. 1.269 du 23/12/2002 portant modification de la loi n° 839 du 23 février 1968 sur les élections nationales et communales, www.gouv.mc/305/legismc.nsf

NEW ZEALAND: Electoral Act, www.legislation.govt.nz/act/public/1993/0087/latest/DLM307519.html?search=ts_act_electoral_resel&sr=1

NIGER: Code électoral, http://democratie.francophonie.org/IMG/pdf/Niger_code_electoral.pdf

PANAMA: Codigo Electoral, www.tribunal-electoral.gob.pa/elecciones/docum_electoral/documentos/codigo-electoral-2003.pdf

PHILIPPINES: Election Law, www.chanrobles.com/electionlawsofthephilippines.htm

SÉNÉGAL: Code électoral, www.elections.sn/code.php?part=1&#p

SEYCHELLES: Constitution, www.cmseducation.org/wconsts/seychelles.html

SOUTH KOREA: Public Officials Election Act, C:\Documents and Settings\massicol\LocalSettings\Temporary InternetFiles\Content.IE5\39BL54IB\Public_Official_Election[1].zip

TAIWAN: The Public Officials Election and Recall Law, www.cec.gov.tw/English/law3.doc

TAJIKISTAN: Constitutional Law on the Election to the Majlisi Oli, www.eurasianet.org/departments/election/tajikistan/tajeleclaw.html

TUNISIA: Code électoral, www.jurisitetunisie.com/tunisie/codes/celect/menu.html

VENEZUELA: Ley organica de Procesos Electorales, www.cne.gov.ve/web/normativa_electoral/ley_organica_procesos_electorales/índice.php

Regional and local election laws:

BADEN-WÜRTTEMBERG: Landeswahlgesetz, www.landtag-bw.de/dokumente/gesetzliche_regelungen/Landtagswahlgesetz.pdf

BAVARIA: Landeswahlgesetz, http://by.juris.de/by/gesamt/WahlG_BY_2002.htm

LONDON: Greater London Authority Act 1999, www.opsi.gov.uk/ACTS/acts1999/ukpga_19990029_en_1

SCOTLAND: Scotland Act 1998, www.opsi.gov.uk/Acts/acts1998/ukpga_19980046_en_1

WALES: Government of Wales Act 1998, www.opsi.gov.uk/ACTS/acts1998/ukpga_19980038_en_1

Default sources:
Election Resources on the Internet, http://electionresources.org/
Interparliamentary Union, www.ipu.org
Wahlen, Wahlrecht und Wahlsysteme, www.wahlrecht.de/landtage/index.htm

chapter seven | preferential vote in party list
Lauri Karvonen

DENMARK

LATVIA

Preferential list systems share two fundamental features: a) By casting a vote for an individual candidate or several individual candidates, the voter has a possibility to affect their chances to become elected; b) Votes are pooled so as to determine the total number of seats a party list receives. To be meaningful, the first point must mean that parties run several candidates on their lists. If a party only puts up one candidate, party choice and candidate choice coincide, and a voter favouring a particular party must either accept its candidate or abandon his/her party preference and vote for the candidate of another party. The second point means that the chances of all candidates to become elected at least to some extent depend on the collective success of the party list. It is on the basis of the collective vote totals of party lists that the number of seats won by each party is determined. A candidate that receives a large number of personal votes but stands on a party list with a low vote total can very well fail to get elected, while a moderately popular candidate on a strong party list may win a seat.

Preferential party list systems thus differ from closed-list systems, where the chances of candidates are determined by their list position in combination with the vote totals won by their respective party lists. Although single-member majoritarian systems are often highly candidate-centred when it comes to campaign focus and organisation, they are also qualitatively different from preferential list systems. In single-seat elections, parties only run one candidate each per electoral district. Consequently, they do not present a choice between different candidates of the same party. While the preferential element is highly present in Single Transferable Vote and Single Nontransferable Vote systems, votes for candidates do not pool on the level of parties in these systems.

There are several aims in this chapter. The dimensions along which preferential list systems may vary are discussed in the next section. It is followed by an empirical account that charts the main varieties of such systems among the democratic countries in today's world. After that the central features in the historical background of preferential list systems will be highlighted. Finally, the strategic incentives inherent in these systems will be discussed both theoretically and in light of some empirical evidence.

VARIETIES OF PREFERENTIAL LISTS

To qualify as a preferential list system (PLS), an electoral system must allow for intraparty candidate choice and contain a mechanism whereby votes pool at the level of parties or lists. Over and above these requirements, PL systems may vary a great deal. It is neither necessary nor indeed possible to discuss and chart all variation among these systems. On the level of technicalities, electoral systems vary almost endlessly, and it would be an immense task to chart this variation in an exhaustive manner. However, even if this were feasible it would not serve an immediate purpose in the present context. It is not the variation at large but variation as concerns the position and conditions of preferential voting that is of relevance. Four dimensions seem of particular interest in this regard; they can all be expressed in the form of dichotomous variables.

The first dimension has to do with whether the preference votes are the sole

Table 7.1: Preferential list systems. Theoretical range of variation

Ballot	Candidate Choice	No. of Votes	Threshold
Open	Compulsory	One	No
Open	Compulsory	One	Yes
Open	Compulsory	Several	Yes
Open	Optional	Several	Yes
Flexible	Optional	Several	Yes
Flexible	Optional	Several	No
Flexible	Optional	One	No
Flexible	Compulsory	One	No
Open	Optional	Several	No
Open	Optional	One	Yes
Open	Optional	One	No
Open	Compulsory	Several	No
Flexible	Compulsory	One	Yes
Flexible	Compulsory	Several	No
Flexible	Compulsory	Several	Yes
Flexible	Optional	One	Yes

All of these theoretically possible combinations do not have equivalents in the empirical world. As is shown in the next section, many of them are nevertheless being used as electoral systems today.

basis on which candidates are elected from a party list or other factors may also influence the order in which candidates are given seats. In the former case, the list can be called *open*: the choice of candidates is left entirely up to the preference ballots of the voters. In the latter case, the rank order of candidates determined by parties frequently plays a role alongside with preference votes. Some candidates may be chosen thanks to list position although their personal votes would not qualify for election. For instance in Belgium (De Winter 2008: 421–2) and Sweden (Holmberg and Möller 1999: 7), most of the elected legislators have a list position that would secure their election irrespective of preference votes. In some other systems, the final composition of the legislative assembly is decided through calculations in several tiers. While preferential votes can be important in one of them, the parties may in others have a decisive influence over which candidates gain seats. This is the case for instance in Estonia (Mikkel and Pettai 2004: 333–4). Where factors other than preference votes influence the order in which candidates are given seats one may speak of *flexible* lists.

Whether preference voting is *compulsory* or *optional* is the second dimension. In some systems, such as in Finland (Kuusela 1995: 25) and the Netherlands

(Andeweg 2008: 494), voters *must* cast a vote for an individual candidate. Denmark (Elklit 2008: 458) and Switzerland (Lutz 2009: 11) are examples of countries where voters have the opportunity to cast a preference vote but are not compelled to do so.

Most countries using PLS follow the maxim 'one man, *one vote*'. However, in some systems the voter has *several* votes at his/her disposal. For instance, voters in Latvia are allowed to mark preference votes for as many candidates on a ballot as they choose (Mikkel and Pettai 2004: 333).

Finally, there may or may not be *thresholds* that preference votes must exceed in order to be effective. In Austria, for instance '[t]o take a seat at the regional district level by virtue of preference votes it is sufficient for a candidate to win either half as many preference votes as the Hare quota, or preference votes amounting to a sixth of the party vote in that district'; otherwise 'the party list prevails' (Müller 2008: 404).

Theoretically, the number of possible variants is 16 (2^4). These possible combinations are shown in Table 7.1.

EMPIRICAL SURVEY

Any exact statement concerning the incidence of different electoral systems tends to become outdated within a short time span. As new countries join the ranks of democratic nations, they tend to reform many of their central political institutions, including electoral systems. Moreover, the group of new democracies has particularly proven to be reform-oriented when it comes to their electoral systems. Typically, changes occur several times during the first phase of democratic politics. As democracy becomes consolidated, electoral institutions are also more likely to remain stable over considerable periods of time. Nevertheless, even long-standing democracies do adjust their electoral institutions from time to time. Several stable democracies have recently adopted mixed-member systems. Moreover, some countries such as Italy have a recent history of several major reforms.

Despite the difficulties in providing exact figures, it is safe to say that varieties of preferential voting are common among countries using proportional list systems. Basically, they are found about as frequently as closed-list systems (Karvonen 2004: 208; Lutz 2009: 2). They are, however, far from evenly spread among the democracies of the world. Their stronghold is clearly in Western Europe from where they have spread to some newer democracies on the European continent. They are basically absent in the English-speaking world. There are a few cases to be found in Latin America. In Africa, by contrast, all democracies with proportional list systems (Benin, Cape Verde, Namibia, Sao Tomé and South Africa) have closed lists. The potential cases in Asia are Indonesia and Sri Lanka. However, both the status of democracy and the stability of electoral rules are still questionable in these states.

Table 7.2 shows the existing varieties of PLS and lists democratic countries that have the corresponding systems.

Table 7.2: Existing variants of preferential list systems

Ballot	Candidate Choice	Number of Votes	Threshold	Cases
Open	Compulsory	One	No	Finland, Chile
Flexible	Optional	Several	No	Switzerland, Luxembourg, Lithuania*, Greece**
Flexible	Optional	One	No	Denmark
Open	Optional	Several	No	Latvia
Open	Optional	One	No	Brazil
Flexible	Compulsory	One	Yes	Estonia, Netherlands
Flexible	Optional	One	Yes	Austria, Belgium, Sweden

* For the proportional half of the mixed-member system
** For 48 multi-member constituencies

Finland

All but one[1] of the members of Finland's 200-seat parliament are chosen from multi-member districts, average district magnitude being around thirteen. Parties and party alliances nominate candidates for lists that are normally ordered alphabetically. Voters simply write the number of their candidate of choice on the ballot paper; there is no possibility to cast a mere party vote. The number of seats won by a list is determined on the basis of list vote totals by using the d'Hondt divisor.[2] Candidates are elected from lists on the basis of their personal vote totals. No minimum requirement concerning personal votes is stipulated (Raunio 2008: 476–82).

Chile

The sixty member Chilean Chamber of Deputies is elected from districts with two seats each. Seat allocation from these districts is based on the vote totals of two-candidate lists. Each voter has one vote which he or she must cast for an individual candidate. The d'Hondt divisor method is applied to list totals to determine the number of seats won by each list. Within lists, candidate votes determine which candidates are allocated seats (Cox 1997: 117).

---

1. The autonomous province of Aaland elects its sole representative in a single-member district using the same proportional system as the rest of the country.
2. The total votes cast for each party in an electoral district are divided, first by 1, then by 2, then 3, ettc., until all seats have been allocated in the district.

Switzerland and Luxembourg

The electoral systems of Switzerland and Luxembourg are best known for their use of *panachage*, i.e. the possibility for voters to spread their votes for candidates across party lists. Elsewhere in this volume, panachage or open ballot is presented as a voting system in its own right. As to their central features, however, the Swiss and Luxembourg systems clearly belong to the PLS category, which is why they are included in this presentation.

In both countries, voters have as many votes as there are seats in the electoral district. They can use these votes in a variety of ways. They can choose to simply vote for a party list meaning that their votes are counted as one vote per each candidate on the list in question. They can also delete certain candidates from a list and double the votes given to other candidates on this list. This practice is called *cumulation*. In Switzerland parties can pre-cumulate certain candidates. Party votes for such lists in fact mean that the voters accept the rank-ordering of candidates made by the parties. The third alternative is panachage, which means that votes can compose lists of their own that can contain candidates from several parties. Irrespective of how the voters choose to use their votes, candidate votes are pooled at the level of parties. Casting a vote for a given candidate always means that the party list of that candidate receives a vote as well (Lutz 2009: 2–4; SOU 1993: 21, 43).

Lithuania

The members of Lithuania's unicameral parliament, *Seimas*, are elected with the aid of a mixed-member system. Seventy-one of the legislators are elected in single-member districts with simple plurality rule. The remaining seventy are chosen from party lists in a nationwide constituency. In this list election, voters have the possibility of casting preference votes for a maximum of five candidates. In determining the candidates that are elected from a list, however, the list order decided by the party also plays a role. Moreover, parties may submit a request that preferential voting not be permitted on their particular lists. All in all, the effect of preferential voting is rather limited in Lithuania (Mikkel and Pettai 2004: 333; Chronicle of Parliamentary Elections: 104–5).

Greece

The members of the 300-seat Hellenic Parliament are elected in three different tiers. The clear majority are elected from forty-eight multi-member constituencies with proportional list vote based on the Hagenbach-Bischoff method. However, there are also eight single-member districts that send a representative to parliament by a simple-majority vote. Moreover, the most successful parties also compete for the twelve 'State Deputies' that are chosen from nationwide closed party lists.

In the multi-member districts, voters may cast between one and five preference votes. List votes are also possible, but the election of individual candidates is based solely on preference votes (Chronicle of Parliamentary Elections: 66; Baldini and Pappalardo 2009: 78).

Denmark

The Danish PL system is not easy to classify in particular when it comes to the 'ballot' dimension. According to Danish electoral law, parties can nominate candidates so as to favour some candidates over others; this matches the description of a flexible-list system. On the other hand, they can also nominate candidates so that it is left entirely up to the voters to choose which of the candidates are elected from a given list. Today, an overwhelming majority of the parties choose the latter, open-list format. Nevertheless, the flexible-list option remains open to them as well.[3]

Irrespective of nomination format, voters can choose between a list vote and a preference vote. It is in the distribution of these votes that the two list formats differ from each other. Under the flexible-list option, the party indicates its preferred candidate by placing him or her on the top of the candidate list and printing his/her name in bold type. This candidate will be credited his/her preference votes plus the party list votes in his/her nomination district. There are on average nine nomination districts per constituency, and it is on the constituency level that the lion's share of the seats are allocated.[4] Therefore, top-placed candidates in large nomination districts have a clear advantage over candidates in small districts, because the larger districts will carry more numerous list votes.

Under the open-list option all candidates are entitled to a share of all list votes in each nomination district. In each nomination district, candidates receive a portion of the list votes corresponding to their personal vote in that district. At the constituency level, list votes and preference votes from each nomination district are aggregated to make up each candidate's total votes. Casting a mere list vote therefore means that the voter in question leaves it up to other party supporters to decide which of the candidates should be elected. This list format often helps locally popular candidates to gain major portions of both the preference and list votes (Elklit 2008: 457–65).

Latvia

The 100 members of the Latvian *Saeima* are elected from five multi-member districts. The division of seats among party lists is determined by the Sainte-Laguë formula.[5] Voters have the option of casting preference voters for as many candidates on a party list as they wish. They can both mark preferences for certain candidates and delete other candidates. The number of seats won by a party list is determined on the basis of how many voters have voted for its candidates. The candidates are chosen entirely on the basis of sum totals of preference votes, where the net sum of positive and negative preference votes is decisive (Mikkel and Pettai 2004: 333–4).

---

3. There is also a variant of this list format where parties rank all candidates; this type amounts to a practically closed party list; it is, however, quite rare in modern Danish politics.
4. 135 of the 175 seats; the remaining 40 are national compensatory seats.
5. The Sainte-Laguë formula is an alternative to the d'Hondt divisor. The difference is that while the latter uses sequential whole numbers, Sainte-Laguë uses odd numbers as divisors. Smaller parties fare better in this system, as the vote share of the largest party is reduced more quickly.

Brazil

The 513 members of the Brazilian Chamber of Deputies are elected by proportional list vote with the twenty-seven states of the federation as electoral districts. District magnitude varies between eight and seventy, and the small districts are clearly overrepresented in the chamber. Parties or party alliances present candidate lists with no internal ranking. Voters can either vote for a list as such or for a particular candidate on the list. When the number of seats won by a list has been determined, however, only preference votes decide which candidates are elected from that list. Those voters who do not cast a preference vote thus leave it up to other votes to determine the order in which candidates are elected. An overwhelming majority of Brazilian voters do in fact cast preference votes (Nicolau 2004: 123–5).

Estonia

In the Estonian electoral system, seat allocation takes place in three different tiers. Two of these contain a preferential element, while the third tier amounts to an almost closed party list. Voters must cast a ballot for an individual candidate on a party list. In the first round of calculations, those candidates whose personal votes surpass the Hare quota necessary for a seat are awarded seats. In the second round, unassigned seats are awarded for 'each 0.75 additional Hare quotas (*sic*) the party has received'. These seats are given to those candidates who have the highest personal vote totals among the yet unelected candidates. However, no candidate can be elected unless he or she receives a minimum of 10 per cent of the Hare quota. In the third tier, finally, adjustment seats are awarded to parties at the national level on the basis of their vote totals. Here, separate candidate lists with predetermined ranking are used. However, even in this third tier there is an element, albeit weak, of preferential voting. No candidate who has not received at least 5 per cent of the Hare quota in his/her district can be awarded an adjustment seat ((Mikkel and Pettai 2004: 334).

The Netherlands

Under the Dutch system, voters must cast a ballot for an individual candidate; the option of a pure party list vote does not exist. Still, the formula is not a strongly candidate-centred one, as list order determined by the parties plays a powerful role in deciding which candidates actually get elected (Andeweg 2008: 492–3).

The system is an extremely proportional one, as the 150 members of the Dutch lower house (*Tweede Kamer*) are, in practice, elected with the entire country as a single constituency. The country is divided into nineteen electoral districts, but as parties have a possibility of pooling their district lists, the districts have mainly an administrative function. All parties that field candidates in more than one district utilise the option of combining their lists at the national level. Parties are then allocated seats according to their shares of the vote at the national level (Andeweg 2008: 493–496).

Parties normally place their party leaders on top of the candidate lists, followed by the other candidates in the preference order determined by the parties internally. Total list votes decide the number of seats that a particular party wins. The candidates are elected according to list order. However, candidates whose preference votes amount to at least 25 per cent of the Hare quota necessary for winning a seat will be assigned seats irrespective of list position (Andeweg and Irwin 2005: 88).

Voters who simply want to support a certain party give their preference vote to the first candidate on the party's list. This person is called the 'list-puller' (*lijsttrekker*). Preference votes (*voorkeurstemmen*) in Dutch parlance refer to votes for candidates other than the list-puller (Andeweg 2008: 494). From the end of World War II until 1998, only three MPs were elected at variance with list order. At the 1998 elections, two candidates managed to do this, as did one candidate per election in 2002, 2003 as well as 2006 (Andeweg and Irwin 2005: 88; www.vrouwenbelaagen.nl/politiek/verkiezingen).

Austria
The 183 members of the Austrian parliament (*Nationalrat*) are elected with a proportional list system in three tiers. These consist of forty-three regional electoral districts, nine *Länder* and a nationwide district. First, a Hare quota required for a seat is calculated at the Land level. All candidates that receive enough votes to win a quota are declared elected. Thereafter, all votes are calculated anew at the Land level. Only parties that have won at least one seat at the regional district level or 4 per cent of the valid votes nationwide participate in this second seat distribution. The same threshold is applied when votes are counted once again at the national level. Seats won at a lower level are deducted from those that are won at higher levels. Should calculations at higher levels result in fewer seats than lower-level calculations, the latter prevail.

Voters can indicate a preference for a candidate at both the regional district and Land levels. Party list order prevails unless a candidate at the regional district level wins at least 50 per cent of the Hare quota or at least a sixth of the total party vote. At the Land level preference votes must amount to the number required for a seat to disturb party list order. In practice, candidates have rarely been elected at variance with party list order (Müller 2008: 401–9).

Belgium
The members of the Belgian parliament, the House as well as the Senate, are elected with the same proportional list system where d'Hondt divisors are used. Candidates are presented on party lists in an order of preference determined by the parties internally. If a voter accepts the list order of the party of his choice he can endorse it by simply casting a list vote. Voters may, however, choose to cast a preference vote for a given candidate. To be elected, candidates must reach the electoral quota (the party's total vote in the constituency divided by the number of seats it receives, plus 1). Those candidates whose preference votes exceed the electoral quota are declared elected. If all seats that a party has won cannot be filled this way, list votes are added to the preference votes until all seats have been allocated. These list votes are distributed among the candidates according to their position on the list. Therefore, the list header almost always gets elected irrespective of his or her personal vote. If all list votes have been used before all seats have

been assigned, the remaining seats are given to candidates with the highest preference votes (De Winter 2008: 421).

Sweden

Until 1997, Swedish electoral law prescribed a closed-list system. Parties presented a slate of candidates, and voters cast list votes only. In 1997, an electoral reform allowing for optional preference voting was passed by the Swedish parliament. The system was first applied in connection with the 1998 parliamentary election.[6]

The fact that preferential voting is optional means that voters can continue to cast pure party votes if they so wish. Party votes are distributed to the candidates according to the list order determined by the parties. If voters use the preference vote option, they must mark one of the candidates on the party list with an X. For a candidate to be elected at variance with list order, he or she must have received a minimum of 8 per cent of the party's total vote in the constituency. If the number of candidates whose preference votes qualify them for election is smaller than the total number of seats won by a party in a constituency, the rest of the seats will be filled according to list order. In many ways, the form of preferential voting introduced in Sweden resembles the Belgian preference vote (Holmberg and Möller 1999: 7).

ORIGINS OF PREFERENTIAL LIST SYSTEMS

Do PL systems share important features in their historical background? Are there patterns that help explain why some countries have included a preferential element in their proportional list systems while others have not? In this section an attempt is made to shed some light on these questions.

Electoral system choice has recently emerged as an important field of comparative political science. While the effects of various electoral systems have long interested political scientists (Duverger 1951; Grofman and Lijphart 1986; Sartori 1994), major works on how and why electoral systems get chosen have only started to appear (Colomer 2004; Lundell 2009).

The choice of electoral system affects political parties fundamentally, and parties are more often than not key actors when it comes to reforming the electoral system. Therefore, party constellations are frequently assumed to be of major importance for the outcome of electoral reforms. Josep Colomer (2004a: 3) has argued for the 'Micro-mega rule', according to which 'the large prefer the small and the small prefer the large'. If there are but a few large parties they tend to favour small assemblies and electoral systems with small districts. By contrast, the existence of many small parties leads to large assemblies and proportional systems with multi-member districts. The reason is that parties always look after their own strategic interests when choosing political institutions.

Past institutions affect future institutions. The choice of a new electoral system can hardly be independent of the existing system. How this relationship works in specific cases is, however, not easy to predict. If the old institutions have totally

---

6. It had, however, been tried out in seven municipalities already in connection with the 1994 election.

fallen into disrepute, there may be a need to distance oneself from them by choosing a radically different system. In cases where no such need exists, incremental reforms are more likely.

In the following account, the party systems of countries with PL systems are compared to a number of cases with closed-list systems. Three variables form the basis for this comparison:

1. Timing: when was the present system introduced?
2. Previous system: what kind of electoral system did the present one replace?
3. Party system characteristics: was the party system stable and clearly structured or fluid and unstable immediately before the present system was introduced?

To some extent, these questions are difficult to answer in a precise way, in particular those which concern the party system dimension. Still, it should be possible to detect any overall patterns that may exist. For those cases where the present system succeeded a period of non-democratic practices, the preceding party system and electoral order will be coded as 'non-democratic'.

The results in Table 7.3 are mixed. It is not easy to detect a clear pattern that might explain why some countries have opted for PLS while others have chosen closed-list systems. Both varieties are present among countries that represent the various waves of democratisation from the early twentieth century to the present period. Similarly, both closed-list systems, mixed systems and single-seat two-round systems have been replaced by PLS. Finally, both groups of countries contain examples of structured, fluid and non-democratic party systems prior to the introduction of the present system. Still, one might point to a couple of interesting features in these data:

In nine out of fourteen cases in the PLS category the introduction of preferential voting was preceded by democratic or semi-democratic electoral systems. In the case of closed-list systems, four out of six were preceded by non-democratic systems. It may be that non-democratic precedents are more likely to lead to closed party lists, while preferential systems are easier to introduce if there is a degree of previous democratic experience.

In a fairly large number of PLS cases, the previous party system was clearly structured. Perhaps parties find it easier to open up the party system for further voter influence if the party landscape is fairly established and the parties are used to striking deals with one another concerning the institutional rules of the game.

On the whole, however, these conclusions must be regarded as preliminary indications. They do not point to a set of strategic conditions that lead to a given choice of electoral system, but the results can neither be interpreted as evidence against the importance of strategic calculations. Far from it, such calculations are always on the minds of decision-makers when they contemplate electoral reforms. The absence of clear patterns may simply mean that decision-makers act under imperfect information. Several powerful factors must be taken into account when trying to understand why countries choose institutions the way they do.

Timing is one thing. Majoritarian, PR and mixed systems have each had their golden age (Shugart and Wattenberg 2001: 1–2). In a given period, decision-makers are more prone to opt for a specific institutional solution than alternative solutions less in vogue. Once a choice has been made and institutions have become stabilised, incremental change is more likely than all-out reform.

Cultural dominance frequently plays a role in institutional choice. A large number of former British colonies have opted for the electoral institutions of their former mother country. Cultural similarity and geographic proximity condition the range of alternatives that decision-makers are likely to consider. In a global analysis, Krister Lundell (2009) found patterns of diffusion to be a powerful determinant of electoral system choice.

Just as decision-makers are likely to have *limited knowledge* of existing alternatives they may *not be aware of all consequences* of institutional choice. For example, David Farrell points out that the introduction of STV in Ireland 'may have had more to do with ignorance of other systems than to a preference for one form of PR over another' and that the system was introduced 'almost by accident' (1997, 114–5). The Finnish PL system introduced in 1955 was basically an unintended consequence of a reform that had quite another goal (Törnudd 1968: 56–8).

Table 7.3: The origins of preferential list systems compared with closed-list systems

Country	Present electoral system introduced year	Previous electoral system	Party system prior to introduction of present electoral system
Preferential list systems			
Finland	1955	Closed-list PR	Structured
Chile	1989	Non-democratic	Non-democratic
Switzerland	1918	Two-round run-off	Structured
Luxembourg	1924	Two-round run-off	Structured
Lithuania	1996	Closed-list PR*	Fluid
Greece	1974	Non-democratic	Non-democratic
Denmark	1920	Double vote	Structured
Latvia	1922**	Non-democratic	Non-democratic
Brazil	1945***	Non-democratic	Non-democratic
Estonia	1992	Non-democratic	Non-democratic
Netherlands	1917	Two-round run-off (semi-democratic)	Structured
Austria	1949	Closed-list PR	Structured
Belgium	1899	Mixed (semi-democratic)	Structured
Sweden	1997	Closed-list PR	Structured

Country	Present electoral system introduced year	Previous electoral system	Party system prior to introduction of present electoral system
Closed-list PR systems			
Norway	1917	Two-round run-off	Structured
Spain	1977	Non-democratic	Non-democratic
Italy	2005	Mixed	Fluid
Portugal	1975	Non-democratic	Non-democratic
Argentina	1983	Non-democratic	Non-democratic
South Africa	1993	Non-democratic	Non-democratic

* For list half of the mixed system

** In 1993, Latvia reverted to its 1922 electoral system (Mikkel and Pettai 2004: 338)

*** In 1986 Brazil reverted to its 1945 electoral system (not in use during the authoritarian period 1964–85) (Nicolau 2004, 122)

Table 7.3 Sources:

For all countries, available from www.ipu.org/parline-e/reports

Additional sources: Finland: Törnudd 1968: 56–8. Chile: Scully 1995: 125. Switzerland: Lutz 2004: 279–93; Lutz 2009: 5. Luxembourg: Mackie and Rose 1991: 289–9. Lithuania: Mikkel and Pettai 2004: 332–45. Greece: Mackie and Rose 1991: 186. Denmark: Elklit 2008: 454–6; Mackie and Rose 1991: 87–101. Latvia: Mikkel and Pettai 2004: 338–42. Brazil: Nicolau 2004: 122–7. Estonia: Mikkel and Pettai 2004: 333–41. Netherlands: Andeweg 2008: 492–3; Mackie and Rose 1991: 322–43. Austria: Müller 2008: 398–402; Müller 1984: 83–5; Mackie and Rose 1991: 23–38. Belgium: De Winter 2008: 415–23; Mackie and Rose 1991: 39–65. Sweden: Holmberg and Oscarsson 2004: 177–91. Norway: Narud and Valen 2007: 51–6; Mackie and Rose 1991: 356–71. Spain: Hopkin 2008: 376–7; Mackie and Rose 1991: 385–99. Italy: D'Alimonte 2008: 253–65; Gallagher and Mitchell 2008: xiv-xv. Portugal: Mackie and Rose 1991: 372–5. Argentina: Colomer 2004b: 86, 95. South Africa: Reynolds 2004: 440–9.

Electronic sources: available from www.ipu.org/parline-e/reports, www.val.se, www.vrouwenbelaagen.nl/politiek/verkiezingen.

Finally, *history and tradition* play a role, too. Austria, Brazil and Latvia reverted to electoral systems that had been abandoned when democracy collapsed in these countries. Naturally, the political constellations were quite different than at the time of the original introduction of these systems.

All in all, it is not surprising that a general overview does not point to clear patterns explaining the choice between PLS and closed-list systems. Electoral system choice involves rational calculations on the part of the involved actors, but this rationality is strongly constrained by historical, cultural and cognitive factors.

STRATEGIC INCENTIVES AND BEHAVIOURAL CONSEQUENCES

How do PL systems differ from closed-list systems in terms of strategic incentives for candidates and voters? Do the different variants of PLS influence the strategic calculations and behaviour of candidates and voters to varying extent and in different ways? Unfortunately, empirical research in this area is still rather limited and unsystematic. In this final section attempts are made to shed light on these questions by discussing a few hypotheses based on an assumption of actor rationality. This assumption contains the following expectations:

1. Candidates seek to maximise their chances of election
2. Voters seek to maximise their influence on the outcome of the election in terms of both personal and party representation

For candidates, it is decisive to what extent their chances to get elected depend on the will of voters as compared to the internal preferences of the party in question. Of course, party organisations almost always to some extent influence the nomination process and therefore control who is electable at all. Having won a nomination, however, candidates face widely varying conditions in different electoral systems. In closed-list systems, candidates can enhance their chances of election only by contributing to the list totals of their party. Over and above that, the list order determined by the party determines who gets elected. In PL systems, there are varying incentives to carry out personal campaigns. The more decisive the candidate votes are, the stronger the incentives to conduct individual campaigns. However, as the chance of election of candidates always depends on the total vote of the party, they are well-advised not to compete too fiercely against other candidates of the same party. If a vote for a candidate only benefits that particular candidate, candidates face few restrictions in designing their individual campaigns. This is the case with the STV and SNTV systems in particular (Carey and Shugart 1995: 421–2; Cox 1997: 45–6, 117–20).

Extrapolating from this reasoning, an earlier comparative study by the author (Karvonen 2004) tested the following hypotheses. The expectation was that differences would be detected between closed-list systems, 'weak' preferential list systems, 'strong' preferential list systems and preferential systems without party lists. *Effective preferential voting has negative effects on political stability.* The idea is that preferential voting introduces an additional basis of political legitimacy besides the collective loyalties attached to parties. This weakens internal party discipline, which in turns reduces the parties' capacity to act and makes them less dependable as coalition partners. One consequence might be more frequent cabinet crises than in systems without preferential voting (Petersson *et al.* 1999: 129–31).

Preferential voting makes central control of party finance more difficult. Preferential voting leads to individual campaigning and, in consequence, personal campaign finance. This makes it more difficult for the central leadership of parties and for government to control and regulate party finance (Petersson *et al.* 1999: 140–2; Katz 1980: 90–1).

Preferential voting moderates the fragmentation of the party system. Preferential voting creates alternative career opportunities for ambitious and attractive candidates past the formal party hierarchy. Unlike in closed-list systems and systems with single-member districts, candidates are not entirely at the mercy of party organisations that decide on list order or candidate selection. As soon as they have passed the nomination hurdle they can successfully use their popular appeal to win a seat. In closed-list systems and systems with single-member districts, challenging the party organisation and leadership may be the only way forward for candidates not privileged by the party. In sum, the pressure towards definite party splits should be smaller in preferential systems.

Preferential voting entails high legislative turnover. The possibility of rewarding and punishing individual legislators leads to more legislators being voted out and newcomers being voted in than in systems without preferential voting (Katz 1980: 34).

Turnover as a consequence of preferential voting is related to district magnitude. The greater the number of seats allotted to an electoral district, the greater the number of candidates nominated by the parties; the greater the number of candidates the more difficult it will be for the parties to favour incumbents over newcomers (Katz 1986: 99–100).

Preferential voting leads to lower party cohesion. Individual legislators will feel a pressure to demonstrate their independence in questions of great importance to their voters, as their political future lies primarily in the hands of the voters in their constituencies (Blais 1991: 250; Katz 1980: 34).

Preferential voting leads to high volatility. As voters grow accustomed to reasoning in terms of both candidate and party, party loyalties will gradually weaken. Attractive candidates of other parties may appear as a better choice than less attractive candidates of one's own party (Marsh 1985: 376).

Preferential voting leads to high electoral turnout. Preferential voting gives the voter a high degree of influence over the electoral process. Voting for individual candidates makes the election more personal and concrete. Both elements should function as a stimulus for an active electoral participation (Petersson *et al.* 1999: 127–129; cf. Johnston and Koene 2000: 243).

Although the empirical evidence was sparse, the 2004 study indicated that a strong element of preferential voting renders a central control of campaign finance difficult. The more candidates are prompted to conduct individual campaigns, the more decentralised and less transparent political finance tends to become. Over and above this, the results did not point to significant differences between electoral systems. However, a later study with a larger N (Söderlund and Karvonen 2008) indicated that the candidate-centredness of electoral systems may be *negatively* related to electoral volatility. It seems that voters may be less prone to switch parties between elections if they have the opportunity of choosing between several candidates of the same party.

Interestingly, preferential voting does not seem to inspire citizens to vote more actively than in those systems where a preferential element is not present. But what about the use of preference votes in systems where it is optional rather than compulsory? Do voters utilise this opportunity, and is their propensity to do so increasing? A look at available data once again points to diverging patterns. There are cases where the overwhelming majority of the electorate casts a preference vote. In Brazil only around 10 per cent of the voters cast a mere party vote, and the electoral campaigns are highly centred on individual candidates (Nicolau 2004: 125). In Belgium, two thirds of those voting also cast a preference vote today, as compared to less than 25 per cent in the 1950s (Wauters 2003: 403). In a few other countries preference voting is still a more marginal phenomenon but seems to be on the increase. In the Netherlands, where votes for candidates other than the list-header are regarded as preference votes, merely a small percentage of the voters cast such preference votes in the first postwar decades. Today, roughly 20 per cent do so (Andeweg and Irwin 2005: 88; Hessing 1985; www.vrouwenbelaagen.nl/politiek/verkiezingen). The situation in Austria is quite similar, although the increase in preference voting occurred as late as in 1990. That year, parties began to use the preference voting system to boost the campaigns of their party leaders, and this led to a general increase in preference voting (Müller 1990; Müller 2008: 408–9).[7] By contrast, no increase in preference voting can be noted in the cases of Denmark and Sweden. The Danish case is particularly intriguing, as parties during recent decades have overwhelmingly opted for the open-list variety of candidate nomination, thus leaving it up to the preference votes to decide which candidates are to be elected from their lists. Still only half of the electorate actually does so, and there has been no increase whatever in the past half century (Statistical yearbook). In Sweden, finally, preference voting has *decreased* during its fairly short history. In 1998, 30 per cent cast a preference vote, in 2002 26 per cent, and in 2006 merely 22 per cent (see www.val.se). All in all, these diverging figures do not support the notion that there is a general wish on the part of the voters to maximise the effect of their vote or to affect which individuals gain a parliamentary seat.

Still, it is apparent that cross-national analyses using entire countries as aggregates have definite limits when it comes to detecting strategic effects that may be due to varying degrees of preferential voting. Stable democracies have thus far been too few to permit real statistical controls for other factors that may condition the strategic behaviour of candidates and voters. As more countries join the ranks of democratic nations, the conditions for comparative analyses of institutional variation will continue to improve. In the meantime, one might be well advised to seek alternative research strategies that can help detect varying effects of different preferential voting systems. For countries where relatively recent changes have occurred, it would be interesting to look for patterns prior to and after the introduction of preference voting. More in-depth comparisons of individual cases would also be called for. Last but not least, comparative electoral surveys should start taking the personal vote and candidate appraisals seriously. While the facts concerning institutional arrangements have become ever easier to access cross-nationally, comparative individual-level research has scarcely begun.

---

7. Interestingly enough, 'no official aggregate data are available on the use of preference votes' (Müller 2008: 408–9).

chapter eight | ordinal rank
Michael Marsh

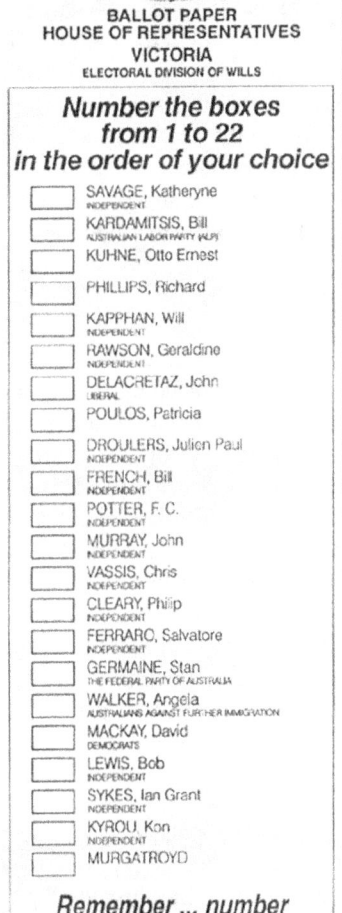

AUSTRALIA   IRELAND

The Republic of Ireland is almost alone in its use of the single transferable vote (STV) system in constituting its national parliament. Of other states only Malta elects its national parliament in this fashion, although the system itself is more widely used for a range of sub-national assemblies as well as in many private associations.[1] STV might be seen as the British system of proportional representation (PR). Long promoted by the Electoral Reform Society (originally the Proportional Representation Society) in the UK, and adopted, or even considered seriously, for the most part only in English-speaking countries it may be seen as combining a property valued in the English parliamentary tradition – the personal representation of districts by individual deputies – with a formula for party representation designed so that the parties nominating the candidates will win a number of seats proportionate to the vote obtained. In this chapter, Ireland's experience of STV is examined and how effectively the balance between personal and party representation has been maintained is considered. It is argued that the balance is problematic in theory, while in practice the system has, at least, encouraged a style of representation that has been widely criticised by commentators on Irish politics in recent years. That said, the public shows little sign that it is keen to see the system changed.

ORIGINS

STV was originally suggested by Thomas Hare in 1857 (and, quite separately, by a Danish politician, Carl Andrea) and his idea was soon lauded by John Stuart Mill who saw it as a means of giving minorities a voice. In 1884 the Proportional Representation Society was founded in Britain (later to become the Electoral Reform Society in 1958) with the purpose of promoting Hare's system. This primary aim was not realised, but the society did play a central role in convincing many people in Ireland, including Arthur Griffith, founder of Sinn Féin (SF), of the merits of the system. STV formed part of the Irish Home Rule Bill in 1912; it was later used in 1919 to elect a town council and the main organ of southern protestant opinion, the *Irish Times*, had written enthusiastically of Ireland's PR experiment. A bill was introduced in the British parliament to prescribe STV in local elections in Ireland, with the aim of reducing the strength of SF, then easily the largest party. Soon after, the Government of Ireland Act 1920 legislated for two parliaments to be elected by STV in Ireland, one in what is now the Republic and one in what is now Northern Ireland.

These elections did nothing to stop the momentum for independence. Irish representatives signed a treaty with Britain at the end of 1921, although the dispute within Ireland over its terms developed into civil war (1922–23) the following year. The new constitution, drawn up while the civil war was in progress, specified the use of PR. O'Leary (1979: 14) argues that the specification of PR was in accord with what was happening across Europe at this time, but more specifically, that the PR society had set the agenda and that Griffith, who led negotiations on the treaty, had promised southern Unionists and the British government that STV

---

1. For more details of variations in STV across different systems see Bowler and Grofman (2000).

would be adopted. Chubb (1970: 146–7) argues in similar fashion: 'That Ireland adopted [STV] was due to the fact that at the time of the Treaty both the leaders of the independence movement and the British Government were in favour if it' . The key point here concerns PR: it was widely appreciated as a means of protecting the interests of the significant protestant minority. STV was seen as the way to facilitate PR. While there was some discussion of the electoral provision to realise PR within the parliament, O'Leary (1979: 15) notes that the 'speeches revealed a complete ignorance of list systems ... and it soon became plain that the constitutional directive was to be interpreted as prescribing STV, the only from of PR of which Ireland had had any experience'.[2] The purely legislative basis for STV provided in 1922 was given constitutional expression in the 1937 Constitution. This specified several significant features of the electoral system, including the use of STV, a minimum of three seats per constituency, and a ratio of seats per head of population of between 1 to 20,000 and 1 to 30,000. While district magnitude initially varied between 3 and 9, large constituencies were soon discontinued. From 1935–44 there were just three with more than 5 seats – there were three 7-seat constituencies – and the range has been between 3 and 5 since 1948.

There was no opposition to the continued use of STV in 1937, although some concerns were expressed about the decision to make constitutional provision for it. However, there have been serious challenges to the system in later years. On two occasions, the largest party, Fianna Fáil (FF), sought a change to first-past-the-post (FPP). Under the current Constitution, any constitutional amendment required popular approval by means of referendum and in both 1959 and 1968 the people opted to reject FPP and stay with STV. FF argued on each occasion that proportional representation encourages a multiplicity of parties and provokes government instability, the classic British arguments against PR. More recently, as will be discussed in more detail below, the system has been criticised as encouraging a focus on so-called 'clientelist' politics – a system in which representatives see their role as providing selective benefits to constituents at the expense of a focus on national affairs and the national interest. Rather than a focus on the proportional representation of parties, this places the emphasis on the personal element of the electoral system. A special report on the electoral system by the non-partisan Constitution Review Group (1996) opened up the debate and suggested the merits of a mixed member system. Change was rejected by the all-party parliamentary committee that investigated the report (All-Party Oireachtas Committee 2002). However, the issue remains topical. The idea of scrapping the electoral system gets a regular airing in the press and in 2010 the Oireachtas Committee on the Constitution produced yet another report on electoral reform which did not recommend change but suggested the issue should be discussed by a citizen assembly.

---

2. The debates are located in Dáil Debates Vol I, 1106–38.

THE SYSTEM

Ballots are ordered alphabetically, with each candidate's occupation and address provided and the party of each candidate clearly designated, although party labels have been provided only since 1965. Party logos and candidate photographs were added in 2002 (see contemporary ballot paper figure on page 135). All a voter is required to do for their vote to be declared valid is to write the number '1' next to the name of a candidate. However, the voter may go on to rank one or more of the remaining candidates in order of preference and is free to rank all of them. The count starts with a validation of each ballot paper and this then permits the calculation of the Droop quota, the number of votes a candidate requires to make certain of election.[3] The serious business then takes place with a count of first preference votes for each candidate. Candidates whose support exceeds the quota are declared elected, and their surplus votes are transferred to other candidates according to the next preference marked.[4] Once this is done, the remaining candidate with the fewest votes is eliminated and her votes redistributed, again according to the next marked preference. Those without another preference are declared to be non-transferable. These processes of election, elimination and transfer continue until all seats are filled, or until no more candidates can be eliminated. In the latter case, all remaining candidates are declared elected despite not reaching the quota (for more details see Gallagher 2005; Sinnott 2010).

Table 8.1 illustrates the process, taking as an example the 2007 general election in the Cork North West constituency. There were seven candidates, three from Fianna Fáil (FF) two from Fine Gael (FG) and one each from Labour and Greens. There were three seats to be filled. 46,620 valid votes were cast, giving a quota of $(46620/(3+1))+1=11,656$. On the first count no candidate exceeded this quota. That being so the candidate with the fewest votes, Caroline Robinson (Greens), was eliminated and her votes were transferred according to the next marked preference. 123 votes had no other marked preference, but the rest were allocated, with 362 to Michael Creed FG), 97 to Michael Moynihan (FF), and so on. As there was still no candidate who had achieved the quota, the candidate with the lowest number of votes after this count, Martin Coughlan (FF), was eliminated and his votes transferred according to the next marked preference on each ballot. 692 of his votes had just come from the eliminated Green candidate, so these votes would be transferred to the third marked candidate. This time 306 votes had no further marked preference (making 429 in all). After Count 3, Michael Creed (FG) now had 12,420 votes, exceeding the quota, so he was declared elected. Donal Moynihan (FF) was then eliminated and his votes made available for transfer to

---

3. This is one more than the number of valid votes divided by the number of seats plus one: in a situation where 10,000 votes were cast and three seats were to be filled it would be 2,501.
4. When the surplus from the first count is being redistributed, actual ballots from the top of the pile, are allocated in such a way so as to reflect the share of second preferences from the first preference votes for that candidate as a whole. When surpluses are redistributed in later counts the ballots from the top the pile are taken without any effort to ensure these are representative. See Farrell and McAllister (2000) for alternatives to this way of counting.

Table 8.1: Election count, Cork NW 2007

Candidate	Party	Count 1	Transfer of Robinson votes Count 2	Transfer of Coughlan votes Count 3	Transfer of Moynihan votes Count 4	Transfer of Moynihan surplus Count 5
Michael Creed	FG	10,516	+362 10,878	+1,542 12,420	12,420	12,420
Michael Moynihan	FF	10,146	+97 10,243	+141 10,384	+3,617 14,001	-2,345 11,656
Batt O'Keeffe	FF	8,040	+173 8,213	+285 8,498	+2,170 10,668	+1,997 12,665
Gerard Murphy	FG	7,397	+148 +7,545	+425 +7,970	+339 +8,309	+348 8,657
Donal Moynihan	FF	6,546	+92 6,638	+281 6,919	-6,919 Eliminated	
Martin Coughlan	Labour	2,288	+692 2,980	-2,980 Eliminated		
Caroline Robinson	Greens	1,687	-1,687 Eliminated			
Non-transferable			123	+306 429	+793 1222	1222
Total valid votes		46,620	46,620	46,620	46,620	46,620

the next marked preference. As an elected candidate, Michael Creed (FG) could not receive any more transfers, but any ballots which would have been transferred to him are transferred to the next marked candidate where there is one still in the race. Of Donal Moynihan's (FF) 6,919 votes all but 793 could be, and were, transferred, the majority going to Michael Moynihan (FF), giving him 14,001 votes. As the latter's total now exceeded the quota he was declared elected. There were then just two candidates left in the fight for the third seat, Batt O'Keeffe (FF) and Gerard Murphy (FG). Murphy (FG) was more than 2,000 votes behind O'Keeffe (FF). However, Moynihan's surplus was 2,345 votes, enough in theory to change the ordering that was established on Count 1 and maintained thereafter. This surplus was transferred according to the next marked preference and the addition of 1,997 votes took O'Keeffe (FF) over the quota. (Had these not been sufficient, there was still a surplus of almost 800 votes available for redistribution from Michael Creed [FG].) There were no non-transferable votes this time. This is because only transferable votes are considered when redistributing at a surplus. FF's candidates won two seats with 53.1 per cent of the vote, FG one seat with 38.4 per cent. Labour, with 4.9 per cent and the Greens, with 3.6 per cent, were unsuccessful in gaining a seat.

There is thus a degree of proportionality, although FF seat share exceeded its vote share by over 13 per cent, while some FG votes might be seen as 'wasted', as was the support for Labour and Green candidates. With only three seats to distribute no mechanism would provide a more proportional distribution of seats at this level, although some list systems employ a second level of allocation and this could provide a more proportionate outcome in terms of *parties*. What the STV system does provide for voters is a say over the *candidates* elected in Cork North West for the FF and FG parties. Both parties nominated more candidates than each had the support to elect. The voters opted for Michael Moynihan and Batt O'Keefe over Donal Moynihan in the case of FF, and for Michael Creed over Gerard Murphy in the case of FG.

The count illustrates also the problematic assumption that votes for candidates are necessarily votes for their parties. When Donal Moynihan was eliminated, most of his votes – 85 per cent in fact – indeed went to FF running mates, but 4 per cent of his votes went to the FG candidate still in the race and 11 per cent were not transferable. Apparently, a significant share of Donal Moynihan's votes was not cast for his party. Again, when Michael Moynihan's surplus was redistributed in Count 5, 85 per cent went to the remaining FF candidate, but 15 per cent to the FG candidate.

In the following sections, we will take up the point about proportionality, and see how effectively STV has delivered proportional outcomes: that is, party seat shares proportional to party vote shares. We will then explore further the extent to which the personal nature as opposed to the party nature of the vote can be estimated and ask on what bases voters distinguish one candidate form another, and what implications this has for the parties themselves.

PROPORTIONALITY

There are a number of ways of looking at the proportionality of outcomes of STV. The most important point to make is that the electoral system has allowed the relatively small Labour Party to maintain a significance presence in the Dáil. While for many years Ireland was described as having a 'two-and-a-half party system' – particularly between the mid 1950s and 1987, it has also allowed the growth of new parties whose strength in the Dáil has at times exceeded what might be expected from their vote. At present there are five parties, plus a number of independent deputies, which is a most unusual feature of a PR system. The most common means of summarising the degree of proportionality is the use of the least squared index (Gallagher 1991). This has a minimum of zero and a maximum of 100. It averages 3.9 over the elections 1923 to 2007, with a range of 1.7 to 6.6 (Sinnott 2010: 124). This compares very favourably with first-past-the-post systems, and is a little better that the average PR system, calculated by Lijphart at 4.3 for 27 countries 1945–90 (Gallagher 2005).

To give a more concrete illustration of the disproportionally, Figure 8.1 shows the percentage seats minus percentage votes in each Irish election for the period 1923–2007 for the two largest parties. For FF the average is +3.6 and for FG it is +1.6, although FF has gone as high as +7.3 in 2002, when FG fell to -3.8. While these two extreme cases fall near the very end of the period, there is no significant trend in either series. In the current Dáil of 166 seats this is worth an average of 6 seats to FF and 2 seats to FG, an advantage that often helped FF to form a single party government, or made that government more stable. There was some concern in 2002 when FF received a 'bonus' of 12 seats and FG 'lost' 6 seats, with commentators expressing some surprise that a PR system could give such an apparently disproportional result. One explanation offered was that FF was much more effective at winning lower preferences in 2002, or at least less unpopular than in the past (Gallagher 2003: 111; see also Marsh *et al.* 2008: 20–2). This raises the question of whether proportionality under STV can be summarised by contrasting only first preference votes with seats won, as the whole point of the system is to accommodate second and third preferences when appropriate. It is the ability to win lower preferences that helps explain why the small Green party could win 6 seats with only 4.7 per cent of the first preference vote in 2007; in contrast, SF obtained only 4 seats with 6.9 per cent of the first preference votes because for most voters it was their least favourite party.

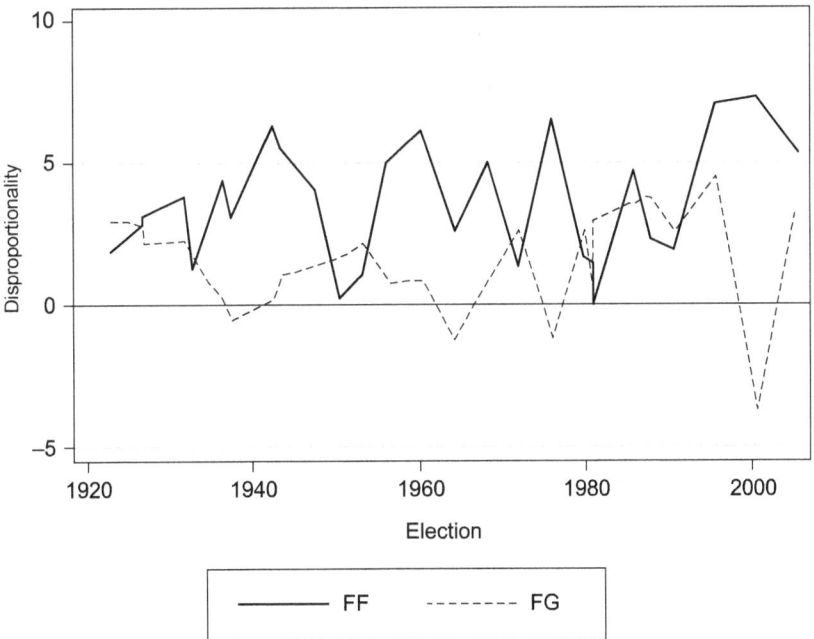

Figure 8.1: Disproportionality for FF and FG 1923–2007

VOTING FOR PARTIES OR CANDIDATES

Analysis of the vote transfers in Table 8.1 show that parties were not able to keep all of their votes. It also shows how their losses could be compensated through winning lower preferences from the candidates of other parties. Analysis of such patterns of transferred votes is a useful way to estimate how important is *party* rather than *candidate* in attracting votes. Obviously the votes transferred are only a sample of all votes and, as we have seen, some votes may be transferred on more than one occasion, so we should be cautious in generalising from the votes we can see transferred to the voting patterns of supporters of all candidates. In the count shown in Table 8.1 there was a high degree of party solidarity, but the most obvious pattern seen in wider analyses of such transfers is a decline in the tendency of votes to transfer within a party. Gallagher (2003) points out that as late as the 1980s, between 80 and 90 per cent of votes stayed within a party when that was possible, but more recent elections have seen no more than about two thirds of votes following party lines. Increasingly it seems that voters are inclined to pick and choose from the candidates offered by a party, and many voters appear to be selecting across party lines.

More evidence on this comes from the 2002 Irish National Election Study (Marsh *et al* 2008), in which voters were asked to fill in mock ballots, replicas of those they would have used in the 2002 election. This revealed what anyone who had ever watched ballots being sorted and counted already knew: that most voters made use of the option to rank candidates. In fact, the study suggested that in 2002 only 6 per cent plumped for a single individual and only 18 per cent restricted their votes to the candidate(s) of a single party. The average constituency had eleven candidates nominated by six parties. The typical voter ranked four candidates, from two parties, and 48 per cent of voters were willing to indicate some degree of preference for the candidates of three or more parties (Marsh *et al.* 2008: 19–20).[5] For many voters – particularly those supporting the minor parties – there would have been only one candidate from the party of their first choice candidate so it is not possible to see if they voted a 'straight ticket', but for all FF voters, almost all FG voters and about half of all Labour voters there was more than one candidate of their party on the ballot. Only 45 per cent of such voters cast a straight party vote. The figures for the individual parties are 51 per cent for FF, 38 per cent for FG and 31 per cent for Labour (Marsh *et al.* 2008: 24). However, a majority of each party's voters did rank all of the candidates of their first preference candidate's party. The typical pattern for such voters was the ranking of a single candidate from another party between the candidates of their first preference party, thus breaking the party sequence. A similar pattern occurred in 2007. This is arguably party voting, and levels would be higher again with a softer definition – such as casting first and second preferences for the same party. Even so, it is evident that most voters are not willing to let party be the sole criterion when filling in their ballot paper.

---

5. See Laver (2004) for supportive analysis using the full electronic records from three constituencies. Bowler and Farrell (1991) reached similar conclusions when studying polls from European Parliament elections.

It might be argued that while *party* is crucial for most voters in determining their initial preferences, the *candidate* carries more weight for lower rankings. If this were to be true, voting a straight ticket would be an overly strong and so misleading indicator of the importance of party. There may be a degree of truth in the argument, but the evidence is far from clear. Asked to rate all candidates and parties, the average voter placed their first choice candidate ahead, if narrowly, of her party, but rated party ahead of candidate for those ranked in the lower places (Marsh 2007). This suggests that, if anything, candidate is particularly important when it comes to the first choice. The direct evidence from the voters supports this. When asked to say whether the party or the candidate is the most important factor in their first preference vote, a clear majority of voters say it is the candidate. However, many of these also said they would be unwilling to support the same candidate if they were standing for a different party. Summing up all the evidence Marsh *et al.* (2008: 158) suggested that as many as 40 per cent of voters could be said to be influenced primarily by the candidate.

Counter to these arguments is the enduring strength and stability of the party system. Gallagher points out that the party label still provides the best explanation for the success or failure of candidates at the polls (2003: 90). FF candidates on average not only win more votes, but very few of them do so badly as to fall below a funding threshold – a fate that befalls a substantial minority of candidates from minor parties. How can this be reconciled with a significantly candidate centred electorate? The answer must be that the label, and the standing and resources linked to that label, help to define a 'good' candidate. 'Good' candidates have an incentive to stand for a major party, and the parties also have an incentive to recruit those who have significant electoral appeal. Analysis of the ratings of candidates and parties abased on data from the 2002 election study shows us that for most voters the most highly rated or 'best' candidate came from the most highly rated or 'best' party (Marsh *et al.* 2008: 155).

While the party label is necessary for many candidates, it is rarely sufficient as all parties nominate more candidates than they win seats. Parties now nominate fewer candidates in individual constituencies than they once did, but they still tend to put up more candidates than the number that they expect to be successful. Typically FG and FF will field more than one candidate in each constituency, and Labour have done so in many districts, whereas SF, Progressive Democrats (PDs) and Greens typically ran only one candidate in each district. This gives rise to significant competition within the larger parties. Indeed, for many candidates, and perhaps particularly for those in the largest party, FF, a candidate's chief rival for the seat is his running mate. A survey of candidates carried out after the 2007 election asked them to say whether the main competitor for a seat lay in their own party or another, or both equally.[6] The majority, 64 per cent, said the main competition was from outside the party, but 22 per cent saw it in a running mate with a further 14 per cent identifying the joint threat. A minority of both FF and FG candidates saw their main threat as lying outside the party.

---

6. This survey was carried out by the author. The data is lodged with the Comparative Candidate Study Archive at MZES, at the University of Mannheim: www.comparativecandidates.org/

Table 8.2: How did incumbents lose? (1927–2007)

	Outgoing TDs (number)	Retiring (%)	Con-testing (%)	Re-elected as % of those in parliament at dissolution	Defeated as % of those in parliament at dissolution	Re-elected as % of those contesting current election
FF	1,824	8.7	91.3	78.7	12.5	86.2
FG	1,285	8.3	91.7	73.7	17.9	80.5
Lab	402	7.2	92.8	74.4	18.4	80.2
Others	444	12.6	87.3	58.6	28.8	67
Total N	3,955	351	3604	2,943	661	2,943

Based on Gallagher 2000, supplemented by 2002 and 2007 election data.

They have good reason to feel that way. Over the last eighty years a significant source of parliamentary turnover has been the electoral defeat of incumbents by challengers from within their own parties as the voters collectively used their preferential votes to make a difference. As Table 8.2 shows, 82 per cent of all deputies standing for re-election over the period 1927–2007 have been successful, suggesting there is some advantages to incumbency. One-third of those who were unsuccessful were ousted by a running mate. FF deputies have been most at risk, with a majority of those losing being displaced by a FF rival. Gallagher (2000) calculated that just over one in five of all Teachta Dála (Dáil deputies, TDs) entering the Dáil in the twentieth century did so by defeating a party running mate in a general election. The electoral system is thus a source of turnover *within* parties, as well as between them.

THE NATURE OF INTRA-CANDIDATE COMPETITION

What is it then that candidates compete about? On what basis can voters choose between them? Clearly it is not just party, although party competition itself is also problematic. (What do parties compete about?) We will start with candidates. On their own admission, personal attributes are very important to their campaigns. Candidates were asked after the 2007 election to indicate the focus of their recent campaigns on an 11 point scale where zero was 'to attract as much attention as possible for me as a candidate' and 10 was 'to attract as much as possible attention for my party'. The mean position was 4.5, with almost 40 per cent of all candidates scoring 0–3 and 22 per cent scoring between 7–10.

Voters have been asked in a number of ways what they want from a candidate, what makes a good candidate. The 2002 Irish National Election Study asked them about three possible criteria: being close to your own views, being good a contributing to national political debate and being good for *this* area. The last of these won hands down. While only 43 per cent were willing to place one above all others, three quarters of those who did so placed working for the area in first place. Furthermore, scores given to candidates on that criterion are much more closely associated with general candidate evaluations (Marsh *et al.* 2008: 155–6, 184–8).

An item used in opinion polls since the 1980s has asked voters to say which of the several criteria are most important in determining their vote, inviting them to choose between voting for a taoiseach, a set of ministers, a set of policies and voting for someone to represent their area. The last of these is most popular, typically selected by between 40 and 50 per cent of respondents. The 2007 Irish National Election Study asked people which of several qualities they thought it particularly important for TDs to have. The results are shown in Table 8.3. By far the largest proportion, almost three quarters of all respondents, say it is very important that a TD speaks up for his or her area. Only 22 per cent thought party loyalty was very important. However, more people thought speaking their own mind was important than rated as important the classic constituency service role, helping individual voters sort out their problems.

Table 8.3: Who should TDs represent?

	Average ranking
All voters in the constituency	2.1
All those in the constituency who voted for the TD	2.9
All those in the constituency who voted for the TDs party	3.2
All voters in the country	3.3
All those in the country who voted for the TDs party	4.0
Members of a particular social group	5.2

Irish National Election Study 2007: www.tcd.ie/ines

Note: 'There are different opinions about which people a TD should primarily represent. What is your opinion? Please rank all of the options below in importance. Mark the most important as 1, the next most important as 2 and so on.'

All this points to the primacy of territory in political representation. Deputies are expected to serve local concerns. The definition of what is 'local' is generally relative, but apart from the constituency as a whole, most deputies have a geographical basis of support within a constituency, their so-called 'bailiwick'. This may have its origins in their own background. Candidates are almost universally local people, often born in the area they represent and with a background of activity in their community. It is also encouraged by the way parties deal with internal party conflict in election campaigns, which they do by laying down boundaries within which each candidate's campaigning tends to be concentrated. Nomination strategies, at least outside the most urbanised constituencies, will typically manifest due concern to balancing the slate of a party's candidates in geographical terms. Incumbent and often aspiring deputies may also make themselves available at a number of locations within the constituency on a regular basis – often weekly – to deal with individual representations. These meetings are usually known as 'clinics', the analogy being with a doctor's surgery hours. Candidates will tend to be more active in those areas where they see their personal support as concentrated. Even those candidates who have no running mate will tend to view their support in geographical terms.

Election results are counted only at the level of the constituency as a whole, but there is ample evidence that geography matters when it comes to elections. It has been shown through the use of 'tallies', the unofficial record made by parties of the voting patterns in each local ballot box (see Parker 1984) that inform campaign strategies at subsequent elections. It is also very apparent in the transfer of votes, although geography here is much less important than party (Marsh 1981). However, when constituencies straddle county boundaries, transferring to running mates from a different county is often much lower than elsewhere. Gorecki and Marsh (2009) have also shown using the 2002 Irish National Election Study that geographical proximity to a candidate is a very significant factor in first preference voting. All this underlines the localism of Irish political life, summarised aptly by the title of Carty's (1981) book on Irish electoral politics: *Party and Parish Pump*.

For many years, many deputies combined their jobs in the national parliament with another on a local council. This dual mandate enabled them to maintain a high profile in dealing with local matters, as well as making it more difficult for a local rival to establish their own reputation. Most deputies have started their political lives on such councils, establishing a record of being able to 'get things done' before moving on to higher things. This practice came to an end before the 2002 election as part of changes designed to give a higher profile to the work of the parliament, with more sitting days and a stronger emphasis on committee work. Arguably this has put even more pressure on deputies to tend to their own backyards for fear that someone else will be doing it, although to lessen the competition, many succeeded in getting family members or close associates elected to the seats they once held.

Deputies have been much better resourced to carry out their roles in recent years, with funds to employ staff to work in the offices. Most have spent this money maintaining a good constituency base. In one of the first academic studies of the life of a TD, Chubb (1963) quoted a politician as characterising their role as 'going about persecuting civil servants', dealing with minor administrative matters on behalf of constituents and most observers would see this as equally true today.

Twenty-one per cent of respondents to the 2002 election study claimed to have contacted their TD in the last five years. While this may not sound a lot, it translates into some 630,000 people, contacting 166 deputies: roughly 3,800 each. Fifty per cent of such contacts were made through clinics, although with the increasingly widespread use of email, this may be declining as people use other channels of contact.

The impetus to change the electoral system in the middle of the last century came largely from FF's wish to strengthen its own position, but over the last few decades the criticism –most of it from outside the parties– has focused less on proportionality, and the party system, and more on the impact of inter-candidate competition within the constituency on the role of the representative. Deputies are considered to spend too much time on constituency work, processing and defending local interests and concerns, rather than dealing with legislation on national affairs. Parliament consequently is not doing its proper job, which is considering and passing legislation.

There are two broad responses to this criticism. The first is to question how far the behaviour of the typical Irish TD is a function of the electoral system, as opposed to a consequence of other institutions, or of the prevailing political culture. The second is to question whether there is anything much more useful that backbench deputies could do with their time given the general weakness of government backbenchers and the opposition in Ireland's parliamentary system. Gallagher and Komito (2010; see also Sinnott 2010), who deal extensively with these arguments, make the point that the perception that Irish TDs in particular are burdened with constituency work is a false one, thus casting doubt on the impact of the voting system on their behaviour. Gallagher and Komito (244–6) cite a number of studies of deputies across diverse systems all of which indicate that representatives spend a great deal of time on constituency work. There are also other possible reasons why the public might require their TDs to engage in this sort of work. One is that the system of public administration is centralised and not very responsive to citizens concerns: people need a TD's help to obtain their entitlements because of inefficiencies in the system (see Roche 1982). This is certainly a view that some TDs are keen to promote, but it may have been true more of the past than it is of the present, as the public services grasp new technology and adopt some of the norms of client-directed organisations. More generally though, as Chubb (1970: 217) argues 'For generations, Irish people saw that in order to get the benefits that public authorities bestow, the help of a man with connections and influence was necessary. All that democracy has meant is that such a man is laid on officially, as it were, and is no longer a master but a servant.''

In general, the public expects, and seems to want, their representatives to be very responsive to both individual and collective constituency concerns, and deputies themselves see that as normal, even desirable, and something that does not necessarily conflict with a legislative role. Bertie Ahern, who maintained a very strong presence in his constituency when Taoiseach, always argued that this was necessary to keep him, and his government, in touch with the public's needs. There can be no doubt that the electoral system provides a strong incentive to encourage incumbent and aspiring politicians to do what their constituents demand of them, but it is hard to make a convincing case that such parochial demands must be universal. Politicians don't have to compete in terms of who can best deliver benefits to the area. They could, for instance, appeal to different groups within their party, defined in ideological, or group terms, rather than geographical ones. That they do not may say more about the embedded political culture than it does about electoral institutions.

THE MEANING OF PARTY REPRESENTATION

Irish *party* competition appears quite unusual in established democracies because the parties, unlike those in Western Europe, or most Anglo-American democracies, do not appear to be the manifestation of class and religious cleavages. As in the USA, the major parties originated in a civil war, but unlike the USA, there is not even a clear liberal-conservative dimension to political life that substitutes for what is generally seen as a left-right divide elsewhere. Irish parties, and particularly the two major parties are probably closer ideologically than are any major parties in comparable countries. The initial division between FF and FG concerned the nature of the relationship between Ireland and Britain, but that could hardly sustain a party system long after independence, even if the status of Northern Ireland remained unresolved. This is not to say that Irish politics is an issue-free zone. People take different positions on many of the broad themes that characterise politics elsewhere, but it is not always easy to see parties as taking positions on such issues.

The 2007 Irish National Election Study sought to explore policy representation through parties by asking people to place themselves and each party on a number of policy dimensions: taxations vs spending, abortion, the role of Britain in Northern Ireland (NI) and the environment, as well as an undefined left-right scale.[7] Figures 8.2a – 8.2e show the placement of each party and its supporters on these scales. We start with the left-right scale and then superimpose each other issue on that scale in turn. What we are looking for here is for parties to be located on the main diagonal, indicated by the line running from bottom left to top right. This is where parties would be located if positions on these issues reflected those of their voters. The left-right dimension does conform quite well to this expectation, but the two largest parties, FF and FG, and their voters are located very close to one another between points 6 and 7, centre right, on the scales. Labour is centre left, at 4. SF is the only party straying far from this main diagonal, as its voters seem to be more centrist than the party.

This left-right dimension is of course without defined content, and it might be argued that the relative absence of these concepts in Irish political debate mean voters have no agreed frame of reference. If so, the fit apparent in the first chart may mean no more than that Labour voters know they are left wing because they vote Labour. Some support can be given to that interpretation in the next chart, in the upper right corner of Figure 8.2b, which indicates the pattern on the dimension of taxing more vs spending less. The differences between parties is tiny, with all grouped between points 4 and 5 on the party scale and 3 and 5 on the voters scale, with only the very small PD party – which carved out its niche in the system as a party committed to cutting tax – differentiated from the rest. The picture is little different on abortion, an issue which remains unresolved in legislation after several referendums between 1983 and 1992 (see Figure 8.2c). Only the Green party is far from the main diagonal here, but again all parties are closely grouped. There is a bigger range with respect to the environmental issue, which opposed

---

7. See Marsh *et al.* (2008) for the question wording and comparable data for 2002.

environmental controls and economic growth, but only with respect to how voters viewed the parties. The voters for all parties lie between points 3 and 4 – well to the pro-environmental side of most parties. Finally the party system's defining issues, Northern Ireland. Apart from SF, and that party is well above the diagonal, indicating that its voters take a softer line that the party is perceived as taking, the parties are again grouped closely.

These charts might be taken to show that there is a reasonable fit between the positions of parties and their voters on these issues. After all, few points are very far from the main diagonal. However, the main conclusion that should be drawn is that on most of these issues there is little difference between the parties, or their voters. This is not to say that voters are of one mind on each of these issues, as they are not. Opinion is spread, with the inter-quartile range typically of the order of 2–3 points. However, views on these issues were not associated with party support in 2002 (see Marsh *et al.* 2008: 161–79) and do not appear to be associated in 2007 either. While it could be accepted that the parties more or less represent the median voter – although not on the environment – they generally give inadequate voice to differences in the electorate.

As with the roles of deputies, this can be argued to be a consequence of the electoral system. The logic is as follows: candidates and their parties need transfers – lower preferences – to succeed and so avoid a clear stance on any divisive issues. They prefer to compete, as do candidates, on filling the pork-barrel and on issues which focus less on what should be done than on who can do it best. These are issues on which there is broad consensus on objectives, such as less unemployment, greater prosperity and so on. This is even more pronounced as the power of parties to structure the vote declines, as voters range freely across the ballot when compiling their preferences. Governments are elected, but such governments have little basis on which to claim a mandate for any particular policy direction. As with the arguments against giving causal recognition to the electoral system for what candidates do, we can also make a case that the nature of Irish party competition and the policy representation that we see here is due to factors other than the single transferable vote. The main point would be that the traditional weakness of the left has historical origins, at independence, or even before. The power of the church, the absence of an industrial working class, the unresolved 'national question', and Labour's decision not to contest the 1918 election, thus surrendering the advantage in a critical election, have all been seen as significant (Mair 1992; see Weeks 2010 for a summary). The reality of valence politics is also hardly confined to Ireland. Even so, the degree to which the parties are undifferentiated does seem remarkable.

150 | personal representation

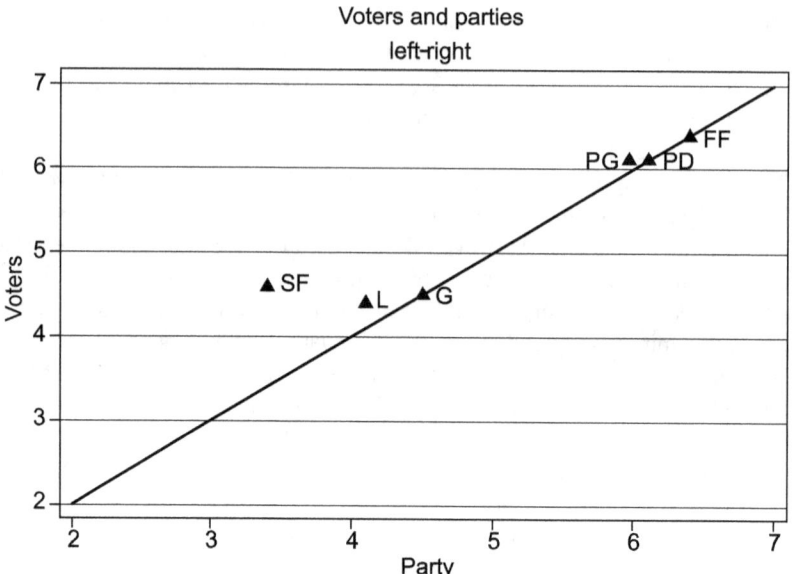

Figure 8.2a: Policy representation in 2007

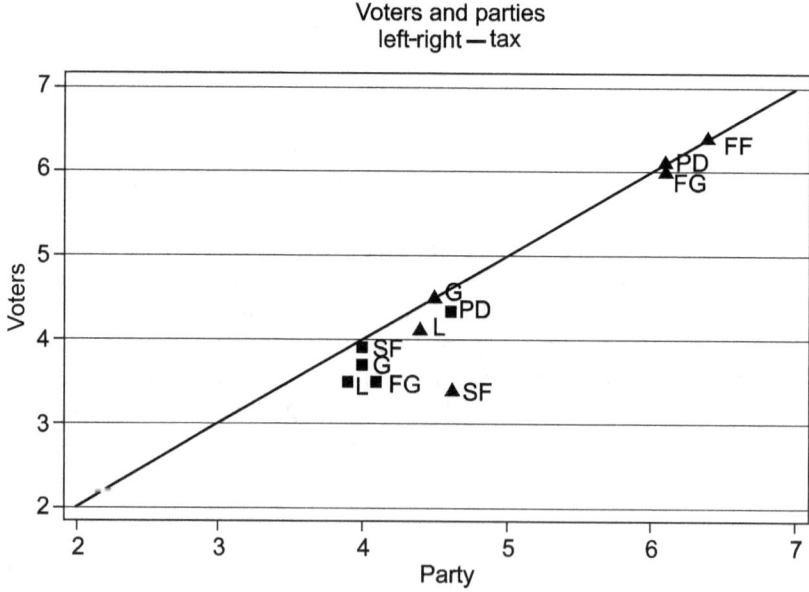

Figure 8.2b: Policy representation in 2007 – tax

ordinal rank | 151

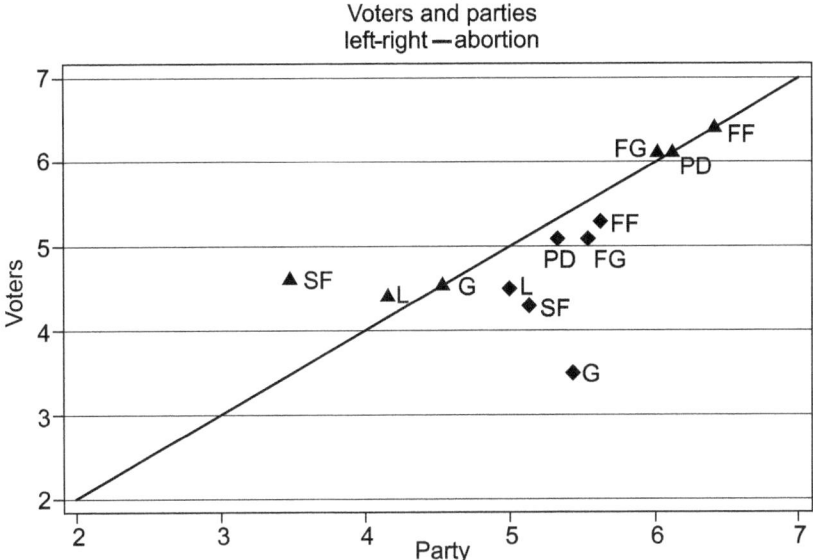

Figure 8.2c: Policy representation in 2007 – abortion

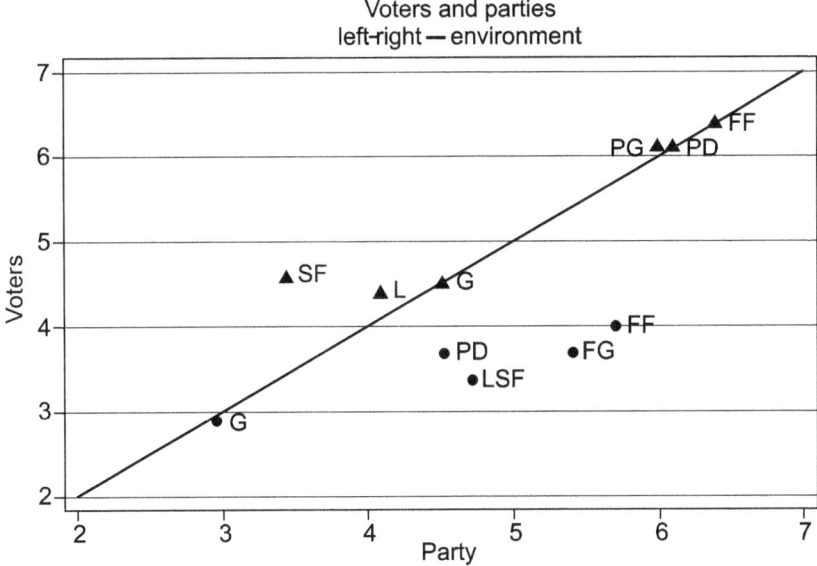

Figure 8.2d: Policy representation in 2007 – environment

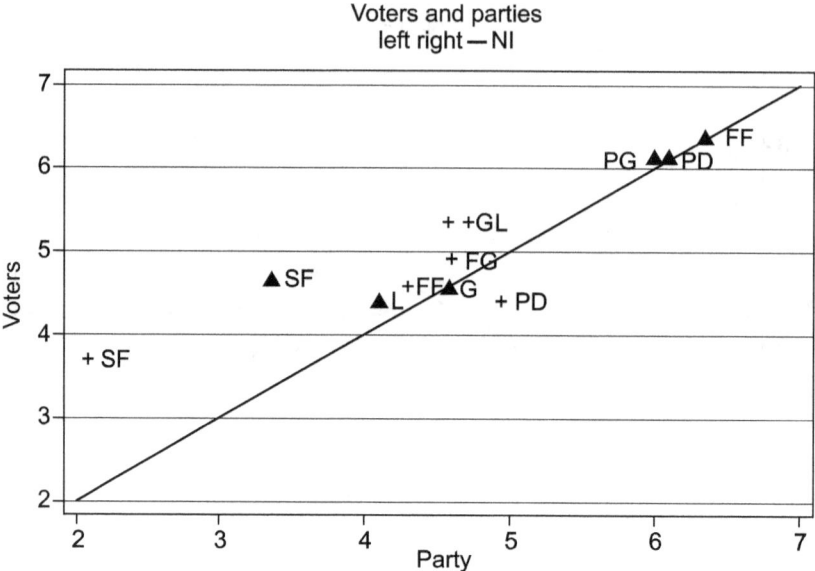

Figure 8.2e: Policy representation in 2007 – National Insurance

CONCLUSION

Under the Irish electoral system voters have a choice of party as well as person. Many take full advantage of that and for at least a significant minority, the candidate seems to matter more than the party. In choosing a candidate, voters want someone to represent local area in an essentially extractive fashion. Where does that leave parties? Parties are certainly not peripheral in electoral politics and the overall stability of the party system would seem to point to their dominance, but parties are almost empty containers with respect to policy. While there is a recognition of which parties are 'left' and which 'right', the concepts have no clear policy reference. On classic left-right issues, economic and social, there is little correspondence between parties and voters.

The electoral system seems to offer a wonderful mixture: representation of minorities without undue fragmentation, and proportional representation along with giving the people a deputy who represents them personally. However, at least in Ireland, where in contrast to the STV experience elsewhere, parties are less powerful in the electoral process, balancing party and personal representation has a cost, in as much as policy representation is unclear. There may be other aspects of policy, such as valence, which do link voters to parties, but, in general, the creation of party representation on the basis of personal representation is achieved with only limited success.

chapter nine | open ballot
Georg Lutz

LUXEMBOURG

154 | personal representation

In this chapter I look at the origin and consequences of the Swiss open ballot system with rules of proportional representation (PR). Such a system allows for a large amount of party *and* personal representation, because voters can not only choose between parties but between candidates within parties. In the Swiss case voters are even allowed to give preference votes to candidates from other parties. I argue that in Switzerland the choice of an open ballot system is linked to the relative weakness of the party leadership compared to ordinary party members. The open ballot system allowed candidates to influence their own fortune independent from the party leadership. There is also a strong continuity between voting in multi-member plurality systems and open ballot PR systems: in both cases, votes write down a large number of candidates on their ballot.

I use data from the 2007 elections in Switzerland, where in 20 PR electoral districts (cantons), 3,089 candidates ran on 311 ballots for the 194 seats, to show the strategic incentives this system creates for parties and candidates. As we will see, parties inflate the number of lists because they believe that more candidates means more preference votes. We can show that for many candidates they have to attract a lot of preference votes from voters from other parties in order to get elected. We can also show that the party leadership hardly ever uses the strongest instruments it has to get desired candidates elected, which is pre-cumulating candidates.

The Swiss electoral system is explained in the first part of the chapter. In the next section, I discuss the origin of the open ballot PR system and try to find reasons why an open ballot system has been favoured instead of a closed ballot system. As far as is known, there is no single study which has looked on why a country had chosen an open ballot instead of a closed ballot PR system in a systematic way. The entire literature on electoral system choices looks almost exclusively at why PR was introduced at some point in time. In the last part I discuss strategic consequences of this system for parties, candidates and voters.

THE SWISS OPEN BALLOT PR ELECTORAL SYSTEM

The system used in Switzerland allows voters to express their preferences in a number of ways. Voters can cumulate candidates, they can add candidates from other parties and also cumulate them (panachage), and they can cross off candidate names. Elections and the distribution of seats take place in electoral districts which are the cantons. The seats for the National Council are distributed to the twenty-six cantons proportionally based on the resident population of a canton. Because of the very uneven population size of the cantons this creates a large variance of district magnitude. The average district magnitude is 7.7, but six cantons have only one seat and the largest canton has thirty-four seats. Plurality elections take place in the cantons with one seat, whilst a PR system is used in cantons with two or more seats.

Some weeks before the elections, voters receive a set of different ballot papers for each election by mail.[1] This set includes an empty ballot paper with a line on

---

1. Voting procedures can vary slightly from canton to canton. For example, in one canton voting is compulsory. All cantons have introduced very easy postal voting. Instead of going to a polling

top for the party name and as many lines as there are seats to fill. In addition, for each party ballot the set includes one pre-printed ballot paper with the party name on the top and the parties' candidate names printed as well. Voters have as many candidate votes as there are seats to be filled, which means that in the largest canton they can cast thirty-four votes, in smaller cantons only two votes.

When filling out their ballot, voters need to make several choices:

- First, voters need to choose between an empty ballot paper or one of the pre-printed ballot papers.
- If they take an empty ballot paper they can write a party name on the top, however this is not necessary. The ballot paper is also valid if no party name appears on the ballot paper. Then they have to put at least one name for a candidate on the ballot paper. A ballot paper with only a party name but no candidate name is not valid. Voters can write down as many candidate names as there are seats to be filled. They have the possibility to write down the same name twice (cumulative vote) and they are allowed to write down names of candidates from other parties (panachage) twice at most.
- If voters use the pre-printed ballot paper they can cast this party ballot without any changes or expressing preferences for specific candidates. They can also cross off candidates on the ballot they don't like and they can also write down the same candidate once again or add candidates from other parties (panachage).

For the distribution of the seats between parties, the individual candidates votes count. This means that all votes received for candidates of a party are summed up. Additional party votes come from empty lines on ballots that have a party name on top but where not all lines are used. The total of these votes is the base to distribute seats between parties using the Hagenbach-Bischoff system, which is the same as the d'Hondt method but another way to calculate the seat distribution.[2]

Such large freedom to express preferences is rare in PR systems. There are several 'strong' preferential voting systems (a term used by Karvonen 2004) which allow to express preferences for candidates of the same party, however only Switzerland and Luxembourg are open ballot PR systems that also allow to express preferences for candidates from other parties.

station voters can send their ballot paper back by mail. The use of postal voting is very extensive. In most cantons a majority of the people that vote use postal voting, in some cantons postal voting exceeds 90 per cent of the votes cast.

2. In Switzerland 'apparentement', which means forming ballot alliances is also possible. First, the seats are distributed between ballot alliances and singe ballots and then in a next step within ballot alliances. This is a feature that has important strategic consequences for parties as well. It creates a huge disincentive to concentrate forces in fewer parties because when small parties run with little chance of winning a seat, this does not weaken the overall block and it allows for parties to present several ballot in the same electoral district.

THE ORIGIN OF THE SWISS OPEN BALLOT SYSTEM

A central argument in the literature to explain why a country introduced PR instead of a majoritarian electoral system has been the strategic considerations of parties and the pattern of political competition in a country (Boix 1999; Blais *et al.* 2004; Colomer 2005). Parties introduce PR when they are worried that they could lose elections under majority rule in the near future. The merit of this argument lies in the simplicity: it is obviously political actors who made such choices and it is almost common sense that motivations to change electoral systems are instrumental for many parties: if they believe that a political reform will mean that they are better off, they are in favour of reform whereas if they believe that they will be worse off, they will be against the reform. This is an important but by far not the only argument brought forward: the choice of electoral systems is a path dependent process influenced by social and structural factors.

Such inter-party competition, anyway, does not help much in explaining why a country then chose an open or a closed ballot PR system. In the absence of any study that focuses on the choice of an open ballot vs a closed ballot electoral system we can not rely on specific theories that could frame the explanation for the introduction of such a system in Switzerland.

The Relative Strength of the Party Leadership

One possible explanation for the introduction of open ballot vs closed ballot systems is the relative strength of the party leadership compared to ordinary party members. Party leadership and ordinary party members, who are thinking about running for election, may have different interests.

Overall, we can assume that the choice of an open vs a closed ballot PR system is related to the relative strength of the party leadership versus ordinary party members. Open ballot PR was introduced where the party leadership was weak relative to the party members.

Party leaders should have an interest in a closed ballot system because this makes it easier to control the party and maintain party coherence. If the parties can steer the candidates' rank order on the party ballot and determine who gets elected, the leadership can easily punish misbehaviour of incumbent candidates and award good behaviour. Theoretically this is possible in an open ballot system too, however it means that you have to exclude an incumbent candidate entirely from the ballot which can create tensions within a party. Closed ballots make candidates more accountable to the party leadership than open ballots systems, which is desirable from a party leadership perspective.

Most candidates however should be in favour of an open ballot system because this gives them a greater opportunity to influence their own fortune. Being elected in an open ballot PR system only partially depends on the party leadership. Candidate selection in Switzerland has always been a bottom up process. Typically local party branches nominate candidates which are then approved by the constituency (cantonal) branch of the party, which again is often a body of delegates from local branches. This process of the nomination of candidates can take place independently from the ballot structure. However if the party leadership then has the influence to determine the rank order on the ballot in closed ballot systems this gives them a great influence on who gets elected. In an open ballot system this is not the case. For an individual candidate to get elected it matters to attract a lot of preference votes, more than other candidates on the same ballot. This can be achieved through personal efforts, while the rank order of party ballots is under control of the party leadership.

Following this line of argument there would be a rather weak party leadership compared to the strength of the ordinary party members in Switzerland. There is only indirect evidence for this. In Switzerland ‚parties had not been structured as strong organisations with a strong leadership for a long time (Gruner 1977, 1978). Parties had only started to form at the national level at the end of the nineteenth century and maybe with the exception of the social democrats, the parties never were strong national organisations until after World War II. Central control over local party branches is still very weak today (Ladner 2004).

It is not only ordinary party members who had an interest in limited control of the party leadership on who gets elected. So did the government. The Swiss government, although elected by parliament for four years, acts rather independently from the parliament because there is no mechanism to remove a member of government from office during its term. In order to continue to act independently the government was not interested in strengthening the role of the party leadership. Once the decision was taken to introduce PR in 1918 (Lutz 2004), it was the government's task to propose a law that specified the details of the new procedure and not surprisingly the government opted for a system which gives voters a lot of control of who gets elected – and as a consequence takes away the party leadership control. The government was open about this intention.[3]

The argument of the national government against PR was that it increases party influence and decreases voters' freedom. The government had been against PR for a long time. Consequently the government opted for the open ballot PR system when forced to design a PR system because this system gives the voters the maximum freedom to express their will. A limitation to casting a party vote only instead of giving votes to candidates from several parties was seen as an unacceptable limitation of the voters' freedom to choose. The government – consisting of party members themselves – also argued that it gives the unpopular parties a far too large influence over MPs and makes MP 'party slaves'. Mistrust of parties was a common features of all debates against the introduction of PR and among the few academics that had written on parties and electoral systems during that time (Braunias 1932). MPs were not supposed to be loyal to the parties but work in favour of the good of a society and PR elections were said to have the opposite effect. This was also the governments' argument why it should be allowed to add candidates from other parties on the ballot. This would increase cross-party vote and stimulate cross-party collaboration.

Why then did parties opt for a system which allows panachage instead of a

---

3. See *Bundesblatt* 16 März 1914, 130.

system which allowed for preferential voting within a single party only? There is an expectation that there will be different interests regarding the introduction of panachage between party candidates. Candidates in line with the parties' main party position should have an interest in an open ballot system with preferential voting but not necessarily with panachage, because they can expect more preferential votes from within the party than from other parties. Candidates not entirely in line with the party may be more in favour of panachage, because a large number of additional votes from other parties ballots make it more likely that they get on the top of the ballot, ahead of the other candidates from the same party.

Why the parliaments in Switzerland voted in favour of panachage is rather puzzling from a rational perspective. It may well be that party leaders expected that they may gain more votes from other parties' voters than they lose through their own supporters adding names on their own party's ballot. Or they feared that some of their potential voters would vote for another party entirely if they could not split their votes among several parties.

To allow voters to add candidates from other parties had consequences on what bases votes are translated into seats. At the cantonal level, two systems were common in Switzerland before PR was introduced at the national level. In the one system, used in several cantons, the votes were distributed to the party based on the list preference votes. In this system there was a disconnection between the party name on top of the list and the preference voting which determined the rank ordering of the candidates.

Although this would have made counting much simpler, the national government stated several times that this system can have undesirable side effects, because it becomes possible that voters can influence the rank ordering of candidates of other parties without weakening their own party. A voter with a strong party preference who does not care about who gets elected from his party can nevertheless give preference votes to candidates from other parties without lowering the chances for his own party.

Therefore the government favoured the system where the sum of a party's candidate votes are the base for the distribution of seats among the parties. Votes for candidates from other parties count as an additional vote for the other party and therefore weaken their own party.

Path Dependency and Continuity
A second reason for the introduction of a specific system may be path dependency. Relying on what is known, is a rational strategy for political actors. One central problem of institutional design that political actors face is uncertainty. Actors are usually not aware of all the available options and they may not be able to compare and assess in a systematic way all the consequences of the different options. Faced with a complex decision, actors are more likely to choose an option with predictable consequences than one with large uncertainties even if the one with greater uncertainty may promise greater gains for an actor.

In many cases, the previous system used influences the choice of a new system. For Switzerland, such path dependent processes matter in two ways, 1) the system cantons which had already introduced PR prior to the introduction of PR at the national level, and 2) the majoritarian electoral system used for the national Council before PR was introduced.

When the introduction of PR was discussed in the national parliament members of parliament and the government made reference to the PR systems already in place in many of the cantons.[4] Because many cantons which had introduced PR already for their elections to the cantonal parliament were open ballot PR systems, the government argued that there was existing experience of this system and therefore it was desirable to introduce the same system at the national level. This leaves, of course, the question open as to why the cantons have chosen an open ballot PR system, which is a question that cannot be answered at this stage.

After the introduction of PR at the national level, the national electoral system had direct consequences on the cantonal system chosen. For example the government of the canton of Bern argued in 1919, one year after PR has been introduced at the national level, that it makes sense to introduce the same system for the cantonal parliamentary elections in order to make it easier for citizens and the parties to get used to the new system.[5]

The system used for the election to the National Council before the introduction of PR was a multi-member majoritarian system. Electoral districts did not overlap cantonal borders, which meant that smaller cantons had a number of seats to be filled in proportion to the number of inhabitants of their cantons. Larger cantons were split into different electoral districts. Drawing district boundaries was a battleground of party interests and long disputes (Gruner 1978). In 1911, when the district structure was adjusted the last time before PR was introduced the average district magnitude was four and the largest district had eight seats to be filled. A two round system was used where in the first round candidates needed an absolute majority and in the second round candidates needed a simple majority only. All first round candidates were allowed to run in the second round and even new candidates could be presented.

Josep Colomer (2007 and the introductory chapter of this book) has argued that if multi-member districts in a country were used, this made it more likely that PR was introduced because the attempt to pool votes and strategically coordinate between different candidates is essential to get many candidates through in multi-member districts. Having larger multi-member districts in majoritarian elections made it more likely that PR was introduced in Swiss cantons too (Lutz and Zila 2008).

This argument can be expanded to the introduction of open ballot systems. Multi-member open ballot systems, whether PR or majoritarian, create incentives for candidates to attract votes from supporters of different party. The change from a multi-member majoritarian system to an open ballot PR system shows remarkable continuity from both a candidate's and a voter's perspective. In fact the ballot paper for both systems looked very similar. In the multi-member majoritarian

---

4. Bericht des Bundesrates an die vereinigte Bundesversammlung 16 März 1914, 121–2.
5. Tagblatte des Grossen Rates 1919: 2008.

system voters could write down as many candidate names from different parties as there were seats to be filled. In the open ballot PR system the voters can write down as many candidates from different parties as there are seats to be filled. The differences are that the new PR system allowed casting two votes for a candidate and of course the way voters were translated into seats differed. However, for the candidates to get elected it was important to be attractive for voters from their own party as well as for voters from other parties in both systems.

Overall we have some indications that an open ballot PR system was chosen over a closed ballot system because of the continuity it created in reference to the systems used at cantonal level in PR elections and to the multi-member majoritarian elections. In addition the system limits the influence of the party leadership on who ends up in parliament. There is not much evidence why this had passed parliament, however it can be assumed that the lack of a strong central party structure at the time when the system was chosen both at the national as well as at the cantonal level was important.

STRATEGIC INCENTIVES FOR PARTIES AND CANDIDATES

The open ballot system used in Switzerland has consequences for the strategic behaviour of parties and candidates.

The main conflict of interest is between the party leadership and the party's candidates. The party leadership mainly has two goals, 1) to increase the party's vote share and 2) to influence who gets elected. To increase the party's vote share, the party leadership should try to stimulate a situation where voters do not change the ballot or at least that voters do not add candidates from other parties. The party leadership wants to run a party-focused campaign or at least a campaign which is focused on party leaders.

Candidates on the other hand, in addition to increasing the overall party's vote share, want to make sure that they get a lot of preference votes from the own party supporters as well as from supporters of other parties in order to get on top of the ballot. Candidates can control the number of seats that a party achieves only to a small degree, but the candidate can influence whether he makes it to the top of the ballot.

Parties and candidates have a number of instruments they can use, as illustrated by the use of data from the 2007 Swiss national election for the National Council (which is the lower house) which is available from the Swiss Statistical Office.[6] In this election, out of the 26 cantons (electoral constituencies), 20 cantons/constituencies had 2 or more seats, which means PR elections took place there. In these cantons 3,089 candidates ran on 311 different lists. The number of candidates varies a lot. In the largest canton of Zurich 804 candidates competed for the 34 seats on 29 lists, in Schaffhausen 14 candidates ran on 7 lists for the two seats.

---

6. See www.bfs.admin.ch

open ballot | 161

Party Strategies
Parties try to make sure that no votes are lost to other parties or at the same time attract many votes for their candidates from other ballots. There are several ways of achieving these objectives:

Inflate the number of candidates through presenting more than one list. In many cases parties present more than one list in the same constituency. This is based on the simple calculation that additional candidates attract additional votes. A further reason is that it may help to increase the level of the campaign because more candidates are directly involved in the campaign.

Different lists can contain candidates from different regions within one constituency, there can be separate lists for female and male candidates or the party's youth organisation may present their own list. This is a possible strategy because parties can create list alliances (apparentement) at different levels. For example they can form a list alliance with parties close to them and within these list alliances they can form a list alliance with all the different lists from their own party. One advantage of presenting several lists for the same party is that it allows for a better representation of different regions or factions within the party. The risk of this strategy is that in some cases it may become even more unpredictable who gets elected because candidates do not only have to attract a lot of preference votes in order to get elected they also has to be on the right list of the party.

Table 9.1 shows the number of lists that was presented by each party in the 2007 election. The larger parties, such as the Peoples Party (SVP), the Liberal Party (FDP) and the Social Democrats (SP) presented list in all cantons, the Christian Democrats (CVP) in all but one and the Greens in all but three. It is very common that large parties present more than one list in the same constituency. On average the larger parties and the Greens had more than 2 lists per canton. In the canton of Valais the Christian Democrats presented a total of 6 lists.

However, this includes in many cases separate lists of the parties' youth branch which is not so much a strategic decision but to allow the parties' youth their own political space. 76 of the 311 lists were from the parties' youth branch, most of which came from the larger parties. Nevertheless, even without the youth list, presenting more than one list is very common. Parties often choose regionally separate lists within the same constituency. Other criteria are used as well, such as separate lists for male and female candidates or separate lists for Swiss people living abroad.

Pre cumulating and avoiding empty lines. Another feature to influence who gets elected is the possibility to pre-cumulate some candidates. Voters can write down the same candidate twice on a ballot paper and so can parties on the pre-printed ballots. This is a strong tool to influence who gets elected because many voters use the pre-printed ballot without any changes or with only minimal changes and for a non-cumulated candidate it is very difficult to receive more votes than a pre-cumulated candidate.

Pre-cumulating candidates is a rather efficient tool in order to increase the chances of a candidate. Parties hardly ever use this possibility. Of 311 lists, 262 did not add names twice (84.2 per cent); 43 did so but not for strategic reasons but

Table 9.1: Number of ballots presented by parties in the 2007 election

Party	No. ballots	No. cantons	No. of ballots per canton	
			Mean	Non-youth ballots
People's party (SVP)	45	20	2.25	1.50
Liberal party (FDP)	48	20	2.40	1.50
Social-democrat (SPS)	44	20	2.20	1.52
Christian-democrat (CVP)	40	19	2.11	1.43
Green	34	17	2.00	1.55
Evangelical	19	14	1.36	1.19
Federal democratic union	12	10	1.20	1.09
Other	69	17	4.06	1.03
Total	311	20	15.55	1.32

Source: *Federal office of statistics.*

to fill all the lines of a ballot when the party did not have a sufficient number of candidates.

Only on 6 lists was a smaller number of candidates listed twice on the pre-printed ballots in advance. If a candidate was pre-cumulated and the list managed to gain a seat it was always a successful strategy to get elected. In one case this did not work because either more candidates were pre-cumulated than the list won seats or the list did not win any seat at all.

If voters find empty lines on a ballot paper they may be more likely to add candidates from other parties. There are two ways to avoid this. Parties, especially in large cantons sometimes have problems filling their list. Since parties are also allowed to pre-cumulate candidates on a pre-printed ballot they can still present a full ballot through pre-cumulation. Until recently the parties were also allowed to spread their parties' candidates all over the ballots. A ballot with fewer candidates than seats still looked full because there was not a large empty space at the end of the ballot paper. This practice was stopped because it confused voters.

In the 2007 elections, 98 of the 311 lists presented had fewer candidates than seats to be filled (31 per cent). 44 per cent of those lists (43) did pre-cumulate all or most candidates in order to fill their ballot. 6 lists pre-cumulated one or only a few candidates strategically in order to give them an advantage over the other candidates on the list. 49 of those 98 lists did not fill up their lists by pre-cumulating candidates for several reasons. Some had only one or two candidates less than seats to be filled. In these cases, if only one or two candidate were pre-cumulated it would have created tensions within the party. Leaving one or two lines on the ballot free decreases the intra-party competition and the possible harm done to candidates on the bottom of the ballot because voters can add names of candidates from other parties without having to cross off candidates from their own party.

There are several usually smaller lists where the number of candidates was less than half of the seats to be filled. In these cases not pre-cumulating candidates is rather stupid. It is likely that the parties presenting those lists were not aware of the possibility to pre-cumulate candidates.

Ballot order. Parties are entirely free to choose the order of the candidates on the ballot. How those rank orders are determined on the ballot is subject to intense debates within many parties and a reasons for internal party conflict. There are several criteria which can be taken into account:

- Alphabetical order
- Incumbent candidates at the top of the ballot
- Women first, followed by men
- 'Zipper ballots': men and women alternate on the ballot
- Specific candidates the party wants to favour on top of the ballot
- Past performance in elections

Several criteria can be used at the same time. For example on a ballot the incumbent candidates appear first, followed by men and women alternated in alphabetical order.

The simplest criteria to structure a ballot is to use the alphabetical order. In order to determine how ballots are structured we calculated Spearman's rank correlation coefficient for each ballot between the actual ranking and the ranking on a ballot if it had been in purely alphabetical order. This coefficient has a value of 1 if the ballot is purely alphabetical and -1 if the names appear from Z to A on the ballot. We only included ballots with five or more candidates which also means that four cantons were excluded entirely because they have fewer seats.

The most frequent order is alphabetical order, however many lists choose another way of ordering their ballots than alphabetical order (Figure 9.1). There exist strong cantonal traditions how ballots are structured (Figure 9.2). In cantons like Tessin and Lucerne ballots are structured purely alphabetically with only few exceptions. In other cantons, many ballots include alphabetical order as a criteria somehow but they utilise other criteria matter too. In several cantons like Zurich, Aargau or Geneva, alphabetical order is not a strong criteria at all.

It is not entirely clear whether this matters. Research from other countries suggests an effect of rank ordering on the ballot and the candidates success in an election; candidates that appear higher on the ballot should have higher chances of getting elected. However this is only true for ballots which follow some other order than alphabetical order (Ortega Villodres 2003) and in this case it is not known whether the likelihood of getting elected is already taken into account in the rank order.

Focus campaigns on specific candidates and force candidates to make their funds available to the party. Parties will want to connect faces to party programmes.

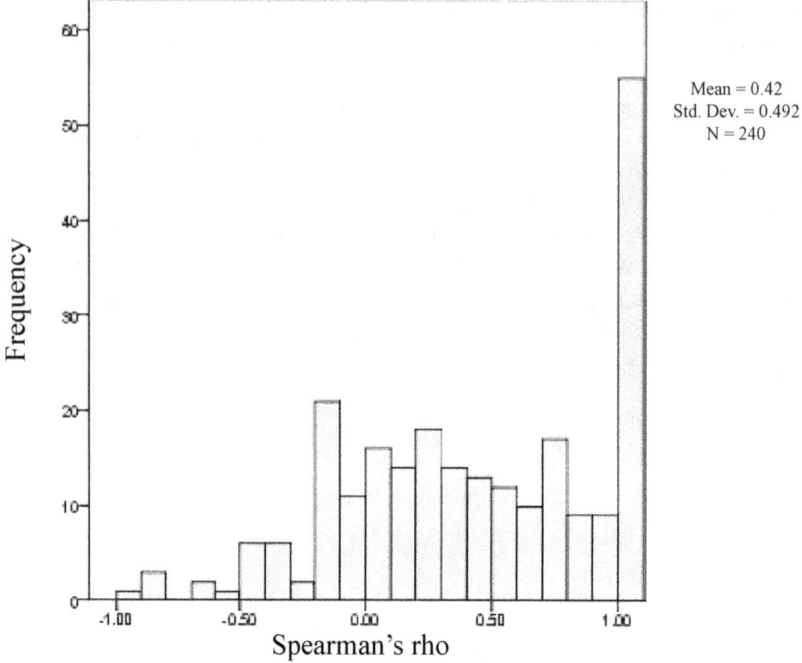

Only ballots with 5 or more candidates included in the graph.

Figure 9.1: Frequency of rank correlations between alphabetical order and actual order of candidates on the ballot

Since they control parts of the campaign they can focus their campaigns on specific candidates.

Some parties have rules, that candidates need to make contributions to the party's funds in order to appear on a party ballot. This lowers the relative advantage of candidates with a lot of funds against those with no funds and strengthens parties vs single candidate campaigns.

In Switzerland there are no rules to disclose information on campaign finances by parties and/or candidates and therefore it is not possible to give any figures if and how this is done.

Candidate Strategies

The open ballot system has a number of strategic consequences for candidates. From a candidate's perspective, to be elected depends on two factors 1) to be on a list which gets one or more seats, 2) and then to be on the top of that ballot.

One of the key problems of the open ballot system is that in order to get elected, candidates from the same party are in strong competition with each other. For an individual candidate the intra-party competition is far more important than the inter-party competition. In order to get elected, candidates have to attract more

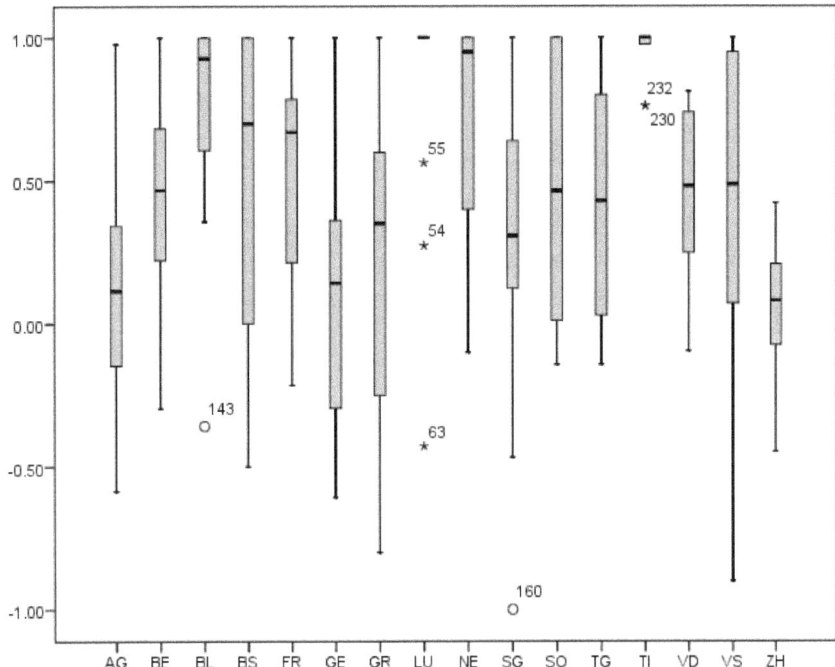

Figure 9.2: Box-plots of Spearman's rho alphabetical order of the ballot per cantons

preferential votes than other candidate from the same party. It is known to a substantial degree how many seats a list may get especially in Switzerland where volatility is rather small compared to other countries (Ladner 2004).

In order to do so, candidates can choose different strategies:
- Attract preferential votes within their own party which can also mean to make sure that you don't lose too many votes from supporters of your own party.
- Attract preferential votes from voters from other parties. In this case a candidate has a strong incentive to run an independent campaign which would be attractive to voters from other parties.

In reality it may often be difficult to distinguish between the two strategies and the candidates main effort is to make themselves known to all potential voters because this makes it most likely that somebody adds a name to the ballot. In order to do so, candidates try to get support from various organisations and they try to run their own campaigns. However, there are always some candidates who try to position themselves at the edge of a party in order to attract a lot of votes from other parties.

In the 2007 Swiss elections for the National Council 171 incumbents ran again. Of those 147 were elected again (86 per cent) and 24 did not get elected (14 per cent). Of those 24 not elected, 9 lost against candidates of the same party which won a seat instead (inner-party defeat), 15 lost a seat because the list they ran on did not make a sufficient number of seats in order to secure the seat (partisan defeat).

In all cases, the question was what kind of preference votes made the difference? In order to get elected candidates have to make it to the top of the ballot which means that they have to get ahead of other candidates. There are two ways to do that 1) either to make sure that many people cumulate a candidate or do not cross him off or 2) to attract preference votes from voters from other parties.

The official candidate statistics allow this distinction to be made and the opportunity to detect how many candidate votes came from unchanged ballot, how many came from changed ballots of their own party and how many preference votes came from other party ballots.

In order to detect what matters more, we compared the preference votes from a candidate's own party ballot to the preference votes received by a candidate from other parties' ballots. We did this for each pair of candidates on ballots where any candidate got elected for the candidate who was last among the elected and the candidate who was first among the not elected on that particular ballot. This gives us a total of 99 pairs of candidates from our dataset. We checked for each pair of candidates what the advantage of the elected candidate was compared to the one who was not elected for both preference votes from own party ballots and preference votes from other party ballots.

Table 9.2: Relative advantage of preference votes for candidates between last elected on a ballot and first not elected on a ballot

Advantage of preference vote from own party ballot	Advantage on preference votes from other party ballots		
	no	yes	Total
no		15	15
yes	2	82	84
Total	2	97	99

In 82 out of 99 cases the candidate who was just about elected had an advantage in both preference votes from other ballot and preference votes from their own party's ballot (see Table 9.2). In 15 out of 99 votes, the candidate who got elected had an advantage in preference votes from voters from other parties and only in two cases the advantage came from their own party ballots. This is an indication that in order to get elected it can matter more to attract votes from other parties than to attract preference votes from one's own party voters.

Overall, the great incentive for candidates to run their own campaigns, and in some cases even with only limited connection to the party, makes it more difficult for the party to run a coherent and focused party campaign.

THE CONSEQUENCES OF PREFERENTIAL VOTING IN SWITZERLAND

In the last part, we analyse some consequences of parties and candidates. First we will look what influences party coherence and second we will look at what influences electoral success of candidates.

Party Coherence

Parties will want to try three things: 1) they prefer if voters don't change their ballot 2) they want to make sure that they attract a lot of extra votes or 3) at least to make sure that they don't lose many votes. We will look now how successful parties have been with regard to those strategies.

In order to do so, we look at different indicators. The first indicator is the number of unchanged party ballots. Out the of 2.1 Mio voters, 46 per cent cast a party ballot without any changes. There was, however, substantial variation between the highest figure of 95 per cent of unchanged ballots and 7.4 per cent as the smallest figure (see Figure 9.3).

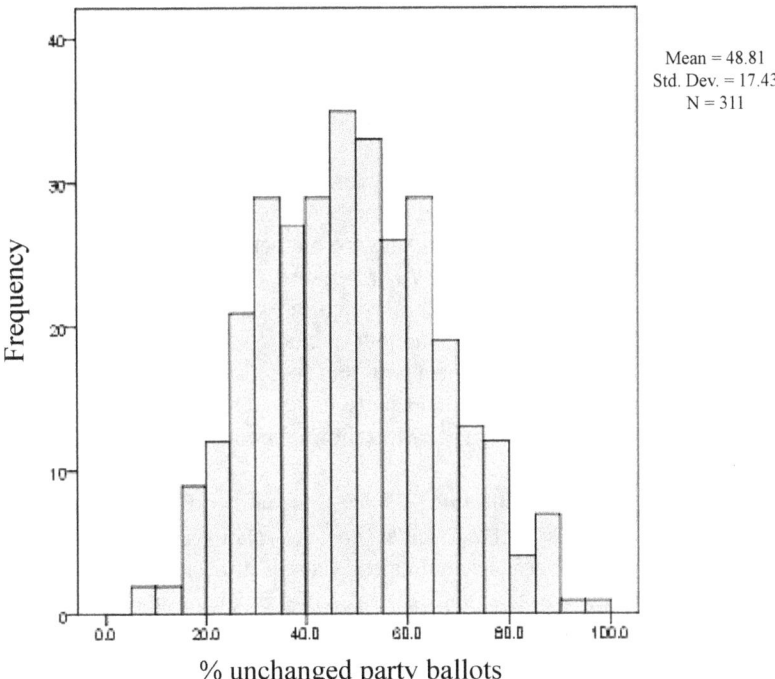

Figure 9.3: Frequency of percentage of unchanged party ballots per ballot

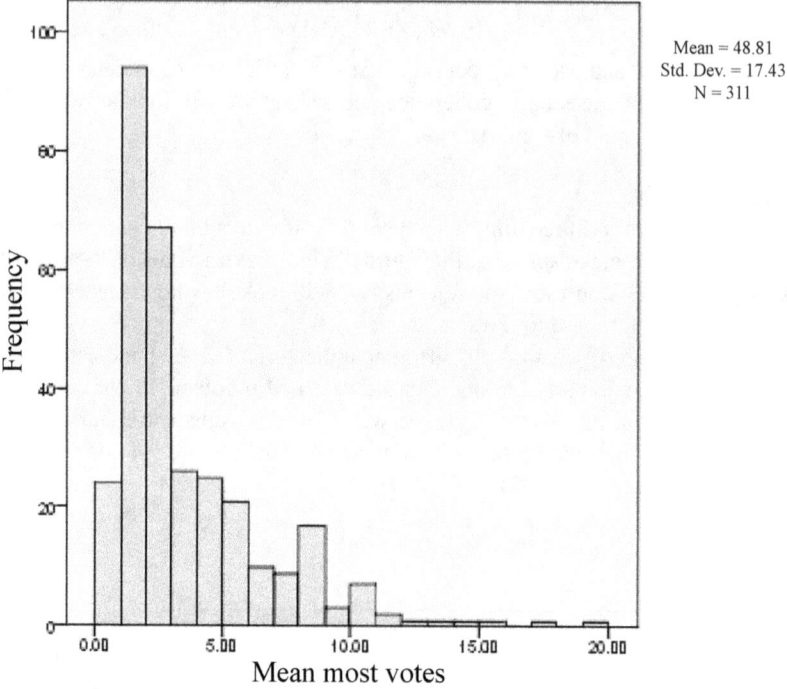

Figure 9.4: Frequency of mean lost votes to other party per ballot

Another set of indicators relates to the amount of preference voting. A party does well when the candidates in total attract a lot of preference votes and when the voters do not add very many candidates from other parties to the ballot paper. Gains and losses can amount to positive or negative figures. We calculated three figures i) votes won, ii) votes lost. All these figures were adjusted to the number of changed party ballots because the number of changed party ballots determines to a great degree the number of votes won and lost. For illustration, Figure 9.4 shows the number of votes lost to other party ballots. On average 3.6 candidates from other parties appeared on party ballots, however with a lot of variation again (see Figure 9.4).

How can we explain this variation? We tested a number of hypotheses:

- *District magnitude* is expected to have a positive relationship with the number of unchanged ballots because candidates in larger districts are less connected to voters than candidates in smaller districts. District magnitude should also be positively related to the number of votes lost *and* won, simply because in larger districts voters have more votes.
- The *overall vote share* of a list in a constituency may have a negative impact on the number of unchanged ballots because voters who support larger parties are usually more sophisticated and have a higher likelihood of changing the ballot structure than voters from smaller lists.

- *French speaking cantons* have a stronger party representative tradition than German speaking cantons and therefore we expect the number of unchanged ballots to be higher. We also expect that the number of votes won and lost is lower in the French speaking area due to the same reason.
- We expect some *party differences*. SVP voters are more likely to cast an unchanged ballot because they attracted a large number of previous non-voters with low education and incomes. We also expect party discipline to be higher among left parties. The very established FDP and CVP voters may be more likely to have a lower proportion of unchanged ballots. With respect to seats won and lost we expect that all the main parties lose less votes to small parties and win more from them, because they have better known candidates.
- If the same party presents *several lists* the number of unchanged ballots should go down, because voters may want to add candidates from an other party. At the same time, the number of votes won and lost should go up.
- If there are *empty line*s on the ballot, this could make it more likely that a voter adds candidates from other parties to fill up the ballot so we expect a negative relationship between empty lines and the percentage of unchanged ballots. Empty lines on the ballot should increase the number of votes lost to other parties, because voters are tempted to fill up their ballots with names. For votes won, we would not find a positive effect.
- The *number of incumbent candidates* on a list should be positively related to the number of votes won by a party, we would however not expect much of an effect for the number of votes lost.

We calculated a multilevel model because we believe that some clustering takes place at the constituency (cantonal) level. Table 9.3 shows the different results and many of the hypotheses are confirmed. The result is different from what we expected, district magnitude is not related to the number of changed ballots of a list. We do, however, find a significant positive relation between the number of votes won and lost and district magnitude, which confirms our hypothesis. Voters of successful lists did change the ballot more often. They were also more likely to lose panachage votes to other parties. Voters in French-speaking areas are much less likely to change the ballot and the level of panachage is lower there too.

We find some interesting party differences. Voters from the FDP and CVP are more likely to change the ballot, voters from the SVP much more often cast an unchanged party ballot. This shows, that SVP voters are much more loyal to their party and also as other studies have shown less sophisticated than the voters from the other parties. The main parties tend to gain from the open list system. The dummy variables for the five largest parties all have positive signs in the model with votes lost and positive signs in the model with votes gain, although there are some differences.

If a party presents more than one list, it is more likely that a voter changes the ballot, which makes sense because voters may want to add candidate names from an other list from the same party. If other party lists exist, a list loses votes too, which makes sense because of the same mechanism. However it does not have much of a positive effect on the votes won by a party.

Table 9.3: Multi-level model explaining the number of unchanged party ballots, mean votes lost and won per list

	Percentage unchanged ballots			Mean votes lost			Mean votes won		
	Coef.	SE		Coef.	SE		Coef.	SE	
District magnitude	0.047	0.247		0.244	0.018	***	0.481	0.036	***
List votes %	-0.450	0.078	***	-0.046	0.011	***	-0.347	0.043	***
French speaking canton	10.320	4.331	**	-0.307	0.327		-1.451	0.716	**
FDP	-5.896	1.951	***	-1.057	0.280	***	1.791	1.054	*
CVP	-7.111	2.059	***	-0.635	0.296	**	1.249	1.114	
SP	2.420	2.000		-0.449	0.288		2.184	1.088	**
Green	1.807	2.052		-0.048	0.296		2.084	1.122	*
SVP	11.752	2.155	***	-1.132	0.309	***	3.096	1.159	***
Total of list per canton	-2.934	0.645	***	0.423	0.087	***	0.051	0.276	
Empty lines on the ballot	0.093	0.152		0.045	0.022	**	0.043	0.082	
Constant	56.379	3.823	***	0.600	0.342	*	2.337	0.942	**
sigma_u	8.067			0.534			0.000		
sigma_e	9.571			1.429			5.554		
rho	0.415			0.123			0.000		
N	311			311			311		
R-sq: within	0.339			0.229			0.213		
between	0.257			0.932			0.953		
overall	0.269			0.740			0.531		

*GLS multi-level estimates, significant at * .1, ** .05, *** .01 level.*

If a party presents more than one list, it is more likely that a voter changes the ballot, which makes sense because voters may want to add candidate names from an other list from the same party. If other party lists exist, a lists loses votes too, which makes sense because of the same mechanism. However it does not have much of a positive effect on the votes won by a party.

If a list has empty lines on the ballot, it does not more likely that a voter changes a ballot, however it makes it more likely that a list loses votes. On winning votes, we don't find a positive effect.

Successful Candidate Strategies
In the last part, we now turn to some explanations of candidate success. To measure candidate success, we use the number of preference votes for each candidate. However, the way changed ballots can be filled out and the system of panachage allows us to distinguish between different kinds of preference votes which follow different logics as to what a preference vote means:

1. *Preference votes from own party voters.* These are preference votes that are given to candidates which appear on the ballot the voter has chosen. Being on a list of a voters own party ballot, however, does not necessarily require a very active decision from a voter. If a voter takes a pre-printed party ballot, he will leave many candidates names unchanged and in this case it is not clear whether this was a voluntary act or just that a voter didn't care about those candidates. We only have aggregated preferences and can not distinguish on how many ballots a candidate's name has been struck off the list and on how many ballots a candidate appeared twice, we only have the net gain or losses of each candidate.

2. *Preference votes from voters from other parties (panachage votes).* Those preference votes do in all cases need an active decision by a voter. Voters have to choose another party list, look through the candidates and write a candidate on their ballot by hand. This is a clearer candidate preference and therefore we should be better able to find effects of attractiveness on electoral success and other campaign-related activities than with the candidate votes for candidates from a voter's own party list.

We used the separate measures of preference votes as well as the total number of preference votes in different models. We took the log value of the number of preference votes since the distribution is skewed because of the many candidates from smaller parties.

- *Number of changed party ballots.* This control variable has to be included because when voters use a pre-printed party ballot, they may not actively cast preference votes for all of the candidates but they may only add some candidates, cross off some candidates but leave most of the ballot unchanged. Therefore the number of candidates' votes is highly dependent on the number of ballots cast for a party. We also took the log value of this variable to correct for the skewed distribution.

- *List vote share* as a percentage. We believe that in line with the finding in Table 9.3, candidates on a list which won a lot of votes also won more preference votes.
- *District magnitude.* The higher district magnitude, the more votes a voter has, however in large districts we expect that voters will cast on average fewer preference votes. So we expect a negative relationship between district magnitude and preference votes.
- *Total number of party lists.* If there is more than one list from a party this should have a positive effect on the number of preference votes per party, mainly on panachage votes.
- *Incumbent* candidates have a large advantage in many elections and are more likely to attract preference votes because they are better known to the voters.
- Some candidates are *pre-cumulated*, which means that their names already appears twice on the pre-printed ballot paper. Those candidates are more likely to receive preference votes especially from voters of the same party, because those voters may not change the entire party ballot but only add or cross off a few candidates.
- *Ballot position.* Ballot position may have a positive effect for two reasons. 1) Candidates which are higher on the ballot are more likely to attract additional votes than candidates at the bottom of a ballot. 2) Candidates that are on the bottom of the ballot are more likely to be crossed off than candidates on the top of the ballot because voters who want to add candidates from other party ballots (panachage) or want to cumulate candidates tend to add them from the bottom on their ballot and have to cross off candidates accordingly. We used the relative position on the ballot as a measure for candidate success which is division of the ballot position through the district magnitude. We also changed the sign to make sure that a positive sign indicates a positive influence of a higher ballot position.
- We also control for *age and sex*.

Because of the hierarchical structure (candidates nested in lists) of the data we applied a linear multilevel regression model again. Table 9.4 shows the result of the regression models. The first model includes preference votes from own party ballots votes, the second model only preference votes from other party ballots (panachage votes) and the third model the total preference votes.

Table 9.4 shows a number of interesting results. First of all, the models explain a large amount of variance. Most of the variance is at the candidate level, however not so surprisingly for the preference votes from a candidate's own list, a substantial amount of variance is also explained at the list level.

The log number of changed ballots has a positive effect in all three models, which is expected. The strength of the list in a constituency has mixed effects. Candidates running on strong lists, receive more preference votes from their own party than candidates running on weak lists. However for panachage votes, the opposite is true: candidates running on strong list on average receive fewer panachage votes. In large districts voters tend to cast fewer panachage votes on average.

Table 9.4: Multilevel model explaining the number of preference votes for candidates

	Preference votes: own lists (log)		Preference votes: panachage (log)		Preference votes: total (log)	
	Coef.	SE	Coef.	SE	Coef.	SE
Number of changed ballots (log)	0.960	0.011 ***	0.616	0.025 ***	0.769	0.015 ***
List votes %	0.004	0.002 **	-0.030	0.005 ***	-0.002	0.003
District magnitude	0.001	0.001	-0.024	0.003 ***	-0.005	0.002 ***
Total number of party lists	0.004	0.027	0.305	0.061 ***	0.192	0.035 ***
Incumbent	0.501	0.022 ***	1.373	0.063 ***	0.750	0.039 ***
Pre-cumulated	0.532	0.031 ***	0.527	0.078 ***	0.520	0.046 ***
Ballot position	-0.459	0.017 ***	-1.168	0.048 ***	-0.778	0.030 ***
Sex	0.016	0.010	0.000	0.028	0.005	0.017
Age	0.001	0.000 *	0.001	0.001	0.001	0.001
Constant	-0.110	0.069	2.917	0.161 ***	2.168	0.093 ***
sigma_u	0.171		0.365		0.201	
sigma_e	0.232		0.677		0.418	
rho	0.352		0.225		0.188	
N	3089		3089		3089	
R-sq: within	0.441		0.377		0.379	
between	0.980		0.767		0.943	
Overall	0.965		0.647		0.903	

GLS multilevel estimates, significant at * .1, ** .05, *** .01 level.

If a party presents more than one list, this has a boosting effect on panachage votes. Incumbents have a large advantage and so do pre-cumulated candidates. We also find a positive effect of ballot position: the lower a candidate is on a ballot, the fewer preference votes he/she receives. Sex or age have no strong effect.

CONCLUSION

This paper on preference voting in Switzerland shows that the introduction of an open ballot system with extensive possibilities to express candidate preferences is closely linked to the previous system: voting in multi-member majoritarian districts is not so different from voting in an open ballot PR system because in both systems voters have the choice to write down names from as many candidates from different parties as there are seats to be filled. It is likely that political elites did not have the political courage to decrease the possibilities of voters and increase the influence of party elites on who gets elected.

Parties and candidates have a number of strategic possibilities to maximise their interest. Parties can present more than one list in the Swiss system, they can determine the order in which candidates appear on the ballot and they can add some candidates twice on a ballot. They can also focus their campaign on specific candidates.

Party elites use the possibilities to influence who get elected on a party list very selectively. They present several lists in many cantons in order to increase the overall party vote share and they influence the rank order on the ballot.

However they hardly ever impose hard measures to influence who gets elected for the parties. The most efficient way to get desired candidates into parliament is to pre-cumulate specific candidates on the ballot, which is something the party leadership hardly ever does. The party leadership does not try to limit individual candidate campaigns either which makes it difficult for most parties to run a coherent campaign nationally or even in a single constituency.

Candidates enjoy a great amount of freedom to run their own campaign. The most important consequence of a system with preference voting to other parties is the relative importance and visibility of candidate instead of party campaigns. This is rational from a candidate perspective because competition does not so much take place between candidates from different parties but between candidates from the same party. Successful candidate campaigns do not only focus on the voters from the own parties: in many cases, candidates were successful because they manage to attract more preference votes from other parties' voters than the candidates from the same party.

bibliography

Andeweg, R. B. (2008) 'Netherlands: The Sanctity of Proportionality', in M. Gallagher and P. Mitchell (eds) *The Politics of Electoral Systems*. Oxford: Oxford University Press: 491–510.

Andeweg, R. B. and Irwin, G. A. (2005) *Governance and Politics of the Netherlands*. Basingstoke: Palgrave Macmillan.

André, A. Depauw, S. and Deschouwer, K. (2009) District Magnitude and Legislators' Personal Vote-Seeking. *5th ECPR General Conference*. Potsdam.

Aragonés, E. and Palfrey, T. (2004) 'The Effect of Candidate Quality on Electoral Equilibrium: An Experimental Study', *American Political Science Review* 98, 1.

Atkeson, L. R. (1998) 'Divisive Primaries and General Election Outcomes: Another Look at Presidential Campaigns', *American Journal of Political Science* 42, 1: 256–71.

Aznar, J. M. (2004) *Ocho años de gobierno: una visión personal de España*. Barcelona: Planeta.

Baldini, G. and Pappalardo, A. (2009) *Elections, Electoral Systems and Volatile Voters*. Basingstoke: Palgrave Macmillan.

Baughman, J. (2004) 'Party, Constituency, and Representation: Votes on Abortion in the British House of Commons', *Public Choice*, 120: 1–2.

Beck, N. and Katz, J. N. (1995) 'What To Do (and Not To Do) with Time-Series Cross-Section Data', *American Political Science Review* 89, 3: 634–47.

Bengtsson, A. and Wass, H. (2009) 'Focus of Political Representation: Voters' Expectations for the Scope of MPs' Representation Role', *5th ECPR General Conference*. Potsdam.

Berg, J. E., Forsythe, R., Nelson, F. D. and Rietz, T. A. (2003) 'Results from a Dozen Years of Election Futures Markets Research', in C. A. Plott and V. Smith (eds) *Handbook of Experimental Economic Results*. Amsterdam: North Holland.

Berg, J. E., Nelson, F. D. and Rietz, T. A. (2003) 'Accuracy and Forecast Standard Error of Prediction Markets,' Working Paper, Tippie College of Business.

Bille, L. (2001) 'Democratizing a Democratic Procedure: Myth or Reality? Candidate Selection in Western European Parties 1960–90.' *Party Politics* 7, 3: 363–80.

Birch, S. (2006) 'Electoral System Change in New Democracies', paper presented at a working session of the Ontario Citizens' Assembly, Toronto, 11 November.

Blais, A. (1991) 'The Debate over Electoral Systems', *International Political Science Review*, 12, 3: 239–60.

- (1988) 'The Classification of Electoral Systems', *European Journal of Political Research* 16, 1: 99–110.
- (2000) *To Vote Or Not To Vote? The Merits and Limits of Rational Choice*. Pittsburgh: University of Pittsburgh Press.

Blais, A., Dobrzynska, A. and Indriadson, I. H. (2004) 'To Adopt or Not to Adopt Proportional Representation: The Politics of Institutional Choice.' *British Journal of Political Science*, 35:182–90.

Blais, A. and Lago, I. (2009) 'A General Measure of District Competitiveness', *Electoral Studies*, 28, 1: 94–100.

Blais, A. and Massicotte, L. (1996) 'Electoral Systems,' in L. LeDuc, R. G. Niemi and P. Norris (eds) *Comparing Democracies: Elections and Voting in Global Perspectives*. London: Sage: 49–81.

Blumenthal, M. (2008) 'Polling a Semi-Open Primary as Closed'. Pollster. com. March 2. Online. Available: <www.pollster.com/blogs/polling_a_semiopen_primary_as.php>.

Bogdanor, V. (1983) 'Introduction,' in V. Bogdanor and D. Butler (eds) *Democracy and Elections: Electoral Systems and Their Political Consequences*. Cambridge: Cambridge University Press: 1–19.

Boix, C. (1999) 'Setting the Rules of the Game: The Choice of Electoral Systems in Advanced Democracies', *American Political Science Review*, 93, 3:609–24.

Bowler S. and Farrell, D. M. (1991) 'Voter Behaviour Under STV-PR: Solving the Puzzle of the Irish Party System', *Political Behavior* 13: 303–20.

Bowler, S. and Grofman, B. (2000) 'Intorduction: STV as an embedded institution' in S. Bowler and B. Grofman, Elections in *Australia, Ireland, and Malta under the Single Transferable Vote*, Ann Arbor: University of Michigan Press: 1–12.

Brady, D. W., Han, H. C. and Pope, J. C. (2005) 'Primary Elections and Candidate Ideology: Out-of-step with the Primary Electorate?', Working paper.

Brams, S. J. (2008) *Mathematics and Democracy. Designing Better Voting and Fair-Division Procedures*, New Jersey: Princeton University Press.

Brams, S. J. and Sanver, M. R. (2006) 'Voting Systems That Combine Approval and Preference', NYU ms.

Braunias, K. (1932) *Das parlamentarische Wahlrecht*. Berlin and Leipzig: Walter de Gruyter and Co.

Butler, D. and Kavanagh, D. (1988) *The British General Election of 1987*. London: Palgrave Macmillan.

Cain, B. E., Ferejohn, J. A. and Fiorina, M. P. (1987) *The Personal Vote: Constituency Service and Electoral Independence*. Cambridge: Harvard University Press.

Calabrese, S. (2000) 'Multi-member District Congressional Elections', *Legislative Studies Quarterly*, 25, 4, 611–43.

Canache, D. and Mondak, J. J. (2000) 'Voters and the Personal Vote: A Counterfactual Simulation', *Political Research Quarterly* 53, 3: 663–76.

Carey, J. M. (2009) *Legislative Voting and Accountability*. Cambridge: Cambridge University Press.
Carey, J. M. and Polga-Hecimovich, J. (2006) 'Primary Elections and Candidate Strength in Latin America.' *Journal of Politics* 68(3): 530–43.
— (2008) 'The Primary Elections 'Bonus' in Latin America', in M. Levi, J. Johnson, J. Knight and S. Stokes (eds) *Designing Democratic Government*. New York: Russell Sage Foundation Press: 227–47.
Carey, J. M. and Shugart, M. S. (1995) 'Incentives to Cultivate a Personal Vote: a Rank Ordering of Electoral Formulas.' *Electoral Studies* 14, 4:417–39.
Carty, K.R. (1981) *Party and Parish Pump: Electoral Politics in Ireland*. Waterloo, Ontario: Wilfrid Laurier University Press.
Carty, K.R. and Cross, W. (2006) 'Can Stratarchically Organized Parties be Democratic? The Canadian Case,' *Journal of Elections, Public Opinion and Parties* 16, 2:93–114.
Chang, E. C. and Golden, M. A. (2006) 'Electoral Systems, District Magnitude and Corruption', *British Journal of Political Science* 37: 115–37.
Chronicle of Parliamentary Elections 1 January – 31 December 2004, Volume 38, Geneva 2004: Inter-Parliamentary Union.
Chubb, B. (1963)'Going About Persecuting Civil Servants', *Political Studies* 11, 3: 272–86.
— (1970) *The Government and Politics of Ireland*. Oxford: Oxford University Press.
Clark, T. D. (1998 'The 1996 Elections to the Lithuanian Seimas and their Aftermath', *Journal of Baltic Studies*, 29(2), 135–48.
Colomer, J. (M. 2003) 'Las elecciones primarias presidenciales en América Latina y sus consecuencias políticas', in M. Cavarozzi and J. M. Abal Medina (eds) *Los partidos latinoamericanos en la era neoliberal*. Buenos Aires: Altamira/Konrad Adenauer.
— (ed.) (2004) *Handbook of Electoral System Choice*. Basingstoke: Palgrave Macmillan.
— (2004a) 'The Strategy and History of Electoral System Choice', in J. M. Colomer (ed.) *Handbook of Electoral System Choice*. Basingstoke: Palgrave Macmillan: 3–80.
— (2004b) 'The Americas: General Overview', in J. M. Colomer (ed.) *Handbook of Electoral System Choice*. Basingstoke: Palgrave Macmillan: 81–109.
— (2005) 'It's Parties That Choose Electoral Systems (or Duverger's Laws Upside Down)', *Political Studies* 53: 1–21.
— (2007) 'On the Origins of Electoral Systems and Political Parties: The Role of Elections in Multi-member Districts', *Electoral Studies* 26 (2):262–73.
Cook, R. (2007) *Winning the presidency: Race for the 2008 nomination*. Washington, DC: Congressional Quarterly Press.
Cowley, P. (2005) *The Rebels: How Blair mislaid his majority*. London: Politicos.

Cowley, P. and Stuart, M. (2005) Parliament: Hunting for Votes, *Parliamentary Affairs*, Vol 58 No 2, 258–71.

Cox, G. W. (1984) 'Strategic Electoral Choice in Multi-Member Districts, Approval Voting in Practice?', *American Journal of Political Science* 28: 722–38.

— (1997) *Making Votes Count. Strategic Coordination in the World's Electoral Systems*. Cambridge and New York: Cambridge University Press.

Cox, K. E. and Schoppa, L. J. (2002) 'Interaction Effects in Mixed-member Electoral Systems. Theory and Evidence from Germany, Japan, and Italy', *Comparative Political Studies*, 35 9, 1027–53.

Crisp, B. F. (2007) 'Incentives in Mixed-Member Electoral Systems. General Election Laws, Candidate Selection Procedures, and Cameral Rules', *Comparative Political Studies*, 40, 12: 1460–85.

Crisp, B. F. and Desposato. S. W. (2004) 'Constituency Building in Multimember Districts: Collusion or conflict?', *Journal of Politics* 66, 1: 136–56.

Crisp, B. F., Escobar-Lemmon, M. C., Jones, B. S., Jones, M. P. and Taylor-Robinson, M. M. (2004) 'Vote-Seeking Incentives and Legislative Representation in Six Presidential Democracies', *Journal of Politics* 66, 3: 823–46.

Cross, W. (2008) 'Democratic Norms and Party Candidate Selection: Taking Contextual Factors into Account', *Party Politics* 14, 5: 596–619.

Crotty, W. and Jackson III, J. S. (1985) *Presidential Primaries and Nominations*. Washington, DC: Congressional Quarterly Press.

Curtice, J. (2010) 'The Last Post', *Parliamentary Brief*, 19 May Online. Available: <www.parliamentarybrief.com>.

D'Alimonte, R. (2008) 'Italy: A Case of Fragmented Bipolarism', in M. Gallagher and P. Mitchell (eds) *The Politics of Electoral Systems*. Oxford: Oxford University Press: 253–76.

Dalton, R. J. and Wattenberg, M. P. (2000) *Parties without Partisans: Political Change in Advanced Industrial Democracies*. Oxford: Oxford University Press.

De la Calle, L. and Orriols, L. (2010) 'Explaining the Electoral Effects of Public Investments: The Case of the Expansion of the Underground in Madrid, 1995–2007.' *European Journal of Political Research* 49: 393–417.

De Luca, M., Jones, M. P. and Tula, M. I. (2002) 'Back Rooms or Ballot Boxes? Candidate Nomination in Argentina.' *Comparative Political Studies* 35, 4: 413–36.

De Winter, L. (1988) 'Belgium: Democracy or Oligarchy?', in M. Gallagher and M. Marsh (eds) *Candidate Selection in Comparative Perspective: The Secret Garden of Politics*. London: Sage: 20–46.

De Winter, L. (2008) 'Belgium: Empowering Voters or Party Elites?', in M. Gallagher and P. Mitchell (eds) *The Politics of Electoral Systems*. Oxford: Oxford University Press: 417–32.

Democratic National Committee. (2008) Memo: The Democratic Surge. May 8.

Online. Available: <www.democrats.org/a/2008/05/memo_the_democr. php>.
Desposato, S. W. (2006) 'The Impact of Electoral Rules on Legislative Parties: Lessons from the Brazilian Senate and Chamber of Deputies.' *Journal of Politics* 68, 4: 1018–30.
Dowse, R. (1963) 'The MP and his Surgery', *Political Studies*, II.
Dunleavy, P., Margetts, H. and Weir, S. (1997) *Making Votes Count: Replaying the 1990s General Elections under Alternative Voting Systems*. London: Democratic Audit.
Dutton, W. H., Helsper, E. and Gerber, M. 2009. *The Internet in Britain: The Oxford Internet Survey* (OxIS) 2009, Oxford: Oxford Internet Institute.
Duverger, M. (1951) *Les partis politiques*. Paris: Armand Colin.
— (1954) *Political Parties, their Organization and Activity in the Modern State*. London: Methuen.
Edwards, M. S. and Thames, F. C. (2007) 'District Magnitude, Personal Votes, and Government Expenditures', *Electoral Studies* 26: 338–45.
Elklit, J. (2008) 'Denmark: Simplicity Embedded in Complexity (or is it the Other Way Around)?', in M. Gallagher and P. Mitchell (eds) *The Politics of Electoral Systems*. Oxford: Oxford University Press: 452–71.
Epstein, L. D. (1964) 'A Comparative Study of Canadian Parties.' *American Political Science Review* 58, 1: 46–59.
de Esteban, J. and López Guerra, L. (1985) 'Electoral Rules and Candidate Selection', in H. R. Penniman and E. M. Mujal-Leon (eds) *Spain at the Polls 1977, 1979 and 1982*. Washington, DC: American Enterprise Institute: 48–72.
Eulau, H. and Karps, P. (1978) 'The Puzzle of Representation: Specifying Components of Responsiveness', *Legislative Studies Quarterly*, 2, 3: 233–254.
Faas, T. and Schoen, H. (2006) 'The Importance of Being First : Effects of Candidates' List Positions in the 2003 Bavarian State Election', *Electoral Studies*, 25: 91–102.
Farrell, D. M. (2001) *Electoral Systems: A Comparative Introduction*. New York: St. Martin's Press.
Farrell D. M. and McAllister, I. (2000) 'Through a Glass Darkly: Understanding the world of STV', in S. Bowler and B. Grofman (eds) *Elections in Australia, Ireland and Malta under the Single Transferable Vote*. Ann Arbor: University of Michigan Press: 131–54.
— (2006) 'Voter Satisfaction and Electoral Systems: Does preferential voting in candidate-centered systems make a difference?', *European Journal of Political Research* 45.
Ferrara, F., Herron, E. S. and Nishikawa, M. (2005) *Mixed Electoral Systems. Contamination and its Consequences*. Basingstoke: Palgrave Macmillan.
Fisher, S. (2010) 'The 2010 General Election', presentation to Seminar and Round Table on UK General Election outcome. University of Oxford: Lecture Theatre, Manor Road Building, 10 May.

Fitzmaurice, J. (2003) 'Parliamentary Elections in Lithuania, October 2000', *Electoral Studies*, 22: 161–65.
Gaines, B. J. (1998) 'The Impersonal Vote? Constituency Service and Incumbency Advantage in British Elections, 1950–92', *Legislative Studies Quarterly* 23, 2: 167–95.
Gallagher, M. (1988a) 'Introduction', in M. Gallagher and M. Marsh (eds) *Candidate Selection in Comparative Perspective. The Secret Garden of Politics*. London: Sage: 1–19.
— (1988b) 'Conclusion', in M. Gallagher and M. Marsh (eds) *Candidate Selection in Comparative Perspective. The Secret Garden of Politics*. London: Sage.
— (1991) 'Proportionality, Disproportionality and Electoral Systems', *Electoral Studies* 10: 33–51.
— (2000) 'The (Relatively) Victorious Incumbent under PR-STV: Legislative Turnover in Ireland and Malta' in S. Bowler and B. Grofman, *Elections in Australia, Ireland, and Malta under the Single Transferable Vote*. Ann Arbor: University of Michigan Press, 81–113.
— (2003) 'Stability and Turmoil: Analysis of the Results', in M. Gallagher, M. Marsh and P. Mitchell (eds) *How Ireland Voted 2002*. Basingstoke: Palgrave: 88–118.
— (2005) 'The Discreet Charm of STV', in M. Gallagher and P. Mitchell (eds) *The Politics of Electoral Systems* Oxford: Oxford University Press, pp. xx–xx.
— (2007) 'Stability and Turmoil: Analysis of the Results', in M. Gallagher and M. Marsh (eds) *How Ireland Voted 2007*. Basingstoke: Palgrave Macmillan.
Gallagher, M. and Komito, L. (2010) 'The Constituency Role of Dáil deputies', in J. Coakley and M. Gallagher, *Politics in the Republic of Ireland*. London: Routledge: 230–62.
Gallagher, M. and Mitchell, P. (eds) (2008) *The Politics of Electoral Systems*. Oxford: Oxford University Press.
Gamm, G. and Huber, J. (2002) 'Legislatures as Political Institutions: Beyond the Contemporary Congress' in I. Katznelson and H. V. Milner (eds) *Political Science: The State of the Discipline*. Washington, DC: American Political Science Association.
Gaviria, A., Panizza, U., Stein, E. and Wallack, J. (2003) 'Political Particularism Around the World', *World Bank Economic Review*, 17, 1, updated 2007 (with Joel W. Johnson) Online. Avaiable: <http://dss.ucsd.edu/~jwjohnso/espv.htm>.
Gay, O. and Jones, S. (2009) 'Candidate Selection Primaries', *Parliamentary Brief*, Parliament and Constitution Centre and International Affairs and Defence Section, SN/PC/05168, 23 September.
Golden, M. A. (2003) 'Electoral Connections: The effects of the personal vote on personal patronage, bureaucracy and legislation in postwar Italy', *British Journal of Political Science* 33: 189–212.

Gorecki, M. and Marsh, M. (2009) 'Not Just Friends and Neighbours: The Effects of Canvassing on Vote Choice in Ireland', presented at panel 'Citizens And Their Representatives: Renewed Ties?', *European Consortium for Political Research General Conference*, Potsdam.

Grofman, B. (1999) 'SNTV, STV, and Single-member District Systems: Theoretical Comparisons and Contrasts', in M. Grofman, S-C. Lee, E. A. Winckler and B. Woodall (eds) *Elections in Japan, Korea and Taiwan under the Single Non-transferable Vote*, Ann Arbor: University of Michigan Press.

— (2005) 'Comparisons Among Electoral Systems: Distinguishing between Localism and Candidate-centered Politics', *Electoral Studies*, 24.

Grofman, B. and Lijphart, A. (eds) (1986) *Electoral Laws and their Political Consequences*. New York: Agathon Press.

Grofman, B. and Selb, D. (2009) 'A Fully General Index of Political Competition', *Electoral Studies* 28, 2: 291–96.

Gruner, E. (1977) *Die Parteien der Schweiz*. Bern: Francke Verlag.

— (1978) *Die Wahlen in den Schweizerischen Nationalrat 1848–1919*. 3 vols. Bern: Francke Verlag.

Gschwend, T., Johnston, R. and Pattie, C. (2006) 'Split-Ticket Patterns in Mixed-Member Proportional Election Systems: Estimates and Analyses of Their Spatial Variation at the German Federal Election, 1998', British Journal of Political Science, 33: 109–27.

Gschwend, T., Shugart, M. S. and Zittel, T. (2009) 'Assigning Committee Seats in Mixed-Member Systems: How Important is "Localness" compared to the Mode of Election?', *European Consortium for Political Research General Conference*, Potsdam.

Hacker, A. (1965) 'Does a "Divisive" Primary Arm a Candidate's Election Chances?', *American Political Science Review* 59, 1: 105–10.

Hainmueller, J. and Lutz Kern, H. (2008) 'Incumbency as a Source of Spillover Effects in Mixed Electoral Systems: Evidence from a Regression-Discontinuity', *Electoral Studies*, 27, 2: 213–27.

Hallerberg, M. and Marier, P. (2004) 'Executive Authority, the Personal Vote, and Budget Discipline in Latin American and Caribbean Countries', *American Journal of Political Science* 48, 3: 571–87.

Hankla, C. R. (2006) 'Party Strength and International Trade: A Cross National Analysis', *Comparative Political Studies* 39, 9: 1133–56.

Hansard Society. (2010) *Audit of Political Engagement 7: The 2010 Report*. London: Hansard Society, Ministry of Justice and House of Commons.

Hattersley, R. (2005) 'MPs in a Spin', *The Guardian*, 19 November 2005.

Hazan, R. Y. (2002) 'Candidate Selection,' in L. Leduc, R. Niemi and P. Norris (eds) *Comparing Democracies 2: New Challenges in the Study of Election and Voting*. London: Sage Publications: 108–26.

— (2003) 'Does Cohesion Equal Discipline? Towards a Conceptual Delineation', *Journal of Legislative Studies* 9, 4:1–11.

Hazan, R. Y. and Pennings, P. (eds) (2001) 'Democratizing Candidate Selection Methods: Causes and Consequences', *Party Politics*, 7, 3.

Hazan, R. Y. and Rahat, G. (2001) 'Candidate Selection Methods: An Analytical Framework', *Party Politics*, 7, 3.

— (2006) 'Candidate Selection: Methods and Consequences', in R. S. Katz and W. Crotty (eds) *Handbook of Party Politics*. London: Sage: 109–21.

Hazan, R. Y., and Voerman, G. (2006) 'Electoral Systems and Candidate Selection', *Acta Politica* 41, 2: 146–62.

Heinz, D. (2008) 'Electoral Rules and Committee Assignment in the German Bundestag', *2nd ECPR Graduate Conference*. Barcelona.

Heithusen, V., Young, G. and Wood, D. M. (2005) 'Electoral Context and MP Constituency Focus in Australia, Canada, Ireland, New Zealand, and the United Kingdom', *American Journal of Political Science* 49, 1: 32–45.

Henry B. Tippie College of Business. (2008) 'Frequently Asked Questions.' Iowa City: Iowa. Online. Available: <www.biz.uiowa.edu/iem/about/>

Herron, E. S. (2002) 'Electoral Influences on Legislative Behavior in Mixed Electoral Systems: Evidence from Ukraine's Verkhovna Rada', *Legislative Studies Quarterly*, 27, 3, 361–82.

Hessing, R. C. (1985) 'Bij voorkeur: een onderzoek naar het gebruik van voorkeurstemmen', *Acta Politica* 20 1985/2: 157–76.

Hicken, A. and Kasuya, Y. (2003) 'A Guide to the Constitutional Structures and Electoral Systems of East, South and Southeast Asia', *Electoral Studies*, 22: 121–51.

Hicken, A. and Simmons, J. W. (2008) 'The Personal Vote and the Efficacy of Education Spending', *American Journal of Political Science* 52, 1: 109–24.

Hirano, S. (2006) 'Electoral Institutions, Hometowns, and Favored Minorities: Evidence from Japanese electoral reforms', *World Politics* 59, 1: 51–82.

Hix, S. (2004) 'Electoral Institutions and Legislative Behavior: Explaining Voting Defection in the European Parliament', *World Politics* 56, 1: 194–223.

Holmberg, S. and Möller, T. (1999) 'Premiär för personval', in S. Holmberg and T. Möller, (eds) *Premiär för personval*. Stockholm: Elanders Gotab: 7–15.

Holmberg, S. and Oscarsson, H. (2004) *Väljare. Svenskt väljarbeteende under 50 år*. Stockholm: Norstedts juridik.

Hopkin, J. (1999) *Party Formation and Democratic Transition in Spain. The Creation and Collapse of the Union of the Democratic Centre*. London and New York, MacMillan Press and St. Martin's Press.

Hopkin, J. (2001) 'Bringing the members back in? Democratizing Candidate selection in Britain and Spain', *Party Politics*, 7, 3: 343–61.

— (2008) 'Spain: Proportional Representation with Majoritarian Outcomes', in M. Gallagher and P. Mitchell (eds) *The Politics of Electoral Systems*. Oxford: Oxford University Press: 375–96.

Iversen, T. and Rosenbluth, F. (2008) 'Work and Power: The Connection Between Female Labor Force Participation and Female Political Representation', *Annual Review of Political Science* 11: 479–95.

Irvine, W. P. (1982) 'Does the Candidate Make a Difference? The Macro-Politics and Micro-Politics of Getting Elected', *Canadian Journal of Political Science*, 15, 4: 755–82.

IDEA. (2005) *Electoral System Design: The New International IDEA Handbook*. Stockholm: International Institute for Democracy and Electoral Assistance.

James, P. (1999) 'The 1998 Bavarian State Election', *Representation*, 36, 1: 97–104.

John, P., Ward, H. and Dowding, K. (2004) 'The Bidding Game: Competitive Funding Regimes and the Political Targeting of Urban Programme Schemes', *British Journal of Political Science*, 34, 3: 405–28.

Johnson, J. W. and Wallack, J. S. (2008) *Electoral Systems and the Personal Vote*. Database.

Jones, M. P., Saiegh, S., Spiller, P. T. and Tommasi, M. (2002) 'Amateur Legislators-Professional Politicians: The Consequences of Party-Centered Electoral Rules in a Federal System', *American Journal of Political Science* 46, 3: 656–69.

Johnston, J. P. and Koene, M. (2000) 'Learning History's Lessons Anew', in S. Bowler and B. Grofman (eds) *Elections in Australia, Ireland, and Malta under the Single Transferable Vote. Reflections on an Embedded Institution*, Ann Arbor: The University of Michigan Press: 205–47.

Jurkynas, M. (2005) 'The 2004 Presidential and Parliamentary Elections in Lithuania', *Electoral Studies*, 24: 770–7.

Karvonen, L. (2004) 'Preferential Voting: Indices and Effects.' *International Political Science Review* 25, 2: 203–26.

Katz, R. (1980) *A Theory of Parties and Electoral Systems*. Baltimore: Johns Hopkins University Press.

Katz, R. S. (1986) 'Intraparty Preference Voting', in B. Grofman and A. Lijphart (eds) *Electoral Laws and Their Political Consequences*. New York: Agathon.

— (1994) 'Intraparty Preference Voting', in B. Grofman and A. Lijphart (eds) *Electoral Laws and their Political Consequences*. New York: Agathon.

Kenig, O. (2009) 'Classifying Party Leaders' Selection Methods in Parliamentary Democracies', *Journal of Elections, Public Opinion and Parties*, 19, 4.

Kenney, P. J. and Rice, T. W. (1987) 'The Relationship between Divisive Primaries and General Election Outcomes', *American Journal of Political Science* 31, 1: 31–44.

Key, V.O. (1947) *Politics, Parties and Pressure Groups*. New York: Thomas Y. Crowell.

Kitschelt, H. (1988) 'Organization and Strategy of Belgian and West German Ecology Parties: A New Dynamic of Party Politics in Western Europe?', *Comparative Politics* 20, 2:127–54.

Kiewiet, D. R. and McCubbins, M. D. (1993) *The Logic of Delegation: Congressional Parties and the Appropriations Process*. Chicago: University of Chicago Press.

Klingemann, H.-D. and Wessels, B. (2003) 'The Political Consequences of Germany's Mixed-Member System: Personalization at the Grass Roots?', in M. S. Shugart and M. P. Wattenberg (eds) *Mixed-Member Electoral Systems: The Best of Both Worlds?*. New York: Oxford University Press.

Kostadinova, T. (2002) 'Do Mixed Electoral Systems Matter? A Cross-National Analysis of their Effects in Eastern Europe', *Electoral Studies*, 21, 23–34.

— (2006) 'Party Strategies and Voter Behaviour in the East European Mixed Election Systems', *Party Politics*, 12, 1: 121–43.

Krupavicius, A. (1997) 'The Lithuanian Parliamentary Elections of 1996', *Electoral Studies*, 16, 4: 541–9.

Kunicová, J. and Rose-Ackerman, S. (2005) 'Electoral Rules and Constitutional Structures as Constraints on Corruption', *British Journal of Political Science* 35: 573–606.

Kunicová, J. and Remington, T. F. (2008) 'Mandates, Parties and Dissent. Effect of Electoral Rules on Parliamentary Party Cohesion in the Russian State Duma, 1994–2003', *Party Politics* 14, 5: 555–74.

Kuusela, K. (1995) 'The Finnish Electoral System: Basic Features and Developmental Tendencies', in S. Borg and R. Sänkiaho (eds) *The Finnish Voter*. Tampere: The Finnish Political Science Association: 23–44.

Ladner, A. (2004) *Stabilität und Wandel von Parteien und Parteiensystemen*. Wiesbaden: VS Verlag.

Lago, I. and Ramón Montero, J. (2010) 'Participación y resultados electorales en España.' *Revista Española de Investigaciones Sociológicas* 130: 97–116.

Lancaster, T. D. (1986) 'Electoral Structure of Pork Barrel Politics', *International Political Science Review* 7, 1: 67–81.

Latin America Data Base. (1999) 'Argentina: Governing party gears up for presidential primary', *NOTISUR: Latin American Affairs* 9, 7 February 1999.

— (2005) 'Organization of American States: Saving Nicaragua from itself since 1979.' *Noticen: Central American and Caribbean Political and Economic Affairs* 10, 22. 16 June 2005.

Latinobarómetro. (2009) *Informe 2009*. Santiago de Chile. Online. Available: <www.latinobarometro.org>.

Latner, M. and McGann, A. (2005) 'Geographical Representation under Proportional Representation: The Cases of Israel and the Netherlands', *Electoral Studies* 24: 709–34.

Laver, M. (2004) 'Analysing Structures of Party Preference in Electronic Voting Data', *Party Politics* 10: 521–41.

Leighley, J. E. and Nagler, J. (1992) 'Individual and Systemic Influences on Turnout: Who Votes, 1984', *Journal of Politics*, 54: 718–40.

Lengle, J. I., Owen, D. and Sonner, M. (1995) 'Divisive Nominating Mechanisms and Democratic Party Electoral Prospects', *Journal of Politics* 57, 2: 370–83.

Lijphart, A. (1985) 'The Field of Electoral Systems Research: A Critical Survey', *Electoral Studies* 4, 1: 3–14.

— (1994) *Electoral Systems and Party Systems: A Study of Twenty-Seven Democracies, 1945–1990*. Oxford and New York: Oxford University Press.

— (1999) *Patterns of Democracy: Government Forms and Performance in Thirty-Six Countries*. New Haven: Yale University Press.
Linz, J. J. (1986) 'Consideraciones finales', in J. J. Linz and J. R. Montero, *Crisis y Cambio: electores y partidos en la España de los años ochenta*. Madrid: Centro de Estudios Políticos y Constitucionales: 645–62.
Linz, J. J., Gangas, P. and Jerez Mir, M. (2000) 'Spanish Diputados: From the 1876 Restoration to Consolidated Democracy', in M. Cotta and H. Best (eds) *Parliamentary Representatives in Europe 1848–2000: Legislative Recruitment and Careers in Eleven European Countries*. Oxford: Oxford University Press.
Linz, J. J. and Montero, J. R. (1999) *The Party Systems of Spain: Old Cleavages and New Challenges*. Madrid: Centro de Estudios Avanzados en Ciencias Sociales.
Lundell, K. (2004) 'Determinants of Candidate Selection.' *Party Politics* 10, 1: 25–47.
— (2009) *The Origin of Electoral Systems in the Postwar Era: A Comparative Study*. London: Routledge.
Lutz, G. (2004) 'Switzerland: Introducing Proportional Representation from Below', in J. M. Colomer (ed.) *Handbook of Electoral System Choice*. Basingstoke: Palgrave Macmillan: 279–93.
— (2008) 'Explaining the Introduction of PR: Non-Strategic Actors, Unfair Electoral Competition and the Need for Political Coordination', ms, APSA meeting.
Lutz, G. and Zila, N. (2008) 'Explaining the Introduction of PR in the Swiss Cantons: The Role of Non-strategic Actors and Unfair Electoral Competition', paper presented at APSA meeting, Boston.
Mackie, T. T. and Rose, R. (1991) *The International Almanac of Electoral History*. Basingstoke: Macmillan.
Mair, P. (1992) 'Explaining the Absence of Class Politics in Ireland', in J. H. Goldthorpe and C. T. Whelan (eds) *The Development of Industrial Society in Ireland*. Oxford: Oxford University Press: 383–410
— (1997) *Party System Change: Approaches and Interpretations*. Oxford: Oxford University Press.
— (2005) *Democracy beyond Parties*. University of California, Irvine: Center for the Study of Democracy.
Manin, B. (1997) *The Principles of Representative Government*. Cambridge and New York: Cambridge University Press.
Maravall, J. M. (2007) 'The Political Consequences of Internal Party Democracy', in J. M. Maravall and I. Sánchez-Cuenca (eds) *Controlling Governments*. Cambridge and New York: Cambridge University Press.
Marsh, M. (1981) 'Localism, Candidate Selection and Electoral Preference in Ireland', *Economic and Social Review*, 12: 167–86.
— (1985) 'The Voters Decide? Preferential Voting in European List Systems', *European Journal of Political Research*, 13: 365–78.
— (2000) 'Candidate Centred but Party Wrapped: Campaigning in Ireland

under STV', in S. Bowler and B. Grofman (eds) *Elections in Australia, Ireland and Malta under the Single Transferable Vote.* Ann Arbor: University of Michigan Press, 114–30.
— (2007) 'Candidates or Parties? Objects of Electoral Choice in Ireland', *Party Politics* 13, 4: 500–27.
Marsh, M., Sinnott, R., Garry, J. and Kennedy, F. (2008) *The Irish Voter. The Nature of Electoral Competition in the Republic of Ireland.* Manchester: Manchester University Press.
Massicotte, L. (2009) 'Les citoyens contre les partis? Le nouveau système électoral de Hambourg à l'épreuve des élections de 2008', *Politique et Société*, 28, 2: 157–69.
Massicotte, L. and Blais, A. (1999) 'Mixed Electoral Systems: A Conceptual and Empirical Survey', *Electoral Studies*, 18, 3: 341–66.
— (2000) 'Mixed Electoral Systems', in R. Rose (ed.) *International Encyclopedia of Elections,* Washington DC: Congressional Quarterly: 165–71.
McCann, J. A. (1995) 'Nomination Politics and Ideological Polarization: Assessing the Attitudinal Effects of Campaign Involvement', *Journal of Politics* 57, 1: 101–20.
McGuire, J. (1997) *Peronism without Peron: Unions, Parties, and Democracy in Argentina.* Stanford, Ca: Stanford University Press.
Méndez Lago, M. (2000) *La estrategia organizativa del Partido Socialista Obrero Español (1975–1996).* Madrid: Centro de Investigaciones Sociológicas.
Mezey, M. (1994) 'New Perspectives on Parliamentary Systems: A Review Article', *Legislative Studies Quarterly* 19, 3: 429–41.
Mikkel, E. and Pettai, V. (2004) 'The Baltics: Independence with Divergent Electoral Systems', in J. M. Colomer, (ed.) *Handbook of Electoral System Choice.* Basingstoke: Palgrave Macmillan: 332–46.
Mill, J. S. (1865) Considerations on Representative Government.
Milligan, K., Moretti, E. and Oreopoulos, P. (2004) 'Does Education Improve Citizenship? Evidence from the United States and the United Kingdom', *Journal of Public Economics* 88, 9–10: 1667–95.
Mitchell, P. (2000) 'Voters and their Representatives: Electoral Institutions and Delegation in Parliamentary Democracies', *European Journal of Political Research* 37, 3: 335–51.
Molina, J. (2001) 'The Electoral Effect of Underdevelopment on Government Turnover and its Causes in Latin American, Caribbean and Industrialized Countries', *Electoral Studies* 20: 427–46.
Monroe, B. L., and Rose, A. G. (2002) 'Electoral Systems and Unimagined Consequences: Partisan Effects of Districted Proportional Representation', *American Journal of Political Science* 46, 1: 67–89.
Montero, R. J. (1997) 'El debate sobre el sistema electoral: rendimientos, criterios y propuestas de reforma', *Revista de Estudios Políticos* 95: 9–46.
— (2000) 'Reformas y panaceas del sistema electoral', *Claves de Razón Práctica* 99: 32–8.

Montero, R. J. and Gunther, R. (1994) 'Sistemas Cerrados y Listas Abiertas', in R. J. Montero, R. Gunther, J. Ignacio Wert, J. Santamaría Ossorio and M. Ángel Abad López (eds) *Sobre Algunas Propuestas de Reforma del Sistema Electoral en España.* Madrid: Centro de Estudios Políticos y Constitucionales.

Montero, R, J., and Riera, P. (2009) 'Anexo II: Informe sobre la Reforma del Sistema Electoral', in F. Rubio Llorente and P. Biglino Campos, *El informe del Consejo de Estado sobre la reforma electoral. Texto del informe y debates académicos.* Madrid: Consejo de Estado and Centro de Estudios Políticos y Constitucionales.

Morgenstern, S. and Swindle, S. M. (2005) 'Are Politics Local? An Analysis of Voting Patterns in 23 Democracies', *Comparative Political Studies* 38: 143–70.

MORI. (1993) 'Summer 1993 Survey of MPs', *British Public Opinion*, 16, 10.

Moser, R. G. and Scheiner, E. (2004) 'Mixed Electoral Systems and Electoral System Effects: Controlled Comparison and Cross-National Analysis', *Electoral Studies*, 23, 575–99.

— (2005) 'Strategic Ticket Splitting and the Personal Vote in Mixed-Member Electoral Systems', *Legislative Studies Quarterly* 30(2): 259–76.

Müller, W. C. (2008) 'Austria: A Complex Electoral System with Subtle Effects', in M. Gallagher and P. Mitchell (eds) *The Politics of Electoral Systems.* Oxford: Oxford University Press: 397–415.

— (1984) 'Direktwahl und Parteiensystem', in *Österreichisches Jahrbuch für Politik 1983.* Munich: R. Oldenbourg Verlag: 83–112.

— (1990) 'Persönlichkeitswahl bei der Nationalratswahl 1990', in *Österreichisches Jahrbuch für Politik 1990.* Munich: R. Oldenbourg Verlag: 261–83.

Nishikawa, M. and Herron, E. S. (2003) 'Mixed Electoral Rules' Impact on Party Systems', *Electoral Studies*, 23: 753–68.

Narud, H. M., Pedersen, M. N. and Valen, H. (eds) (2002) *Party Sovereignty and Citizen Control: Selecting Candidates for Parliamentary Elections in Denmark, Finland, Iceland and Norway.* Odense: University Press of Southern Denmark.

Narud, H. M. and Valen, H. (2007) *Demokrati og ansvar. Politisk representasjon i et flerpartisystem.* Oslo: N.W. Damm and Søn AS.

Nemoto, K., Krauss, E. and Pekkanen, R. (2008) 'Policy Dissension and Party Discipline: The July 2005 Vote on Postal Privatization in Japan', *British Journal of Political Science* 38, 3: 499–525.

Nicolau, J. M. (2004) 'Brazil: Democratizing with Majority Runoff', in J. M. Colomer (ed.) *Handbook of Electoral System Choice.* Basingstoke: Palgrave Macmillan, 121–32.

Nie, N. H., Junn, J. and Stehlik-Berry, K. (1996) *Education and Democratic Citizenship in America.* Chicago: University of Chicago Press.

Nielson, D. L. (2003) 'Supplying Trade Reform: Political Institutions and Liberalization in Middle-income Presidential Democracies', *American*

Journal of Political Science 47, 3.
Norris, P. (2004) *Electoral Engineering. Voting Rules and Political Behavior*. New York: Cambridge University Press.
— (2002) 'Ballot Structure and Legislative Behavior', in T. J.Power and N. C. Rae (eds) *Exporting Congress? The Influence of the U.S. Congress on World Legislatures*. Pittsburgh: University of Pittsburgh Press.
— (2010) 'Why the Cameron-Clegg coalition will be a shock to both Tory and Liberal Democrat voters', *LSE Election Experts Blog*, 14 May.
— (1994) 'The Growth of the Constituency Role of the MP', *Parliamentary Affairs*, 47, 4: 705–20.
Norton, P. and Wood, D. (1990) 'Constituency Service by Members of Parliament; Does it Contribute to a Personal Vote?' *Parliamentary Affairs*.
Notisur. (1999) 'Chile: Socialist Ricardo Lagos is Concertacion Candidate for President,' *Latin American Political Affairs* 9, 22 Online. Available: <http://jukebox.ucsd.edu/news/> accessed 11 June.
Obler, J. (1970) 'Candidate Selection in Belgium'. PhD Dissertation, University of Wisconsin, USA.
Ortega Villodres, C. (2003) 'Intra-party Competition under Preferential Ballot Systems: The Case of Finland', Representation 40, 1:55–66.
O'Leary, C. (1979) *Irish Elections 1918–77: Parties, Voters and Proportional Representation*. Dublin: Gill and Macmillan.
Palomo, G. (1990) *Túnel: la larga marcha de José María Aznar y la derecha española hacia el poder*. Madrid: Temas de Hoy.
— (1993) *El vuelo del halcón: José María Aznar y la aventura de la derecha española*. Madrid: Temas de Hoy.
Parker, A. J. (1984) 'An Ecological Analysis of Voting Patterns in Galway West, 1977', *Irish Geography*, 17: 42–64.
Pattie, C. and Johnston, R. (2004) 'Party Knowledge and Candidate Knowledge: Constituency Campaigning and Voting and the 1997 British General Election', *Electoral Studies* 23, 4: 795–819.
Pekkanen, R., Nyblade, B. and Krauss, E. S. (2006) 'Electoral Incentives in Mixed-member Systems: Party, Posts, and Zombie Politicians in Japan', *American Political Science Review* 100, 2: 183–93.
Pereira, P. T. and Andrade e Silva, J. (2009) 'Citizens' Freedom to Choose Representatives: Ballot Structure, Proportionality and "Fragmented" Parliaments', *Electoral Studies*, 28.
Persson, T. and Tabellini, G. E. (2003) *The Economic Effects of Constitutions*. Cambridge: MIT Press.
Petersson, O., von Beyme, K., Karvonen, L., Nedelmann, B. and Smith, E. (1999) *Democracy the Swedish Way. Report from the Democratic Audit of Sweden 1999*, Stockholm: SNS Förlag.
Polsby, N. W. (1983) *Consequences of Party Reform*. New York: Oxford University Press.
Popkin, S. L. (1991) . *The Reasoning Voter: Communication and Persuasion in Presidential Campaigns* Chicago: University of Chicago Press.

Powell, B. G. (1982) *Comparative Democracies: Participation, Stability and Violence.* Cambridge, Ma: Harvard University Press.

Rae, D. (1967) *The Political Consequences of Electoral Laws.* New Haven: Yale University Press.

Rahat, Gideon. 2008a. 'Trial and Error: Electoral Reform through Bypass and its Repeal', *Israel Affairs* 14, 1:103–117.

— 2008b. 'Entering through the Back Door: Non-party Actors in Intra-party (S)electoral Politics,' in David M. Farrell and Rüdiger Schmitt-Beck (eds) *Non-Party Actors in Electoral Politics: The Role of Interest Groups and Independent Citizens in Contemporary Election Campaigns.* Baden-Baden: Nomos: 25–44.

Rahat, G. and Hazan, R. Y. (2001) 'Candidate Selection Methods: An Analytical Framework', *Party Politics* 7, 3: 297–322.

— (2006) 'Political Participation in Party Primaries: Increase in Quantity, Decrease in Quality,' in D. Fuchs and T. Zittel (eds) *Participatory Democracy and Political Participation: Can Democracy Reform Bring Citizens Back In?* London: Routledge: 57–72.

Rahat, G., Hazan, R. Y. and Katz, R. S. (2008) 'Democracy and Political Parties: On the Uneasy Relationships between Participation, Competition and Representation', *Party Politics* 14, 6: 663–85.

Rahat, G. and Sheafer, T. (2007) 'The Personalization(s) of Politics: Israel, 1949–2003', *Political Communication* 24, 1:65–80.

Rallings, C., and Thrasher, M. (2003) 'Explaining Split-ticket Voting at the 1979 and 1997 General and Local Elections in England', *Political Studies* 51, 3: 558–72.

Ranney, A. (1968) 'Representativeness of Primary Electorates', *Midwest Journal of Political Science* 12: 224–38.

— (1981) 'Candidate Selection,' in D. Butler, H. R. Penniman and A. Ranney (eds) *Democracy at the Polls: A Comparative Study of Competitive National Elections.* Washington, DC: American Enterprise Institute: 75–106.

— (1987) 'Candidate Selection,' in V. Bogdanor (ed.), *The Blackwell Encyclopaedia of Political Institutions.* Oxford: Blackwell.

Raunio, T. (2009) 'Finland: One Hundred Years of Quietude', in M. Gallagher and P. Mitchell (eds) *The Politics of Electoral Systems.* Oxford: Oxford University Press: 473–90.

Rawlings, R. (1990) The MPs Complaints Service, The Modern Law Review 53, 2: 149–69.

Reed, S. R. and Thies, M. F. (2001) 'The Consequences of Electoral Reform in Japan', in M. Soberg Shugart and M. P. Wattenberg (eds) *Mixed-Member Electoral Systems. The Best of Both Worlds?* Oxford: Oxford University Press: 380–403.

Reynolds, A. (2004) 'South Africa: Proportional Representation and the Puzzle to Stabilize Democracy', in J. M. Colomer (ed.) *Handbook of Electoral System Choice.* Basingstoke: Palgrave Macmillan: 440–52.

Reuters. (2005) 'Mexico's PRI opens presidential primary to all.' *Reuters.com*. July 12.
Reynolds, A., Reilly, B. and Ellis, A. (2005) *Electoral System Design: The New International IDEA Handbook*. Stockholm: International IDEA.
Roche, R. (1982) 'The High Cost of Complaining Irish Style', *Journal of Irish Business and Administrative Research*, 4 (2): 98–108.
Runner, G. (2009) *Week In Review: California and the Open Primary-Third Time a Charm?* Online. Available: http://cssrc.us/web/17/publications.aspx?id=5531andAspxAutoDetectCookieSupport=1> Accessed February 19
Rush, M. (1969) *The Selection of Parliamentary Candidates*. London: Nelson.
Sartori, G. (1976) *Parties and Party Systems: A Framework for Analysis*. Cambridge: Cambridge University Press (Republished 2005 Colchester: ECPR Press).
— (1994) *Comparative Constitutional Engineering. An Inquiry into Structures, Incentives and Outcomes*. Basingstoke: Macmillan.
Scarrow, S. (2005) *Political Parties and Democracy in Theoretical and Practical Perspectives: Implementing Intra-Party Democracy*. Washington, DC: National Democratic Institute for International Affairs.
Scarrow, S., Webb, P. and Farrell, D. (2000) 'From Social Integration to Electoral Contestation: The Changing Distribution of Power within Political Parties,' in R. J. Dalton and M. P. Wattenberg (eds) *Parties without Partisans: Political Change in Advanced Industrial Democracies*. Oxford: Oxford University Press: 121–56.
Schattschneider, E. E. (1942) *Party Government*. New York: Holt, Rinehart and Winston.
Scully, T. R. (1995) 'Reconstituting Party Politics in Chile', in S. Mainwaring and T. R. Scully, (eds) *Building Democratic Institutions. Party Systems in Latin America*. Stanford, California: Stanford University Press: 100–37.
Scully, R. and Farrell, D. M. (2003) 'MEPs Representatives: Individual and Institutional Roles', *Journal of Common Market Studies* 41, 2: 269–88.
Shomer, Y. (2009) 'Candidate Selection Procedures, Seniority, and Vote-Seeking Behavior', *Comparative Political Studies* 42, 7: 945–70.
Shugart, M. S. (2001) '"Extreme" Electoral Systems and the Appeal of the Mixed-Member Alternative,' in M. S. Shugart and M. P. Wattenberg (eds) *Mixed-Member Electoral Systems: The Best of Both Worlds?* Oxford: Oxford University Press: 25–51.
— (2008) 'Comparative Electoral Systems Research: The Maturation of a Field and New Challenges Ahead', in M. Gallagher and P. Mitchell (eds) *The Politics of Electoral Systems*. Oxford and New York: Oxford University Press.
Shugart, M. S. and M. P. Wattenberg (eds) (2001) *Mixed-Member Electoral Systems. The Best of Both Worlds?*. Oxford: Oxford University Press.
— (2001) 'Introduction: The Electoral Reform of the Twenty-First Century?', in M. S. Shugart and M. P. Wattenberg (eds) *Mixed-Member Electoral Systems. The Best of Both Worlds?* Oxford: Oxford University

Press: 1–6.
Shugart, M. S., Valdini, M. E. and Suominen, K. (2005) 'Looking for Locals: Voter Information Demands and Personal Vote-Earning Attributes of Legislators under Proportional Representation', *American Journal of Political Science* 49, 2: 437–49.
Sieberer, U. (2006) 'Party Unity in Parliamentary Democracies: A Comparative Analysis', *Journal of Legislative Studies* 12 2: 150–78.
Singer, M. M. (2005) 'Presidential and Parliamentary Elections in Panama, May 2004', *Electoral Studies*, 24: 531–37.
Sinnott, R. (1995) *Irish Voters Decide: Voting Behaviour in Elections and Referendums since 1918*. Manchester: Manchester University Press.
— (2010) 'The electoral system', in J. Coakley, and M. Gallagher (eds) *Politics in the Republic of Ireland*. London: Routledge: 111–36.
Söderlund, P. and Karvonen, L. (2008) 'Candidate-Centeredness and Electoral Volatility', Paper presented at the XV Conference of the Nordic Political Science Association, Tromsø, 6–9 August.
SOU. (1993) 'Ökat personval. Betänkande av personvalskommittén'. Stockholm: Norstedts tryckeri AB, 21.
Statistical Yearbook. Copenhagen: Danmarks statistik, various years.
Stratmann, T. and Baur, M. (2002) 'Plurality Rule, Proportional Representation and the German Bundestag: How Incentives to Pork-Barrel Differ Across Electoral Systems', *American Journal of Political Science* 46, 3: 506–14.
Strøm, K. (1990) *Minority Government and Majority Rule*. Cambridge: Cambridge University Press.
— (1997) 'Rules, Reasons, and Routines: Legislative Roles in Parliamentary Democracies', *Journal of Legislative Studies* 3(1): 155–74.
Strøm, K., Müller, W. C. and Bergman, T. (eds) (2003) *Delegation and Accountability in Parliamentary Democracies*. Oxford: Oxford University Press.
Swindle, S. M. (2002) 'The Supply and Demand of the Personal Vote', *Party Politics* 8, 3: 279–300.
Taagepera, R. (2007) *Predicting Party Sizes: The Logic of Simple Electoral Systems*. New York and Oxford: Oxford University Press.
Taagepera, R. and Shugart, M. S. (1989) *Seats and Votes: The Effects and Determinants of Electoral Systems*. New Haven: Yale University Press.
Thames, F. C. and Edwards, M. S. (2006) 'Differentiating Mixed-Member Electoral Systems. Mixed-Member Majoritarian and Mixed-Member Proportional Systems and Government Expenditures', *Comparative Political Studies*, 39, 7: 905–27.
Törnudd, K. (1968) *The Electoral System of Finland*. London: Hugh Evelyn.
Tronconi, F. and Marangoni, F. (2009) 'Looking for Locals? Electoral reforms and intraparty competition in Italy'. *5th ECPR General Conference*. Potsdam.
Turner, J. (1953) 'Primary Elections as the Alternative to Party Competition in "Safe" Districts', *Journal of Politics* 15, 2: 197–210.
Uhlaner, C. (1989) 'Rational Turnout: The Neglected Role of Groups', *American Journal of Political Science,* 33, 2: 390–422.

Urquizu, I. (2008) '9-M: Elecciones tras la crispación', *Claves de Razón Práctica* 181: 48–54.
Van der Kolk, H. (2007) 'Local Electoral Systems in Western Europe', *Local Government Studies*, 33, 2.
Vivyan, N. and Wagner, M. (2010) 'Do Voters Reward Rebellion? The Legislative Accountability of MPs in Britain', Draft Paper, 5 May.
Wauters, B. (2003) 'Het gebruik van voorkeurstemmen bij de federale parlementsverkiezingen van 18 mei 2003', *Res Publica* 2–3: 401–28.
Weeks, L. (2010) 'Parties and the Party System', in J. Coakley and M. Gallagher (eds) *Politics in the Republic of Ireland.* London: Routledge: 137–67.
Wertman, D. A. (1988) 'Italy: Local Involvement, Central Control', in M. Gallagher and M. Marsh (eds) *Candidate Selection in Comparative Perspective: The Secret Garden of Politics.* London: Sage: 145–68.
Williams, P. M. (1966–67) 'Two Notes on the British Electoral System.' *Parliamentary Affairs* 20:13–30.
Williamson, A. (2009) *MPs Online: Connecting with Constituents.* London: Hansard Society.
Winger, R. (2008) *2008 October Registration Totals.* Ballot Access News. Online. Available: <www.ballot-access.org/2008/120108.html#9> Accessed December 1.
Wolfinger, R. E. and Rosenstone, S. J. (1980) *Who Votes?* New Haven: Yale University Press.

index

Abril Martorell, F. 57
Ahern, B. 147
Albania 100
Alternative Vote (AV) 50–2
Andeweg, R. B. 122, 126, 127, *131*, 134
Andorra 101, *113*
André, A. 60
Andrea, C. 136
Aragonès, E. 14, 18
Argentina *11*, 30 n.6, 86 n.2
    closed-list PR system *131*
    Partido Justicialista (PJ) 84
    primary elections in 82, 84
Armenia 101, *113*
Atkeson, L. R. 83
Atmor, N. 8, 18, 56
Australia
    ballot system in 4–5, 12
        ordinal rank 9, 10, *11, 135*
    majority rule system in 10
Austria *11*, 16
    preferential voting in 122, *123,* 127, *130,* 131, 134
Azerbaidjan 100
Aznar, J. M. 64 n.8, 71 n.19

Baden-Württemberg 102 n.2, 104, 106, 111, *112, 114*
Baldini, G. 124
ballot structures 8–11, 30–1, 160–6
    'Australian' 4–5, 12, 13
    candidate order, forms of 163–4, 172
        alphabetical order correlation study *164*
    closed *see* closed list systems
    forms/classification of 8–10
        origins and consequences of 11–18

    two-dimensional *10*
    open 3, 5, 8, 9, 10, *11*, 13, 18, 60, 61, 105–6, 156, 164
        preferential voting and 122, 156, 160
        success strategies 160–6
        see also panachage; Switzerland
    ordinal rank 9, 10, *11*, 14, 163
    semi-open 8, 9, *10, 11,* 13, 18
    women candidates and 110, 111
    see also preferential list systems; proportional rule systems; Single Nontransferable Vote; Single Transferable Vote
Barrionuevo, J. 63
Baughman, J. 47
Baur, M. 61
Bavaria *10*, 101, 104–5, 108–10
    CSU 109, 110
    electoral system 104–5, 108–10, 111, *112, 114*
    women candidates and 110
    Office of Statistics 109
    parties in 109–10
    Social-Democratic Party (SPD) 109, 110
BBC News 49
Beck, N. 67 n.16
Beckstein, G. 109
Belgium
    electoral system in 5, 9, *11*, 16, 60, 127–8
    preferential list voting in 121, *123*, 127–8, 134
    Socialist Party 23–4 n.3
Bengtsson, A. 65
Benin 122
Benn, T. 43
Berg, J. E. 88
Bergman, T. 22 n.1

194 | personal representation

Bille, L. 32
Bingham, G. C. 1
Birch, S. 100
Blais, A. 30, 63, 87, 100, 106 n.7, 133, 156
Boix, C. 156
Bolivia 101, *113*
Bowler, S. 59, 136 n.1, 142 n.5
Brady, D. W. 83
Brams, S. 10, 18
Braunias, K. 157
Brazil 6, *10*, *11*, 16, 86 n.2, *123*, 126, 131, 134
British Election Study 51
Brown, G. 41
Bulgaria *11*
Bundesblatt, 157 n.3
Butler, D. 46

Cafiero, A. F. 84
Cain, B. E. 59
Calabrese, S. 4
Cameron, D. 45 n.2, 50
Cameroon 101, *113*
Canache, D. 61
Canada, electoral system in 5, *10*, *11*, 101
candidate selection 13, 17, 18, 22–35, 64
   ballot structure and 27, 30, 31–2, 160–4, 171–2
      strategic incentives for success 164–6, 172
   candidacy requirements 23–4
   closed list systems 132, 133
   decentralisation and 28–9, 30, 33 n.7
   democratisation of 32–3
   electoral performance and 58
   electoral system and 22, 30–5
   incumbency advantage and 47, 64, 85, 172
   media figures and 64
   personal vote-earning attributes and (PVEA) 58, 61, 62, 63, 65
   multi-party systems and 83
   political experience and 64
   primary elections and 83–98
      economic performance and 85
      Latin American presidential election study 85–6, 87, 97
      US 2008 election study 86–98
   racism and 45 n.2
   selectorate and 24–5, 31, 32, 33
   study of 22, 23, 32
   voting v. appointment 26–7, 30
   women and 45 n.2
   see also personal vote; personal representation; preferential list systems
Cape Verde 122
Cardoso, F. H. 86 n.2
Carey, J. M. 8, 15, 18, 22 n.1, 27, 59, 60, 61, 71, 83 n.1, 85, 86, 132
Carty, K. R. 25, 148
Chad 101, *113*
Chang, E. C. 60
Chavez, H. 86 n.2
Chile *11*
   Christian Democrats 84–5
   Concertación (1999) 84–5
   preferential voting in 123, *130*
Chronicle of Parliamentary Elections 124
Chubb, B. 137, 146, 147
Clark, T. D. 108
Clegg, N. 39, 50
Clinton, H. 88, 90
closed list systems 6, 8–9, 15, 18, 61, 101, 156
   accountability and 156
   candidate selection and 132, 133
   party leaders and 156
   preferential lists and 120, 122, 129, *130–1*
   proportional rules and (CLPR)15, 56, 58, *131*
      electoral performance and 58
      personal representation and 56, 58, 59

voting behaviour and 56, 61, 78
see also Spain, CLPR study
Colombia 86 n.2
Colomer, J. 4, 64, 83, 128, *131*, 156, 159
Comparative Candidate Study Archive (MZES) 143 n.6
Cook, R. 95
corruption, political 60
Costa Rica *11*
Coughlan, M. 138, *139*
Cowley, P. 48
Cox, G. W. 4, 78, 123, 132
Cox, K. E. 100
Creed, M. 138, *139*, 140
Crisp, B. F. 60, 61, 100
Croatia 100
Cross, W. 25, 33
Crotty, 83
Cyprus *11*
Curtice, J. 39, 41
Czech Republic 11

Dáil Debates 137 n.2
Daily Telegraph 52
D'Alimonte, R. *131*
Dalton, R. J. 65
De Esteban, J. 22 n.1
De la Calle, L. 66 n.13
De Luca, M. 30 n.6
De Winter, L. 24 n.3, 121, 128, *131*
Dean, H. 90
democratisation 122
　dictatorships and 13
　waves of 129
Denmark *11*, 16
　electoral system 125
　preferential voting in 122, *123*, 125, *130*, 134
Desposato, S. W. 61, 62
D'Hondt method 66, 123, 127, 155
Dowse, R. 42
Duke, D. 26 n.4
Duncan, A. *49*
Dunleavy, P. 40, 51

Dutton, W. H. 43
Duverger, M. 22 n.1, 64–5, 128

Ecuador 100
Edwards, J. 88, 90
Edwards, M. S. 60 n.7
electoral behaviour
　candidate attributes and 58, 62, 65
　knowledge of candidate and 64–5
　party allegiance/identification and 62, 65, 78
　see also personal representation; personal vote; personal vote-earning attributes (PVEA)
Electoral Reform Society (1958) 136
electoral systems 122, 128
　ballot forms *see* ballot structures
　basic elements of 2, 30
　classifications of 2, 3, 10
　　two-dimensional *10*
　corruption and 60
　district magnitude and 59, 60, 61, 168
　intraparty dimension 58, 59
　mixed *see* mixed electoral systems
　party and personal representation table *11*
　personal vote and *see* personal vote
　reform of 128–30, 156
　　PR introduction of 156
　research and 59
　rules of 2–6, 13
　see also majority rule system; primary electoral systems; preferential list systems; primary electoral system; proportional rule systems
Elklit, J. 122, 125, i131
Ellis, A. 30
Ender, J. 110 n.10
Enten, H. J. 15, 18
Epstein, L. D. 33
Estonia *11*
　preferential voting in 121, *123*, 126, *130*

Eulau, H. 41, 43
European Parliament 59, 60 n.5
　election studies 142 n.5

Faas, T. 109
Farrell, D. M. 30, 32, 59, 60 n.5, 130, 138 n.4, 142 n.5
Fernández de la Vega, M. T. 57
Ferrara, F. 100
Finland 9, 10, *11*
　preferential voting in 121–2, 123, 130
'first past the post' (FPTP) system 41, 51, 137
Fisher, S. 50
Fitzmaurice, J. 108
Forsythe, R. 88
Fraga, M. 64 n.8
France 101, *113*
　multi-member districts, use of 3
　two-round system 9, *10, 11*, 15
Fujimori, A. 86 n.2

Gaines, B. J. 47, 61, 64
Gallagher, M. 22, 31, 32, 35, 64, 138, 140, 141, 142, 143, 144, 147
Gamm, G. 61
Gay, O. 52
Georgia 101, *113*
Germany 61, 101
　double vote in 9, *10, 11*, 16
　electoral system in 105, 109–11, *112, 113, 114*
　　multi-member districts, use of 3
　　personalised PR system in 100, 101, 111
　see also Baden Württemberg; Bavaria
Giuliani, R. 88, 89, 90
Golden, M. A. 60, 61
Googletrends 49
Gorecki, M. 146
Greece *11*
　preferential voting in 124, *130*
Griffith, A. 136

Grofman, B. 8, 63, 128, 136, n.1
Gruner, E. 157, 159
Gschwend, T. 16, 61
Guinea-Conarky 100
Gunther, R. 57, 60, 62, 65, 66, 78, 79
Gutiérrez Mellado, M. 71 n.19

Hacker, A. 83
Hainmueller, J. 100
Hallerberg, M. 60 n.7
Han, H. C. 83
Hankla, C. R. 60 n.7
Hansard Society 41, 44, 45, 48–9, 50
Hare, T. 136
Hattersley, R. 52
Hazan, R. Y. 8, 18, 22 n.1, 23, 25, 31, 32, 33
Heepe, K. 110 n.10
Heinz, D. 61
Heithusen, V. 59
Henry B. Tippie College of Business 88
Herron, E. S. 100
Hessing, R. C. 134
Hicken, A. 60 n.7, 100
Higher Council for Scientific Research (CSIC) 18
Hino, A. 101
Hirano, S. 61
Hix, S. 61
Holmberg, S. 121, 128, *131*
Hopkin, J. 52, 57, 60, 62, 63, 64, 66, *131*
Huber, J. 61
Huckabee, M. 87, 88, 90
Hungary 9, *10, 11*, 101, *113*

Imai, R. 101
Independent, The 45 n.2
India 9
　National Congress Party 30
Indonesia *11*, 122
Iowa Electronic Markets (IEM) 88, *89*, 92
Ireland

civil war (1922–23) 136, 137
electoral system in 9, *11*, 14, *34*, 137, 138–40, 142, 146–9, 152
  ordinal rank ballot 16, 18, *135*, 138–40, 163
  proportionality in 140–3, 146
  reform of 137, 146
  STV in 136 -7, 140, 141, 152
Fianna Fáil (FF) 30, 137, 138, 140, 141, 142, 143, 144, 5, 146, 148
Fine Gael (FG) 138, 140, 141, 144
Government of Ireland Act 1920 136
Green Party 138, *139*, 140, 141, 143, 148
Labour 138, *139,* 140, 142, 143, 144, 148, 149
Oireachtas Committee (2002) 137
party competition 148, 149
party system in 142, 148–9, 152
  candidate nomination 144–6
Progressive Democrats (PD) 148
representation in 41, 44, 147, 146, 152
  Dáil deputies (TD) role of 145, 146–7, 152
  localism of 146, 152
Sinn Féin (SF) 136, 141, 143, 148, 149
2002 Irish National Election Study 142, 144, *145,* 146
  'good candidate' study 144
2007 general election 138, 142–3
  candidate v. party support in 142–4
  Cork election count 138, *139*, 140
  vote transfer analysis 142
2007 Irish National Election Study 145, 148
  Dáil deputy (TD) qualities and 145
  policy representation 149, 152
Irish Home Bill (1912) 136
Irish Times 136

Irwin, G. A. 127, 134
Italy 100
  closed-list PR *131*
  electoral reform 122
  communes in 3
  Communist Party (PCI) 26
Israel
  electoral system *10, 11,* 33–4
    political personalisation study 33–4
  Labor Party 30
  Likud Party 30
Iversen, T. 58

Jackson III, J. S. 83
Japan *11, 34*, 106
  mixed electoral system in 101, 102, 111, *112, 113*
  Parliament 61
John, P. 44
Johnson, J. W. 58
Johnston, J. P. 133
Johnston, R. 47
Jones, M. P. 30 n.6, 56, 61
Jones, S. 52
Jurkynas, M. 108

Karps, P. 41, 43
Karvonen, L. 13, 16, 18, 122, 132, 133, 155
Kasuya, Y. 100
Katz, J. N. 67 n.16
Katz, R. S. 8, 31, 132, 133
Kavanagh, D. 46
Kazakhstan 100
Kenney, P. J. 83
Key, V. O. 83
Kiewiet, D. R. 78
Kitschelt, H. 25
Klingemann, H.-D. 16
Koene, M. 133
Komito, L. 147, 178
Korea *11*
Kostadinova, T. 100
Krupavicius, A. 108

Kunicová, J. 60, 62
Kuusela, K. 121
Kyrgyzstan 100

Labbé-St.-Vincent, S. 106 n.7
Ladner, A. 157, 165
Lago, I. 63, 66 n.13
Lagos, R. 84–5
Latin America 122
   Data Base 84
   presidential election study 83, 84, 85–6, 97
Latner, M. 58
Latvia *11*
   preferential voting in *119*, 122, *123*, 125, *130*, 131
Laver, M. 144 n.5
Lengle, J. I. 83
Lesotho 101, *113*
Lijphart, A. 59, 128, 141
Linz, J. 57, 58, 62
Lithuania 9, *10*, 11
   mixed electoral system in 101, 102–3, 106–8, 111, *112*, *113*, *114*, *115*, 124
   preferential voting in *123*, 124
Lluch, E. 71 n.19
López Guerra, L. 22 n.1
Lundell, K. 22 n.1, 128, 130
Lutz, G. 12, 16, 18, 122, 124, *131*, 157, 159
Lutz Kern, H. 100
Luxembourg *10*, *11*, *123*, 124, *130*, *153*, 155

McAllister, I. 138 n.4
McCain, J. 87, 88, 89, 90
McCann, J. A. 83
McCubbins, M. D. 78
McGann, A. 58
McGuire, J. 84
Mackie, T. T. *131*
Magnet, F. 109
Mair, P. 65, 149
majority rule system 2, 3, 5, 6–7, 10, *11*, 12, 129
Malta 136
Manin, B. 65
Männle, U. 109
Marangoni, F. 61
Maravall, J. M. 64
Margetts, H. 15, 18, 40, 51
Marier, P. 60 n.7
Marsh, M. 14, 16, 18, 35, 61, 133, 141, 142, 143, 144, 146, 148 n.7, 149
Martin, M. *49*
Massicotte, L. 16, 18, 30, 100
Méndez Lago, M. 63
Menem, C. 84, 86 n.2
Mexico 9, *10*, *11*, 101, *112*, *113*
Mezey, M. 65
Mikkel, E. 121, 122, 124, 125, 126, *131*
Miliband, D. 52
Miliband, E. 50, 52
Mill, J. S. 7–8, 136
mixed electoral systems 10, *11*, 16, 18, 61, 99–117, 129
   definition of 100
   personal preferences, effect of 105–10, 111
   personal representation survey 101–5, *112*,
   PR tier in 100
   regional or local level *114*
   state level *113*
   see also under Bavaria; Germany
Molina, J. 85
Möller, T. 121, 128
Monaco 101, 103, 108, 111, *113*
   National Council 103
Mondak, J. J. 61
Monroe, B. L. 66
Montero, R. J. 57, 60, 62, 65, 66, 78, 79
Morgenstern, S. 62
MORI 43, 49
Moser, R. G. 62, 100
Moynihan, D. 138, *139*, 140

Moynihan, M. 138, *139*, 140
Müller, W. C. 22 n.1, 122, 127, *131*, 134
Murphy, G. *139*, 140
MySociety 42

Namibia 122
Narud, H. M. 35, *131*
Nelson, F. D. 88
Nemoto, K. 62
Netherlands, The
  electoral system *10, 11*, 16, 30, *34*, 126–7
    preferential voting in 121–2, *123*, 126–7, *130*, 134
New Zealand
  electoral system in 5, *11*, 101, *112, 113*
Nicolau, J. M. 126, *131*, 134
Nielson, D. L. 60 n.7
Niger *113*
Nishikawa, M. 100
Norris, P. 58
Northern Ireland 136, 149
Norton, P. 42, 43, 46, 47
Norway *11, 131*
Notisur 85

Obama, B. 87, 88, 90
Obler, J. 24 n.3, 26
O'Keeffe, B. 139
O'Leary, C. 136, 137
Open ballot 9, 11, 62, 101, 111, 124, 154-5, 157–8, 169, 171–4
Open list *see* preferential list systems
ordinal rank 9, 10, *11*, 14, 163
  candidate election success and 163
  see also under Ireland
Orriols, L. 66 n.13
Ortega Villodres, C. 163
Oscarsson, H. *131*
Owen, D. 83

Palfrey, T. 14
Palomo, G. 64 n.8

panachage *see* open ballot
Panama
  electoral system 101, 103–4, 108, 111, *113*
  primary elections in 82
Pappalardo, A. 124
Paraguay 82
Parker, A. J. 146
parties, political
  ballots and 4–5
    strategies for success 161–4
  block voting and 4, 5, 12
  candidate selection and 13, 14, 18, 22, 23–35
    personal qualities and 14, 18, 33
    policy positions and 14
    see also candidate selection
  closed party lists and 13, 15
  cohesion of 31–2
  emergence of 2, 4, 7
  factions in 5
  PR use of by 156
  see also ballot structures; electoral systems
PARTIREP project 60
Party and Parish Pump 146
party identification 65, 78
party systems 12, 129
  electoral rules and 12, 129
  fragmentation of 132–3
Pattie, C. 47
Paul, R. 87
Pauli, G. 110
Pedersen, M. N. 35
Pekkanen, R. 61
Pennings, P. 32
Pereira, P. T. 18–19
personal representation 7–8
  ballot forms and 15, 17, 18, 30
  candidate selection and 22–35
    personality and 14, 18
    see also candidate selection
  constituency service and 59, 60
  electoral rules and 5–6, 7, 12
  internet, use of 43

mixed electoral systems and 100, 101–2
origins of 2
political instability and 13
primary competition and 86, 97
tension with party representation 2, 7
women and 17, 58
see also under single-member districts; United Kingdom
personal vote 15, 56 n.1, 58, 59, 61, 62
district magnitude and 59, 60, 61, 65
legislative factionalism and 61
personal vote-earning attributes (PVEA) 58, 61, 62, 63, 65
negative 63
Persson, T. 60
Peru *11*, 86 n.2
Petersson, O. 132, 133
Pettai, V. 121, 122, 124, 125, 126, *131*
Philippines, The 101, *113*
Poland *11*
Polga-Hecimovich, J. 83, 85, 86
Polsby, N. W. 83
Ponsatí, C. 19
Pope, J. C. 83
Popkin, S. L. 63
Portugal 9, *11*, *131*
Powell, B. G. 87
preferential list systems (PLS) 9, *10*, 11, 13, 16, 18, 51, 120–34, 168–9
candidate success strategies 171–2, 174
closed-list systems and 120, 131, 132
district magnitude and 168, 172
empirical survey of 120, 122–8, 134
fundamental features/dimensions of 120–2
existing variations *123*
theoretical variations of *121*
historical background of 120, 128–31
incentives/consequences 132–4
see also under Switzerland
primary electoral system 9, 52, 82, 83
candidate strength study (US 2008 election) 83–98
measures of competitiveness 90–3
consensus generation and 84
presidential nominations and 82, 83, 84
primary bonus hypothesis 84–6
primary penalty hypothesis 83–4, 85, 86
transparency and 84, 86
see also under Latin America; United States
Proportional Representation Society (1884) 136
proportional rule systems 2, 3, 6–7, 10, *11*, 12, 15, 30, 51, 61, 136, 156
assembly elections and 6
ballot systems and 15
see also under Switzerland
closed lists and (CLPR) 58
see also under closed lists
marginality in 63
multi-member districts and 159
personalised PR 100

Rae, D. 30
Rahat, G. 8, 18, 23, 24, 25, 31, 33
Rallings, C. 40
Ranney, A. 22, 32, 35, 64, 83
Raunio, T. 123
Reed, S. R. 102 n.3
Reilly, B. 30
Remington, T. F. 62
responsiveness 41
'symbolic' 43, 44
Reuters 84
Reynolds, A. 30, *131*
Ricart-Huguet, J. 19
Rice, T. W. 83
Riera, P. 15, 18, 65 n.10
Rietz, T. A. 88

Robinson, C. 138, *139*
Roche, R. 147
Rodríguez-Zapatero, J. L. 57
Romania *11*
Romney, M. 87, 88, 89, 90
Rose, R. 66, *131*
Rose-Ackerman, S. 60
Rosenbluth, F. 58
Rule, W. 110 n.10
Rush, M. 31
Russia 100

San Francisco *10*
Sao Tomé 122
Sartori, G. 128
Scarrow, S. 26 n.4, 32
Schattschneider, E. E. 35
Scheiner, E. 62, 100
Schoen, H. 109
Schoppa, L. J. 100
Schultze, R. O. 110 n.10
Scotsman 49
Scully, R. 60 n.5
Scully, T. R. *131*
Selb, D. 63
Senegal *10*, 101, *112, 113*
Seychelles, The 101, *113*
Sheafer, T. 24, 33
Shomer, Y. 33 n.7
Shugart, M. S. 8, 22, 27, 30, 58, 59, 60, 61, 62, 71, 78, 86, 100, 129, 132
Sieberer, U. 61
Silva, J. A. 19
Simmons, J. W. 60 n.7
Singer, M. M. 108
single-member districts 6, 7, 8–9, 10, *11*, 12, 15, 61, 63, 120
 candidate selection and 30, 31, 133
 'safe' seats and 8, 31
single nontransferable vote (SNTV) 61, 120, 132
single transferable vote (STV) 52, 61, 120, 130, 132, 152
 see also under Ireland; United Kingdom
Sinnott, R. 138, 140, 147
Slovakia *11*
Slovenia *11*
Söderland, P. 133
Solana, J. 71 n.19
Sonner, M. 83
SOU 124
South Africa 122, *131*
South Korea 101, *112, 113*
Spain
 CLPR study 56, 62–79, 131
  candidate's attributes (PVEA) and 56, 62, 63, 69, 71
  candidate selection and performance 58, 63–4, *70, 72, 73*, 78
  district magnitude effect *70*, 71, *72*, 74, 78, 79
  personal vote, determinants of *75*, 79
  voter knowledge and 64–5, 79
 Constitution 57
 electoral system in 3, 6, 8, *10, 34*, 62
  closed lists and 9, 10, *11*, 15, 18, 56, 62, 66, 79
  personal vote and 59, 66
  proportional system in 10, 16
  reform of 66
  see also Spain, CLPR study
 multi-member districts, use of 3
 party identification in 62
 personal vote, importance of in 62–3, 74, 78, 79
  candidate PVEA and 63, 69, 71
 Popular Alliance (AP) 65 n.10, 66, *68–9, 70, 75, 77*
 Popular Party (PP) 65 n.10, 66, *68–9, 70,* 71, *72, 73, 75, 77*, 78
 Senate 3
 Socialist Party (PSOE) 57–8, 63, 65 n.10, 66, *68–9, 70,* 71, *72, 73, 75–6,* 78
 Union of Democratic Centre (UCD)

57, 65 n.10, 66, 67 n.14, *68–9,*
70, 71, *72, 73, 75, 77*
Sri Lanka 122
Stoiber, E. 105, 109
Stratmann, T. 61
Strøm, K. 22 n.1, 56
Stuart, M. 48
Suárez, A. 57
Sweden *11*
  electoral system in *11,* 16, 128
    preferential voting in 122, *123,*
      128, *130,* 134
Swindle, S. M. 56 n.1, 62
Switzerland
  Christian Democrats (CVP) 161,
    162, 169
  communes and cantons in 3, 12
  electoral system 154, 157–74
    ballot structures 163–6, 174
    cantons and 159, 160, *165,* 169,
      174
    Hagenbach-Bischoff system 155
    PR, introduction of 157–60
  Evangelical party *162*
  Federal Democratic Union *162*
  Federal Office of Statistics *162*
  Green Party 161, *162*
  Liberal Party (FDP) 161, *162,* 169
  National Council 154, 159, 165–6
  open ballot in 9, *10, 11,* 12, 16, 18,
    154–7, 159–60, 174
    party leadership and 154, 156–7,
      160
  panachage, use of 124, 154, 155,
    157–8, 169, 171, 172, *173,* 174
  party system 154, 157
    ballots, party strategies and
      161–4, 169, 174
    candidate selection 156–7
  Peoples Party (SVP) 161, *162,* 169
  preferential voting in 122, *123,* 124,
    130, 134, 154, 155, 157, 158,
    168–74
    advantage study *166*
    candidate campaigning and 161,
163–4, 166, 166, 174
    district magnitude and 168, *170,*
      172, *173*
    multi-level models 169, *170, 173*
    Social Democrats (SP) 161, *162*
    2007 Election study 154, 160,
      161–3, 165–6
    party lists 161, *162*

Taagepera, R. 30
Tabellini, G. E. 60
Taiwan 100–1, *112, 113*
Tajikistan *113*
Telegraph, The 48, *49*
Thailand 101, *113*
Thames, F. C. 60 n.7
Thies, M. F. 102 n.3
Thompson, F. 88, 90
Thrasher, M. 40
Times, The 45 n.2
Törnudd, K. 130, *131*
Tronconi, F. 61
Tula, M. I. 30 n.6
Tunisia 101, *113*
Turner, J. 31

Ukraine 100
United Kingdom
  British National Party (BNP) 40, 51
  Conservative Party 38, 39, *40,* 42,
    50, 51, 52
    candidate selection 45, 47
    2010 coalition 38, 39, 40, 50
  electoral system 3, 4, 6, *10,* 38–40,
    46
    Alternative Vote referendum
      50–1, 53
    mixed system, use of 39, 101
    ordinal rank ballots in 15
    plurality rule 3, 39, 52
    proportional 39, 42
    reform of 38, 41, 50–3, 136
    'safe seats' and 31
    single-seat system 8–9, *10, 11,*
      15, 18, 38, 41, 45, 52

Single Transferable Vote (STV) 38, 39, 50
European elections and 38
Green Party 40, 51
House of Commons 3, 8–9, 31, 38, 39, 44, 48
  MP rebelliousness in 48, 52
  MP's role and 42–5, 52
  2010 Election 40, 50, 52
Ireland and 136–7, 150
Labour Party 39, *40*, 42, 48, 50, 51
  candidate selection 45–6, 47
Liberal Democrats 38, 39, 40, 50, 51
  candidate selection 46, 47
  2010 coalition 38, 39, 40, 50
local government 39
London Assembly 38, 39, 40, *114*
parties and party system 38, 39, 40, 47
  candidate selection 29, 31, 32, 64
  development of 5
party representation in 38, 39–41
personal representation in 38, 41–6, 47, 48, 49, 52–3
  citizen interaction and 41–4
  Expenses scandal (2009) and 46, 48–50
  MP responsiveness 43, 44, 45, 46, 52
  primary elections and 52, 53
  single-seat system and 45, 52
Plaid Cymru *40*
Scottish National Party *40*
Scottish Parliament 38, 39, 42, 100, *112, 114*
2010 Election 38, 39, 40–1, 50
United Kingdom Independence Party (UKIP) 40, 51
voting behaviour 38, 40, 46, 47, 48, 52
  Expenses scandal fallout 50
  personal voting 46–50
welfare state 43

Welsh Assembly 38, 39, 42, 100, 101, *114*
United States
  Congress 31, 61
  Democratic Party 88
    Democratic National Committee 87
    2008 election turnout 82, 87, 93–4, 95, *96–7*, 98
    2008 primaries 88, *89*, 91, 92–3, 94, 95
  electoral system in 3, 4, *10*, 16
    ballots 5
  House of Representatives 3, 16
    majority rule system and 16
  parties 150
    candidate selection 23, 24, 26, 29, 30, 31, 32, 47, 82
    development of 5, 150
  plurality rule 3
  presidential candidates, selection of 82, 83
    primaries, use of 82, 83, 84, 88–9, 95
  Presidential College 3
  primary elections and 9, 15, 17, 18, 24, 31, 82, 83–98
    competitiveness and participation study 87–98
    primary penalty hypothesis and 83–4
  representation in 44
  Republican Party 87, 88
    2008 election turnout 93, 94–5, *96–7*
    2008 primaries 88–9, 91, 92, 93, 94–5
  state congresses 3
  2008 election 82, 87–98
    electoral turnout 82, 87, 90, 93, 94–8
Uribe, A. 86 n.2
Urquizu, I. 66 n.13
Uruguay *11*, 82
Valen, H. 35, *131*

Van der Kolk, H. 19
Venezuela 86 n.2, 101, *113*
Vivyan, N. 47, 48
Voerman, G. 22 n.1

Wagner, M. 47, 48
Wallack, J. S. 58
Wass, H. 65
Wattenberg, M. P. 65, 100, 129
Wauters, B. 134
Webb, P. 32
Weeks, L. 149
Weir, S. 51
Wertman, D. A. 26
Wessels, B. 16
Williams, P. M. 47
Williamson, A. 42
Winger, R. 90 n.5
Wood, D. 43

Xefteris, D. 19

Zaldívar, A. 84
Zapatero, R. 78
Zila, N. 159
Zimmermann, J. F. 110 n.10